Gathering

Gathering

Bohlin Cywinski Jackson

ORO
EDITIONS

Gathering

We believe in an architecture that springs from the nature of people, places, and the way we make things: the particular individuals involved, the arc of the sun, the warp of the land, the breezes, and the spirit of all materials.

As our practice continues to evolve, the circumstances in which we work become more complex and varied, and this is one of our great fascinations.

Yet we have always recognized the nature of people as a primary influence: how we move, how we touch, how we see, our intellect and our emotions, our dreams, our memories, our aspirations, and how we interact with one another.

This book contains fourteen projects that encourage people to gather—working, learning, living, studying, meeting, or playing—together. Whether in a new civic green for the city of Newport Beach, a modest screened porch and studio for students and teachers at Fallingwater, a cascading and stepped stair in a workplace for Square, or the retail stores for Apple that have become urban centers, we believe it is important for us as humans to come together in exceptional places that foster connection and enhance our sense of shared community. This is *Gathering*.

Each chapter begins with a sequence of photographs and sketches that give insight into our design process, revealing the inspiration and key ideas for the project. Our approach requires interacting, listening, and drawing, not only in the initial concept but throughout the shaping of the building. Our design culture is based in the intuitive and the rigorous, the conceptual and the technical. We do not have a rigid hierarchy, nor do we specialize in one building type. We believe it is far better to work on a diverse range of projects, ever open to new realities and possibilities, honing our senses, intuition, and skills.

We believe this is the way to make a richer, more nuanced, and powerfully human architecture.

Bohlin Cywinski Jackson, 2019

Cherie Flores Garden Pavilion

The Seeds of Grace
Sam Lubell

One word can never sum up the work of an entire design practice. But if I had to choose one to describe Bohlin Cywinski Jackson it would be *grace*. The word has so many definitions, but at its essence, *grace* is the ability to make something extraordinary appear effortless when it is in fact anything but.

I've spent more than a year observing Bohlin Cywinski Jackson's process, buildings, and people, and the firm has proven itself to be one of the most thoughtful and tireless in the architecture profession, creating elegant, dexterous, and often breathtaking work. Yet their labor—combining diligent study with artful intuition—is subtly embedded in their projects. It's not announced with easy gestures or brash gimmicks. This is *grace*.

So how did Bohlin Cywinski Jackson get here? The seeds of this culture were sown more than five decades ago by the firm's founders Peter Bohlin and Richard Powell, who from the beginning focused on the nature of circumstance—what Bohlin often refers to as "the nature of people, the spirit of places, and the way we make things."

In other words, they embraced a layered, richly-investigated approach not superficially based on trends or gestures, but deeply rooted in human experience, place, and material. The firm would not become specialists in a particular building type, and they would not become known for a certain look or approach. Theirs would be a responsive, natural, and humane architecture carefully and intentionally growing out of its context and reflecting the humans it serves.

All these years later, this commitment is still the guiding force for a firm that has grown significantly, both in size and in the variety and scale of its work. Bohlin began by designing single-family residences and small civic projects in northeastern Pennsylvania. Bohlin Cywinski Jackson now has thriving offices in Wilkes-Barre, Pittsburgh, Philadelphia, Seattle, San Francisco, and New York, and is designing corporate headquarters, retail hubs, and university buildings, as well as housing at all scales, serving large, diverse groups of people, both creating and connecting thriving communities.

The projects in this book represent the evolution of Bohlin Cywinski Jackson into a firm that cherishes its core values, but has carried them into a new, more complex time and a radically new set of circumstances. The firm's projects and programs have grown larger and more intricate, as our society's need for collaboration has become more urgent. The practice is now led by a new generation of designers and thinkers who tend to the firm's roots—maintaining that initial sense of richness, articulation and, yes, *grace*—while implementing them in new ways, bridging time and scale, and encouraging this carefully assembled group of dreamers to grow, thrive, and change together. And so Bohlin Cywinski Jackson continues to chart new territory, driven by a clear, shared compass, but eagerly exploring new realms and challenges.

Forest House

Coal Street Park Pool

Camp Louise

High Meadow at Fallingwater Studio

Nurturing Progress

The key to Bohlin Cywinski Jackson's evolution is its talented people, who have embraced Bohlin's message and furthered it, creating a nurturing, collaborative environment ideally suited to designing, and then improving on, extraordinary architecture. Each generation's leaders are as much thinkers as designers; as much mentors as stars. Bohlin likes to call their progression a series of "threads," a moving web connecting people and past projects to the present and the future. These threads can also be seen as intricate, interconnected seeds, allowing new roots to grow slowly, imperceptibly, but with great strength.

I saw a perfect illustration of this embracing, experimental spirit last summer when I visited Bohlin Cywinski Jackson's downtown Pittsburgh office. A group of architects, most of them young, sat around a table discussing new projects, one by one. A smaller group of senior architects, including Bohlin, led the discussion. All weighed in on every aspect of the complex, large-scale work, from massing to materials to facade details to program. Bohlin actively participated, helping drive the direction and continually challenging and questioning. The group worked together like a single organism, pushing forward and back, developing richer solutions.

The next day, on a sunny drive toward one of the firm's newest projects, High Meadow at Fallingwater, Bohlin talked to me about "bridge" projects, which have shifted the focus of the firm to larger scales and new contexts, and, yes, a focus on collaboration and cooperation. Bohlin Cywinski Jackson's leaders have continually reiterated this sentiment to me, stressing how the firm's work has evolved through experiment and discovery, all the while maintaining its values.

Ballard Library and Neighborhood Service Center

Mountain Lake Park Playground

A convincing example of how the firm transitioned its focus on people, places, and materials into a wider context is Seattle's Ballard Library (2005), whose extended front porch, mast-like columns, and overall sense of transparency provide a dramatic public connection and a link to its neighborhood's maritime history and Scandinavian roots. The firm's participatory process drew in neighbors and local officials at every stage of the project. Its expansive material explorations include tapering steel columns supporting a bending green roof, articulated glulam beams reaching skyward, and shimmering galvanized shingles cladding a public meeting room. An authentic focus on community is reinforced through a large, light-filled public meeting room, anchoring the northwest corner of the site, and by a generously landscaped west-facing public plaza.

A deep profusion of sustainable elements—an outgrowth of the firm's long dedication to this topic—comprise enhanced incorporation of natural light through glazed walls and skylights, the use of recycled construction materials, metered photovoltaic panels, and an outdoor computer-controlled irrigation system. The building's green roof is planted with a mix of self-sustaining, drought-tolerant indigenous seedums and grasses, and data about wind, energy use and rainfall is displayed on LED panels as artwork.

Many more transitional projects helped reinforce the firm's approach, drawing on past lessons while allowing for steady growth and change. Bohlin Cywinski Jackson's core values weren't lost due to scale. In fact, they became enhanced: more nuanced, multi-dimensional and of course, team-oriented.

Pocono Environmental Education Center

Frick Environmental Center

New Circumstances, New Challenges

This book is at its core an investigation of the top of this still-growing tree: a new generation of larger scale architecture gathering people to learn, work, meet, and play. Building on the past but remaining focused, collective, and, above all, humane. And always maintaining the core dedication to people, place, and material. With greater scales and new typologies comes an intensified focus on, and facility with, larger, more complex communities, widely different environments, and new technologies.

Furthering the firm's commitment to people and community, the boldly evocative Newport Beach Civic Center and Park has helped shift an entire city's focus toward communal values. Its city hall, whose roofs gracefully shade the glass-dominated mass and emphasize the area's nautical focus, anchor the complex. Outdoor gathering is encouraged by a central lawn and a diverse new park. Indoor areas actively encourage interaction between staff and the public in a transparent and democratic way. Visitors and employees can see right through the building, and those seeking city assistance can sit side by side with local officials.

The firm, expanding on lessons from the Pocono Environmental Education Center, is embracing the natural world in fresh new ways, teaching us about the environment and encouraging us to relate more viscerally to it. Pittsburgh's Frick Environmental Center, a bridge-like structure nestled into the side of a slope, draws visitors inside and educates them about sustainable design practices. A LEED Platinum project, it is the first municipal building to receive rigorous Living Building certification. Its regionally-sourced materials harmonize with the setting, and in the case of its thin, staggered forest-facing steel columns, evoke the forest's forms and shadows.

New academic projects, building on their predecessors at Carnegie Mellon's Intelligent Workplace and Mills College's Lorry I. Lokey Graduate

Pixar Animation Studios

School of Business, work to reinforce and elevate institutions of learning, creating more active, communal environments. At the Colorado School of Mines, the CoorsTek Center draws students inside with its shifting, transparent facade, and creates community through its highly active public spaces that are linked to all classrooms and labs. At UC Davis, the Manetti Shrem Museum's undulating steel canopy not only provides shade and a shimmering new icon, but it dramatically gathers visitors into a welcoming curved-glass entry. It also unifies distinct volumes for education, administration, and art display, bringing all branches of the school's arts infrastructure closer together.

In the workplace, Bohlin Cywinski Jackson is drawing from past successes like Pixar Animation Studios, which facilitated an enhanced culture of cross-pollination, technology and creativity. For Square's new offices in San Francisco, large floorplates are deftly organized through pedestrian thoroughfares—inspired by some of the world's most successful urban planning experiments—strategically positioning communal and private workspaces, and linked by an auditorium stair that fosters gathering and circulation. At Nu Skin's headquarters in Provo, a glowing atrium, ethereally lit via a layered system of louvers and skylights, unifies its worldwide community and reflects the company's ethos of openness, collaboration, and technical sophistication.

Forays into new realms of building have expanded the scope of Bohlin Cywinski Jackson's work, but they haven't changed its values. New commissions for public parks, playgrounds, high-rises, museums, offices, and academic buildings must address new factors and new constituencies, but they still depend on attention to detail, craft, and a focus on human experience.

Square, Inc. Headquarters

Successful Evolution

It's not an accident that the seeds of Bohlin Cywinski Jackson's past, planted more than half a century ago, continue to blossom, evolve, and refine. While styles, tastes, clients, and technologies have changed at an extraordinary rate, the roots that Bohlin laid out—careful attention to the special nature of people, site, and material—have not. They're timeless elements of our existence, distilled to their essence. While these are basic elements, embracing them is by no means simple. It has required a level of rigor, attention, and cooperative, iterative intuition that few firms have been able to sustain.

Each aspect of Bohlin Cywinski Jackson's work has been carefully investigated, steeped over time, and woven into a broader vision. You'll never understand a project through one rendering or photograph.
You must first understand the rich layering of ideas, materials, and investigation that went into it. You must perceive architecture—be it for one family or a company with thousands of employees—not as an object, but as a series of experiences and opportunities.

And more than anything, you need to understand their timeless work as still stemming not from a sketch or a quick thought, but painstakingly drawn from its circumstance. Distilling the essence of site, people, and building with a sense of both rigor and intuition. Bohlin Cywinski Jackson's elusive *grace* is not just woven into its projects, it's woven into its people and its process, growing and evolving out of the past and into the future. It may look easy, but it's anything but.

CoorsTek Center for Applied Science and Engineering

High Meadow at Fallingwater

For years High Meadow at Fallingwater has served as home base for students of the Western Pennsylvania Conservancy Fallingwater Institute's summer residency program in architecture, art, and design. Participants—ranging from high schoolers to teachers—study Frank Lloyd Wright's masterpiece, and the 1,500 acres around it, at close range, taking part in classes, workshops, and on-site design studios.

Spectacularly sited along a rolling expanse of tall grass and golden wildflowers—about a half mile from Fallingwater—the new building is the perfect spot to inspire further exploration.

Location
Mill Run, Pennsylvania

Dates
2014–2016

Client
Western Pennsylvania Conservancy

Size
2,425 SF

The Western Pennsylvania Conservancy's mission is in part "to foster an appreciation of the natural world and showcase how one can live in harmony with nature." In keeping with this ethos, and supporting the client's wish to incorporate the site's panoramic views, the design team pulled the units further away from the existing cabin and positioned them along the forested edge of the meadow, taking full advantage of the opportunity to connect inhabitants to the landscape.

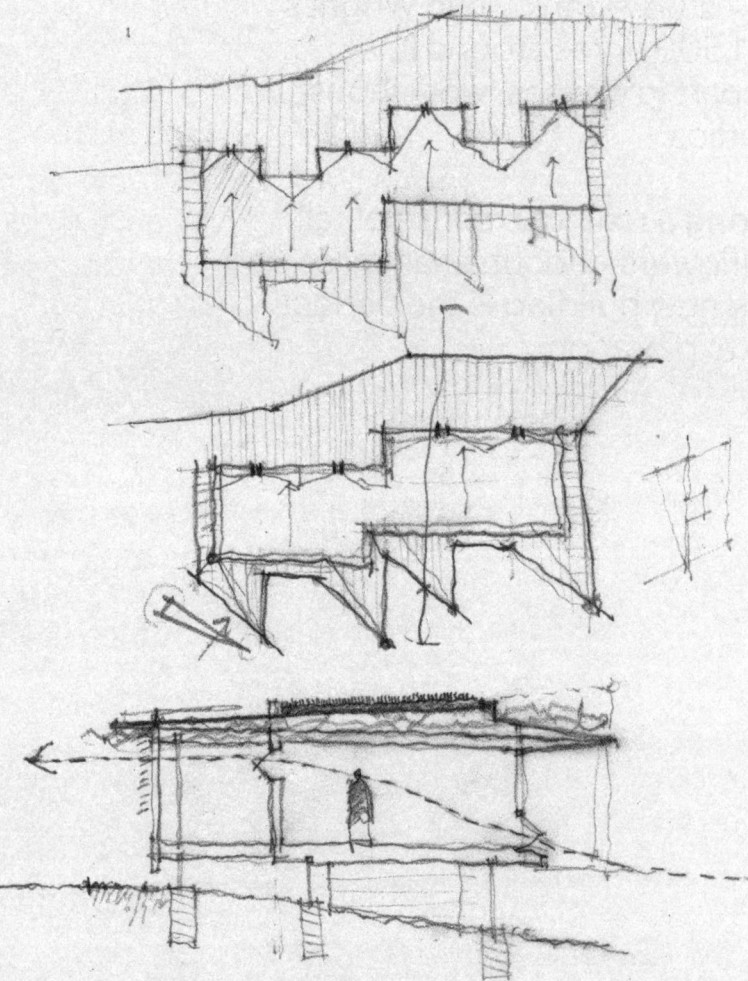

The initial design process alternated between hand drawing and computer modeling. Project manager Bill James, who had stayed at High Meadow as a student, built a detailed digital model of the work in progress. The team spent equal time sketching on site and in transit to and from the firm's Pittsburgh office.

A wood screen wall weaves together the existing cabin and the new screened porch and sleeping units. The tapestry is constructed of nonnative spruce trees, harvested and milled on site.

Through a series of selective cuts, the rough-sawn boards were divided into four distinct profiles, which provide a varied texture to the screen and offer composed openings at a variety of viewing heights. The wood is treated with a pine-pitch and organic linseed-oil mixture that acts as a natural wood preservative, a finish that has protected Nordic ships and structures for centuries.

The diagram below was created by the design team to guide the assembly process.

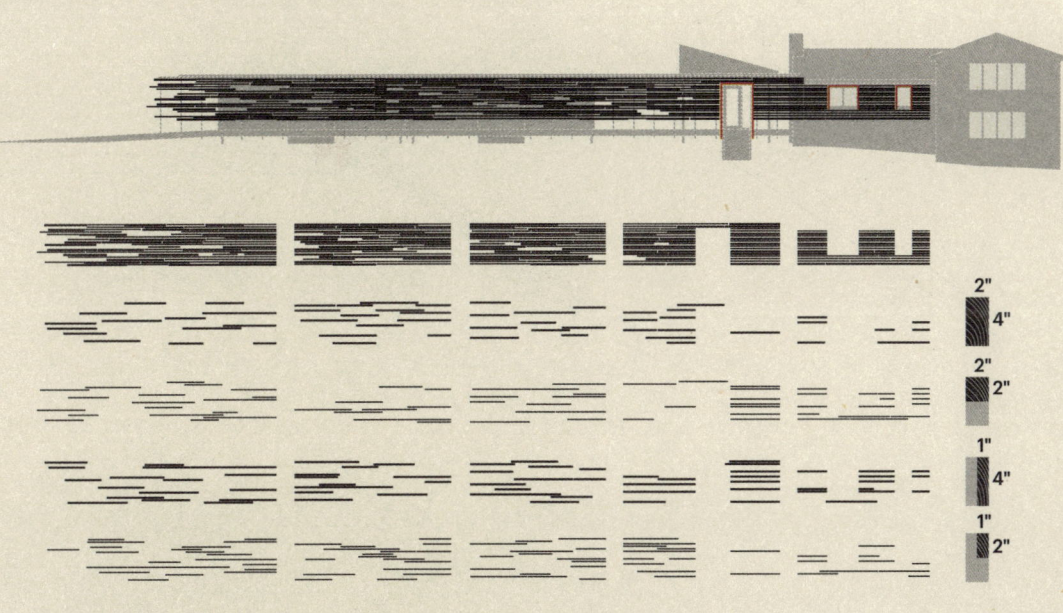

2"
4"

2"
2"

1"
4"

1"
2"

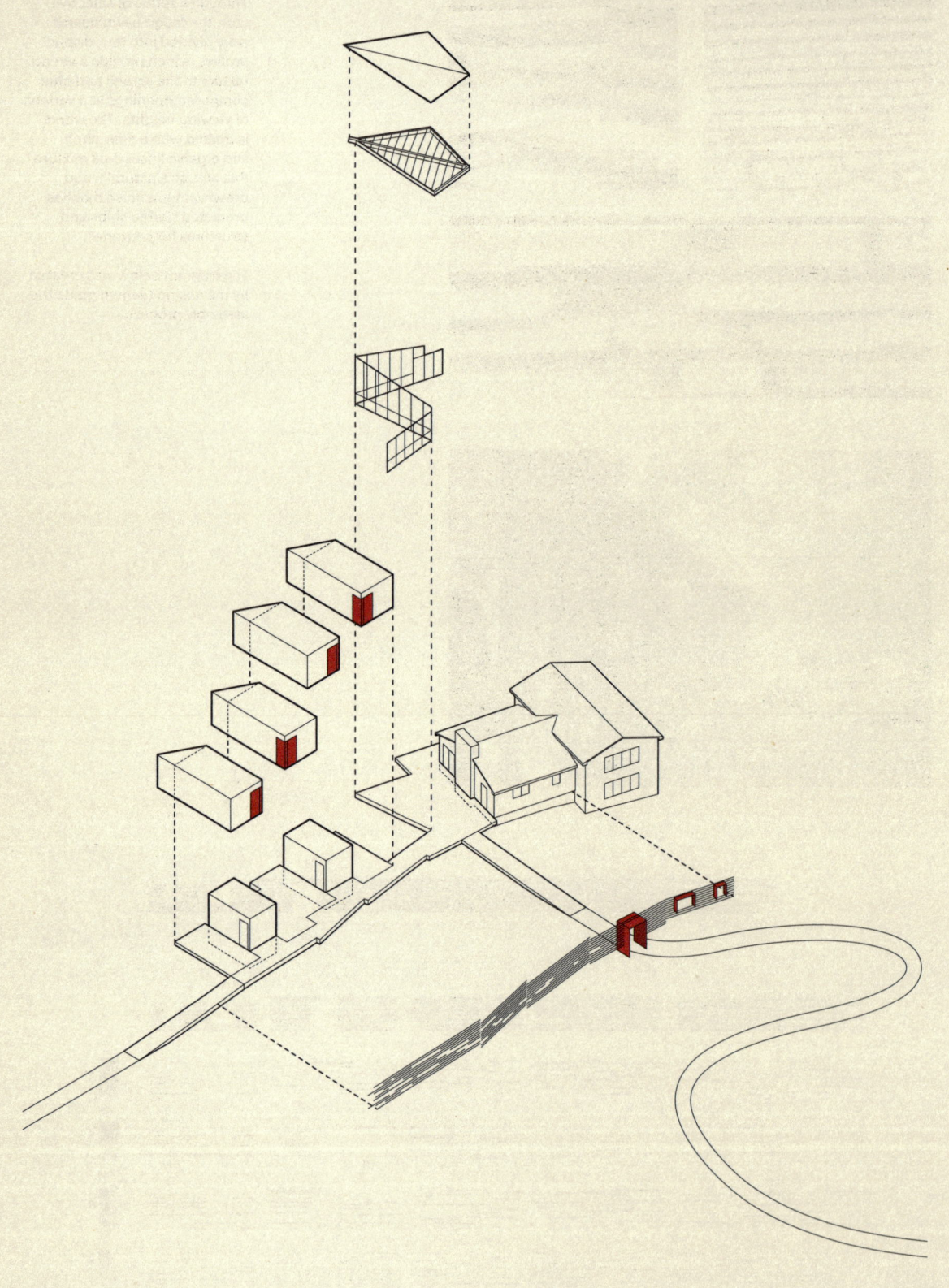

When its original home, a 1960s split-level residence located on a local farm, was proving inadequate for housing and learning, the Conservancy hired Bohlin Cywinski Jackson to expand and update its facilities. No one wanted to imitate Fallingwater, but the Conservancy hoped to create a peaceful, timeless place that would honor its location and sit lightly on the land.

The addition—consisting of four living units and a screened common space—is a linear composition floating gently on thin steel columns. It extends southward from the house, filled with what Western Pennsylvania Conservancy Vice President Lynda Waggoner calls "episodes of delight and light."

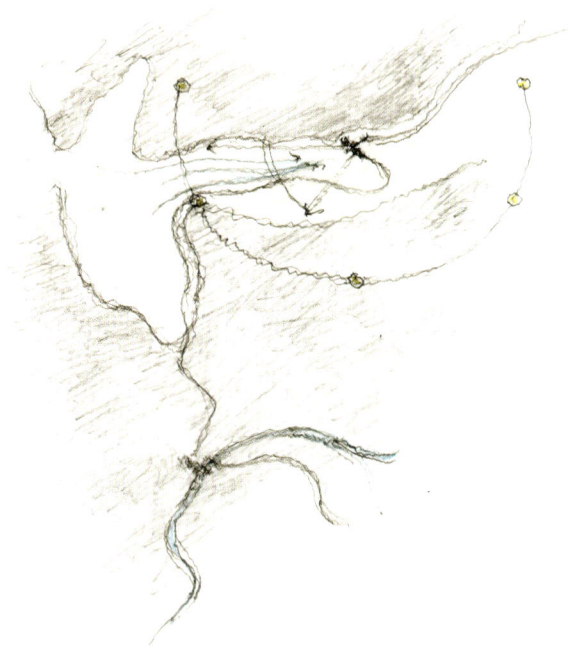

Conceptual site sketch shows
the relationship between
High Meadow and Frank Lloyd
Wright's Fallingwater.

0 5 15 30

Floor Plan
1 Entry Path
2 Porch
3 Deck
4 Existing House
5 Screened Walkway
6 Dwelling Unit
7 Bathroom Core
8 Path to Fallingwater

High Meadow at Fallingwater

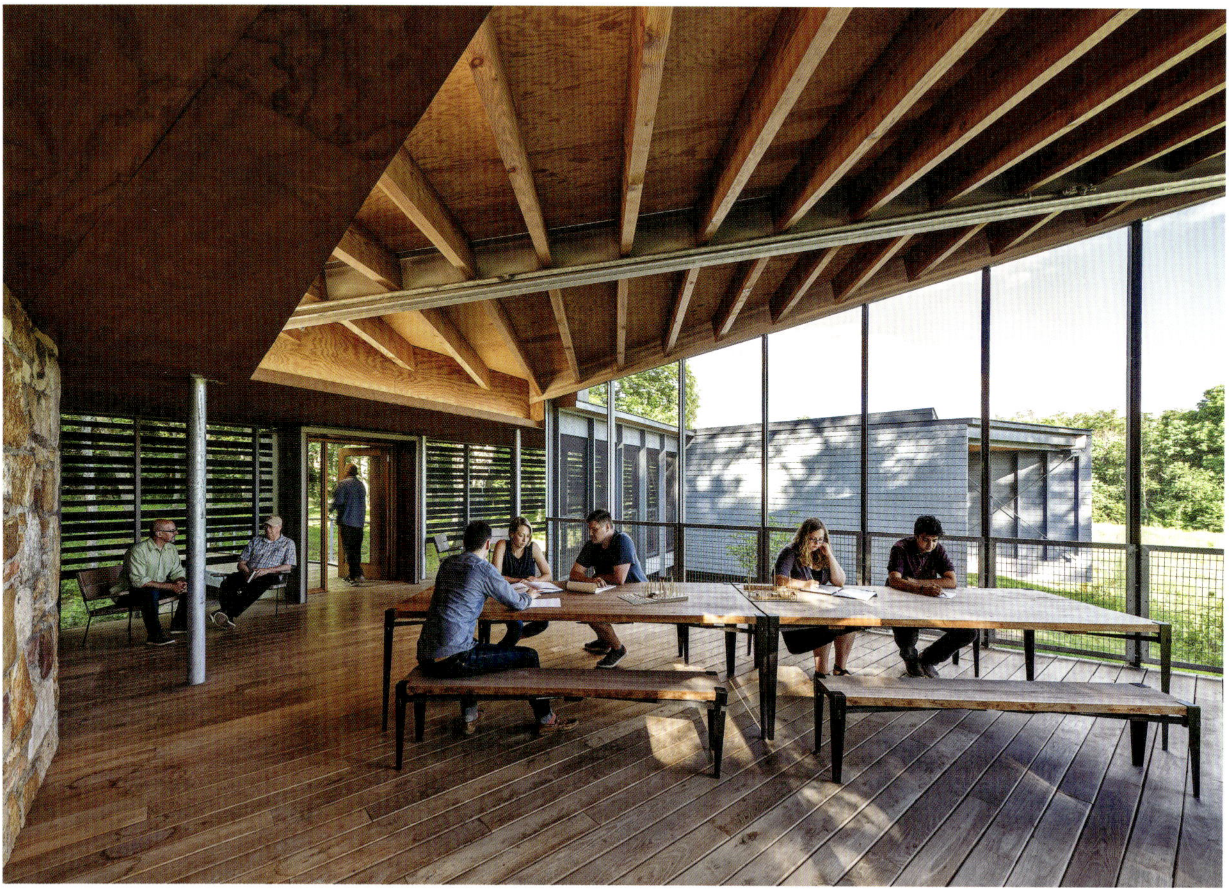

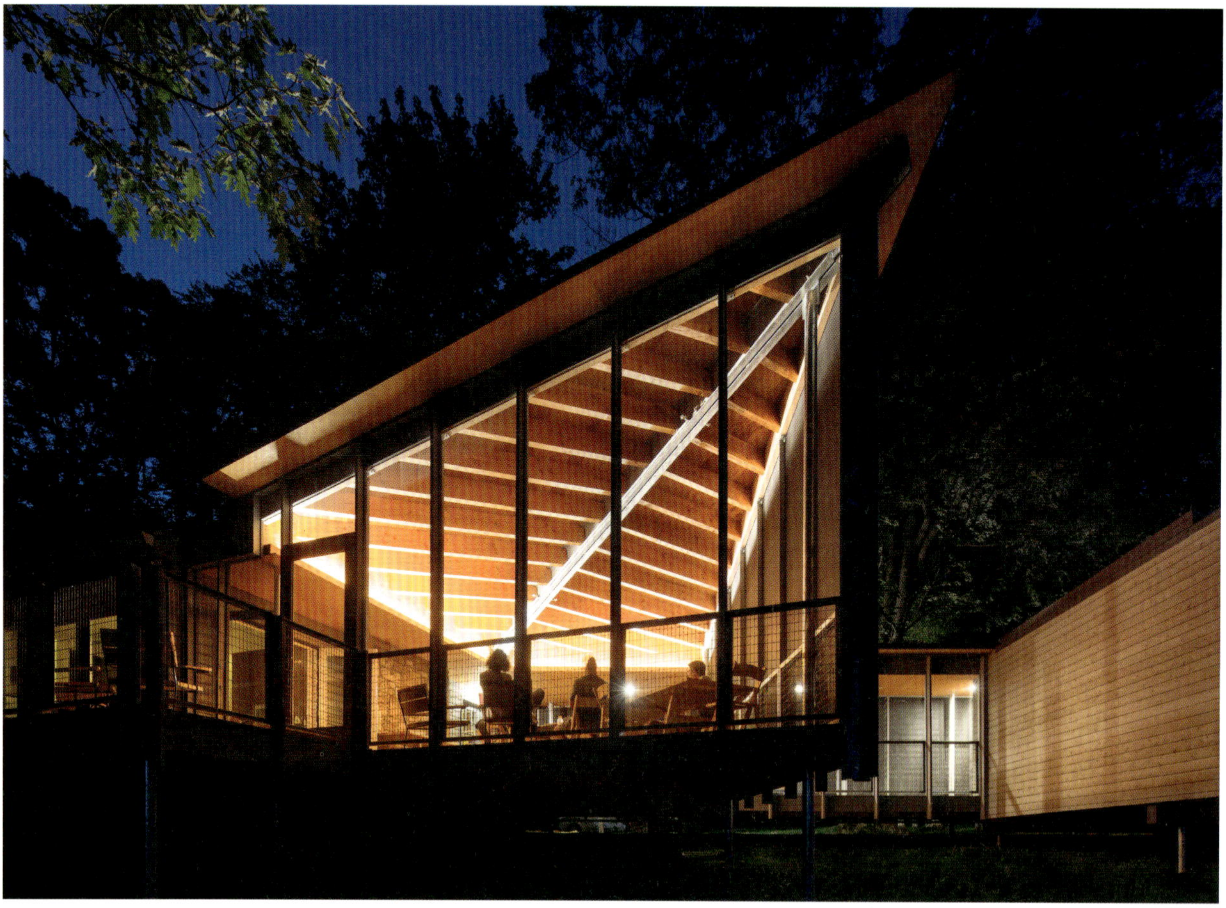

When visitors approach the gray, cedar-wrapped complex from the forest, its rustic, understated nature makes it feel like it's been here for generations. But flashes of red, latticed woodwork and projecting apertures are reminders that it hasn't. One walks a narrow, curving path, then a small elevated boardwalk, up a ramp into the lofty, view-framing common space. Used for gatherings and meals after long days in the field, it angles elegantly into the surrounding landscape. Lightly framed in timber and steel, its exposed rafters lift one's eyes up and out, providing uninterrupted vistas of the rolling meadow below. Breezes and light flow easily through; it's tempting to sit and take in the scene, letting the outside world go.

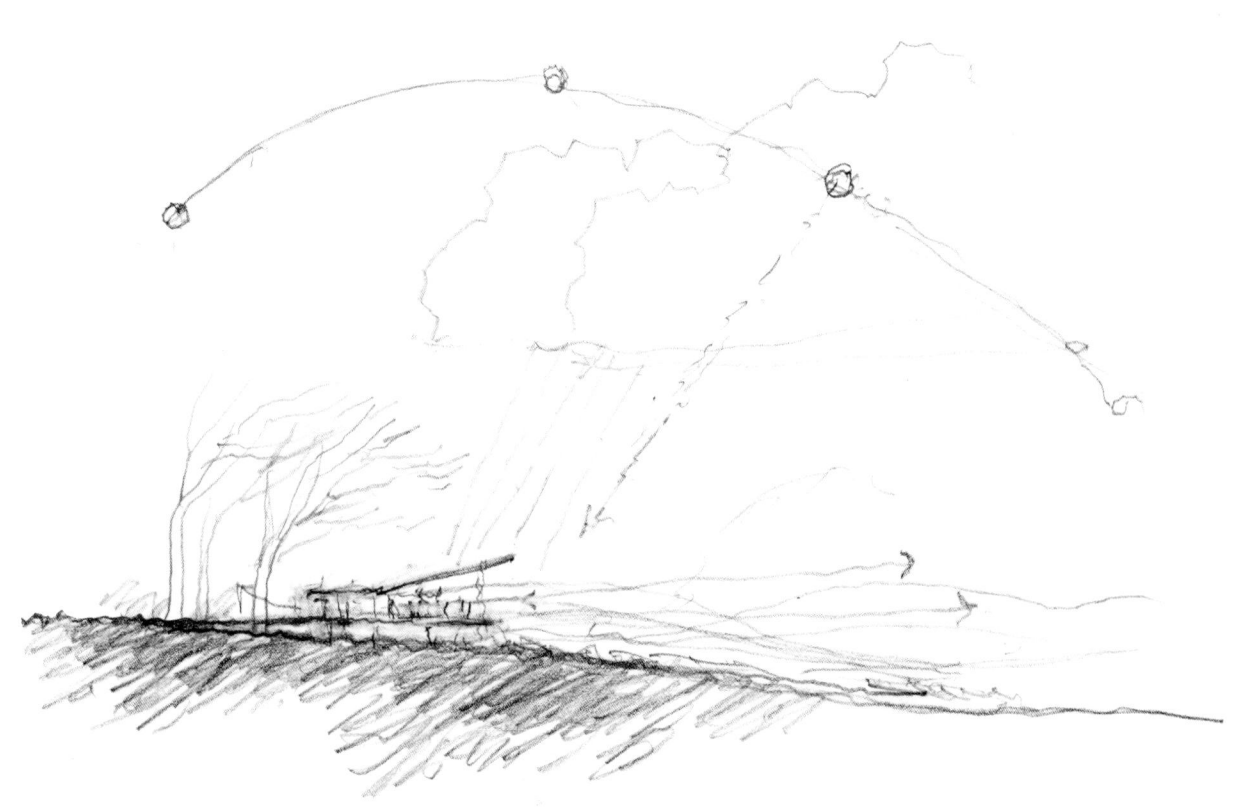

High Meadow at Fallingwater

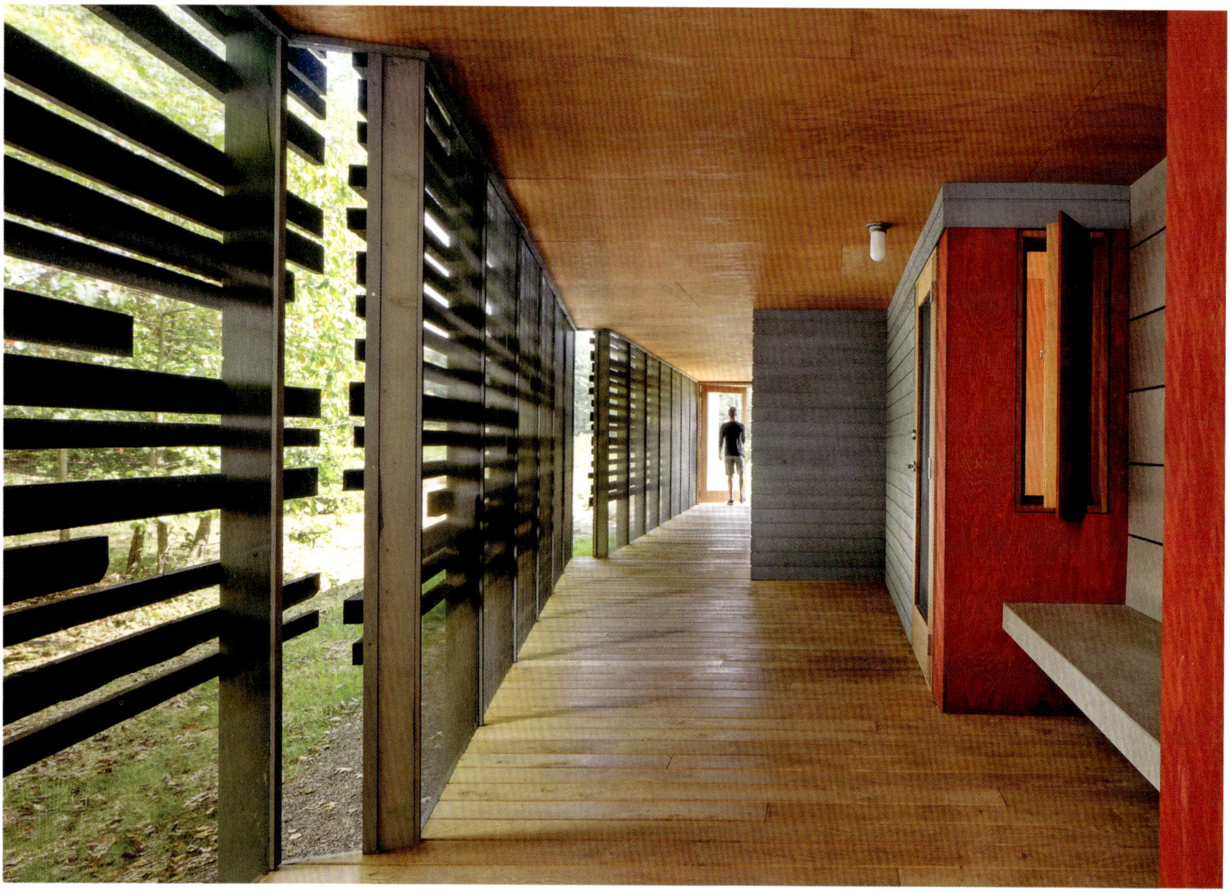

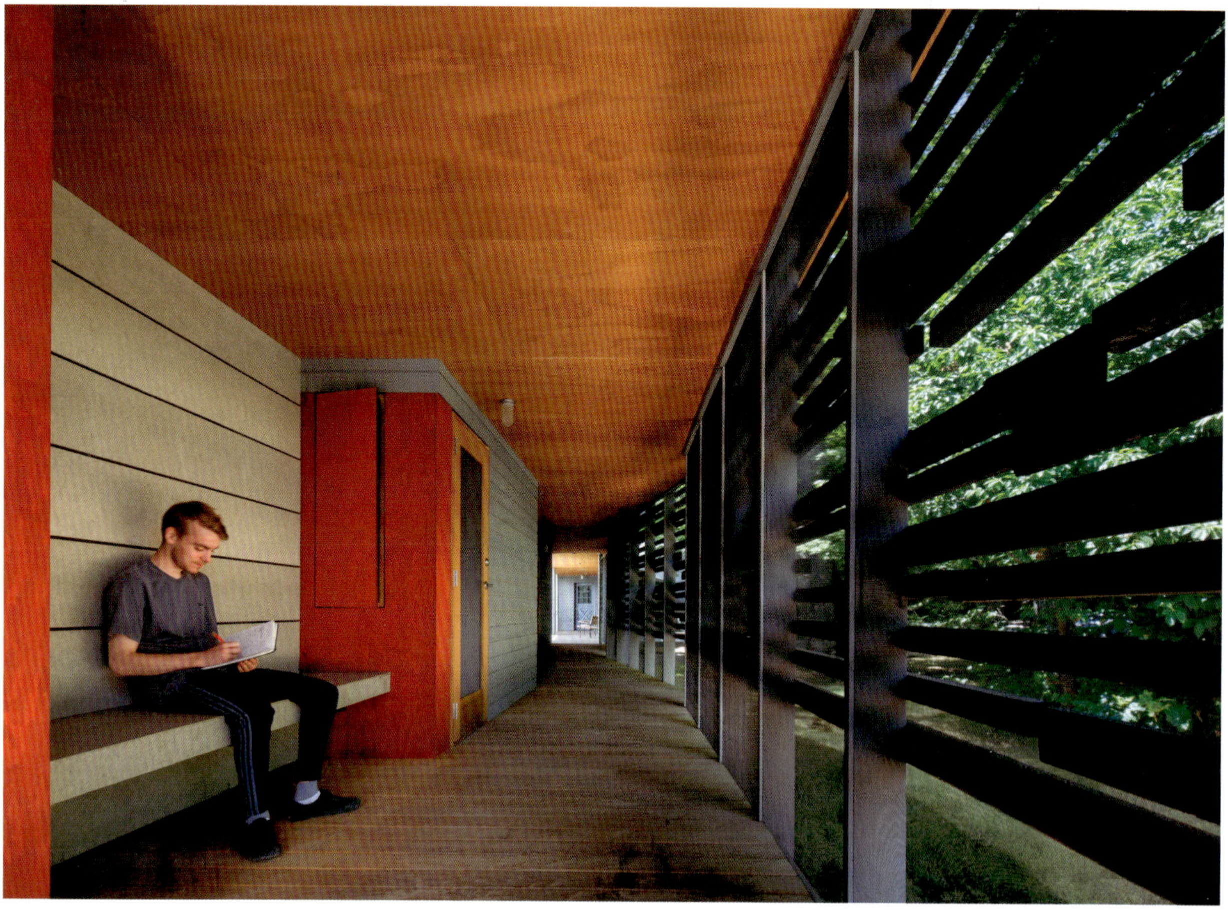

From this gathering place, a slightly canted, plywood-lined walkway peels away, flush with the field, subtly shifting the view and ushering residents to one of the four elemental guest rooms (also clad in plywood). The rooms' large windows—protected from the direct sun by out-stretched, angled timber fins—focus attention on the meadow, without distraction.

The forest side of the hallway subtly fragments as visitors walk along, its loosening pattern of dark wood slats creating a connection to the outdoors. Evoking the experience of progressing through the woods, they subtly filter light and views, as the tree canopy does with the sun. The design team collaborated on this element with the Conservancy's volunteer staff, who affixed the pine tar and linseed oil—coated slats in a gradient pattern—taking ownership of the building in a new way.

Ventilation hatches flag the entries into the units, drawing valley breezes through and across the shaded walkway.

"It's wonderful for any kind of convening," adds Waggoner, who admires the structure's simultaneous assertiveness and soft nuance. "You're immediately relaxed and ready to work. You get energized by the breeze and the sounds."

This elusive combination of calm and vigor, as well as the building's display of organic modernity and compression and release, helps it effectively evoke the spirit of Frank Lloyd Wright, which rightfully pervades this place. Yet it very much maintains a fresh, modern feel.

The sleeping units are compact, highly insulated boxes that are naturally ventilated in the summer and tempered with radiant floor heat in the spring and fall. The shrouds to the south of each unit are shaped to control the summer sun and provide privacy. The window wall contains both a low awning and a tall casement window that welcome the summer breezes.

Within the units, Pennsylvania slate, cork flooring, plywood built-ins, and furniture lend a minimalistic, unadorned quality to the space.

High Meadow at Fallingwater

"Thanks to Bohlin Cywinski Jackson, this once humble little prefab has metamorphosed into a wonderful space that connects to the beauty of its setting in the most delightful way, all without hubris or a heavy hand," says Waggoner. "It is everything we had hoped for."

High Meadow at Fallingwater

Newport Beach
Civic Center and Park

In planning their new Civic Center, city leaders in California's Newport Beach sought a timeless landmark that would become the opposite of their existing facility: a series of outdated, siloed structures that had been pieced together over decades.

Through a design competition, the project— located on a sliver of sloped land in the center of the city—was awarded to Bohlin Cywinski Jackson and PWP Landscape. Instead of focusing on designing a singular object building, their collaborative concept proposed a linear complex of civic buildings centered around a long, grassy green.

Location
Newport Beach, CA

Dates
2008–2013

Client
City of Newport Beach

Size
117,000 SF

Civic architecture has often sought to associate itself with the governing ideals of ancient Greek and Roman culture through the appropriation of its aesthetics—emphasis on symmetry, formal axes and monumentality conveyed stability and longevity. Today, however, citizens demand an open and transparent government that works with and for them which requires an architecture that mirrors and supports these qualities.

The Newport Beach Civic Center draws inspiration from humble industrial shed buildings. With their large floor plates, ample daylighting, and natural ventilation, these buildings provide an inspiring example of openness and flexibility.

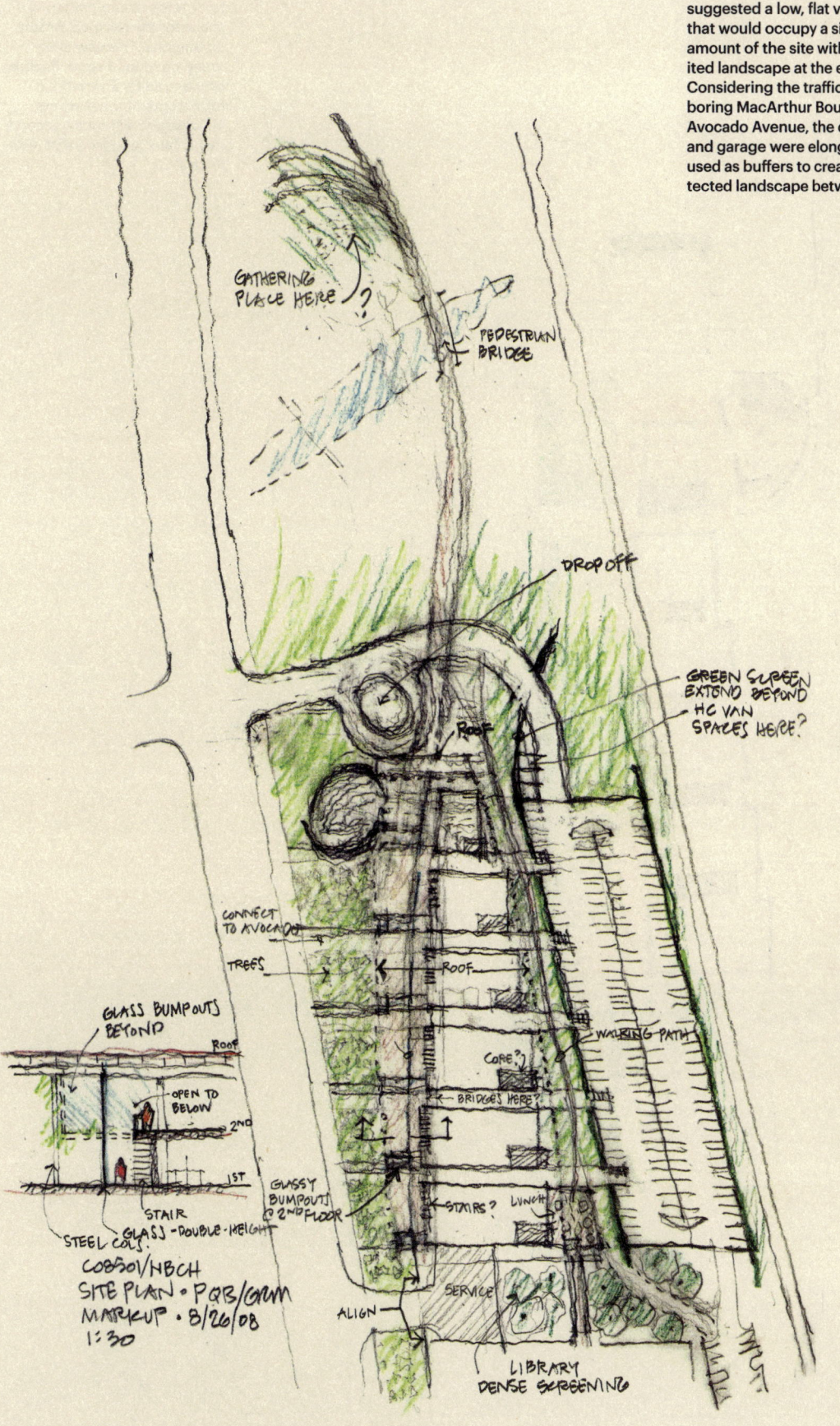

Narrow site boundaries and a height restriction to maintain neighboring ocean views suggested a low, flat volume that would occupy a significant amount of the site with limited landscape at the edges. Considering the traffic on neighboring MacArthur Boulevard and Avocado Avenue, the city hall and garage were elongated and used as buffers to create a protected landscape between them.

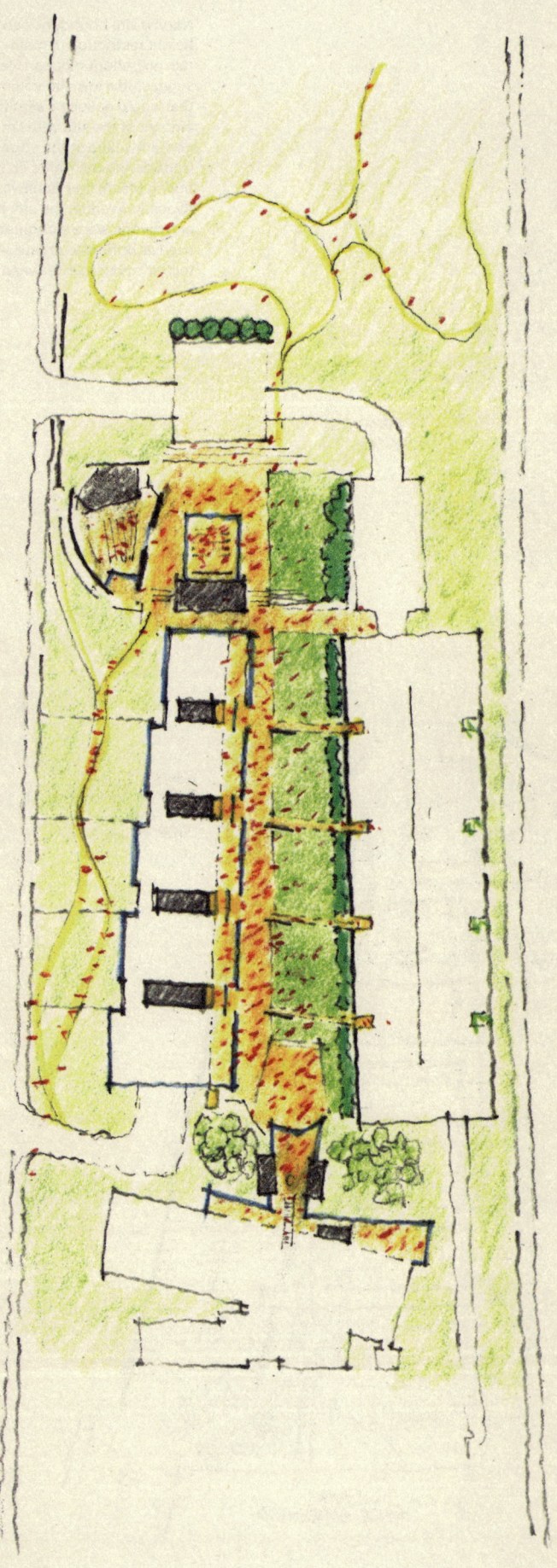

The concept pushes automobile circulation to the perimeter, freeing up the center of the site for a new outdoor gathering space for the Newport Beach community. This new civic green provides a large, flexible space used for a variety of formal and informal events including community concerts, maker fairs, and food and wine festivals.

A sail-inspired council chamber would punctuate one end, and a renovation and addition to the city's existing library the other. Circulation and public events would now take place on the green, perfect for the area's temperate climate, and for officials' desire to enrich the local community.

The design team commenced its research, observing how staff worked, interviewing city workers and citizens, and sketching, modeling, and analyzing the site.

The design concept responds to the nature of life in Newport Beach, where most people move by car. The sequence of arrival is orchestrated as an experience entering the site from a busy suburban boulevard, through an entry drive and auto-court, to a parking structure embedded into the hillside. The parking structure is hidden behind a planted wall and is filled with light. Visitors then proceed along pathways through the green to various city departments across the way.

The Civic Center was designed to be understood at the scale and speed of the car, and to provide a satisfying sense of place for users visiting the city hall, library, and park.

Newport Beach Civic Center and Park

1
2
3
4
5
6
7
8
9
0 100 200 400

NEWPORT BEACH CIVIC CE ER AND PARK

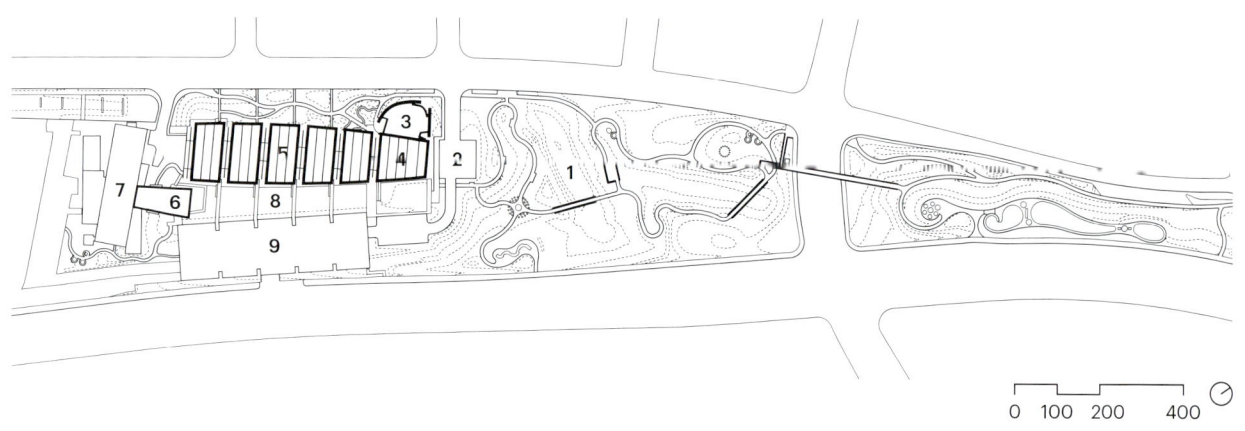

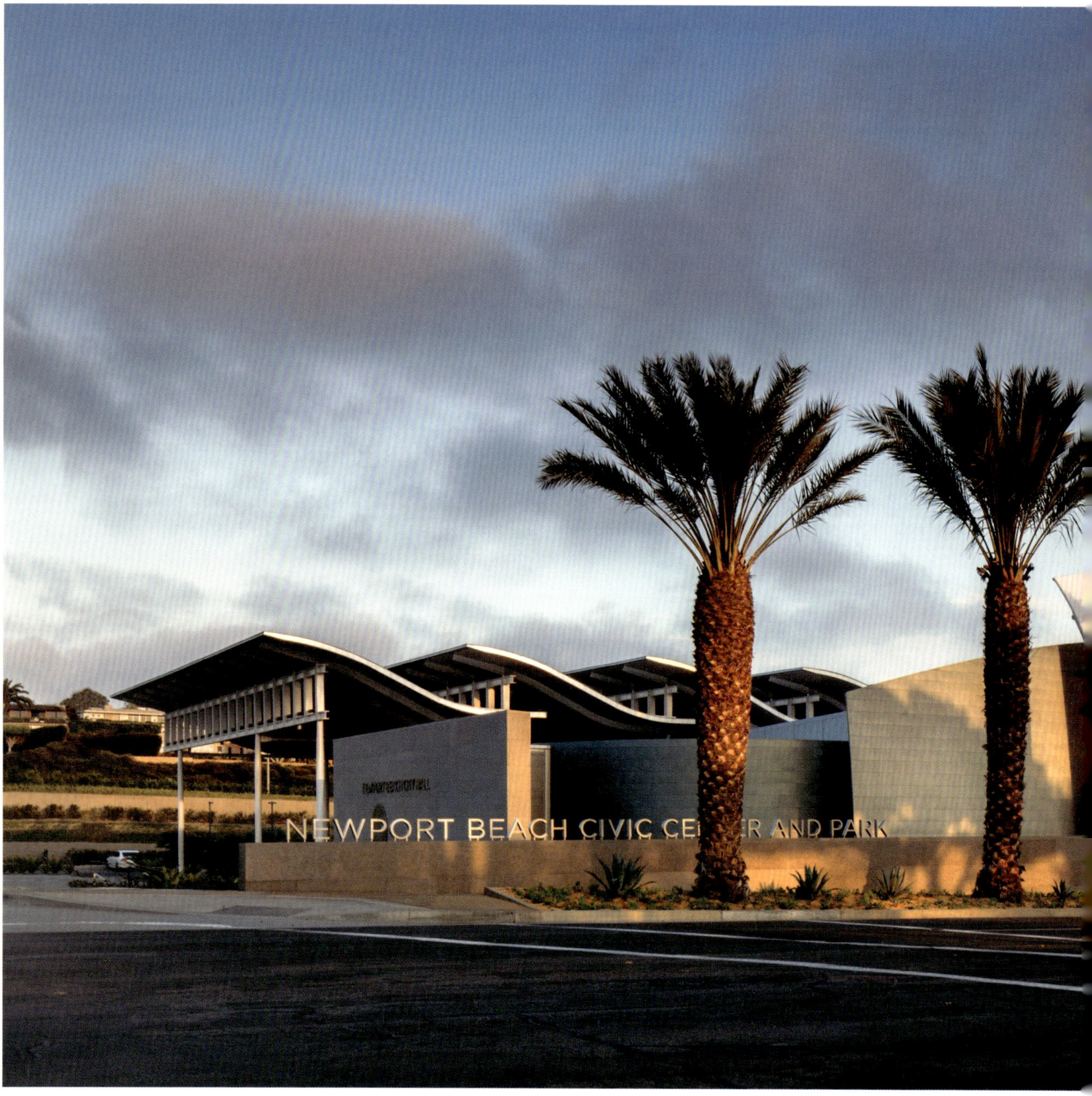

Newport Beach Civic Center and Park

Landscape and architecture have been joined to create an integrated civic center and park experience. Roof forms connect the council chamber and city hall, creating outdoor spaces for large and small events.

Newport Beach Civic Center and Park

The council chamber uses controlled daylight to enliven the space. A sail-like form helps to soften the quality of light, as well as mitigate glare and heat gain.

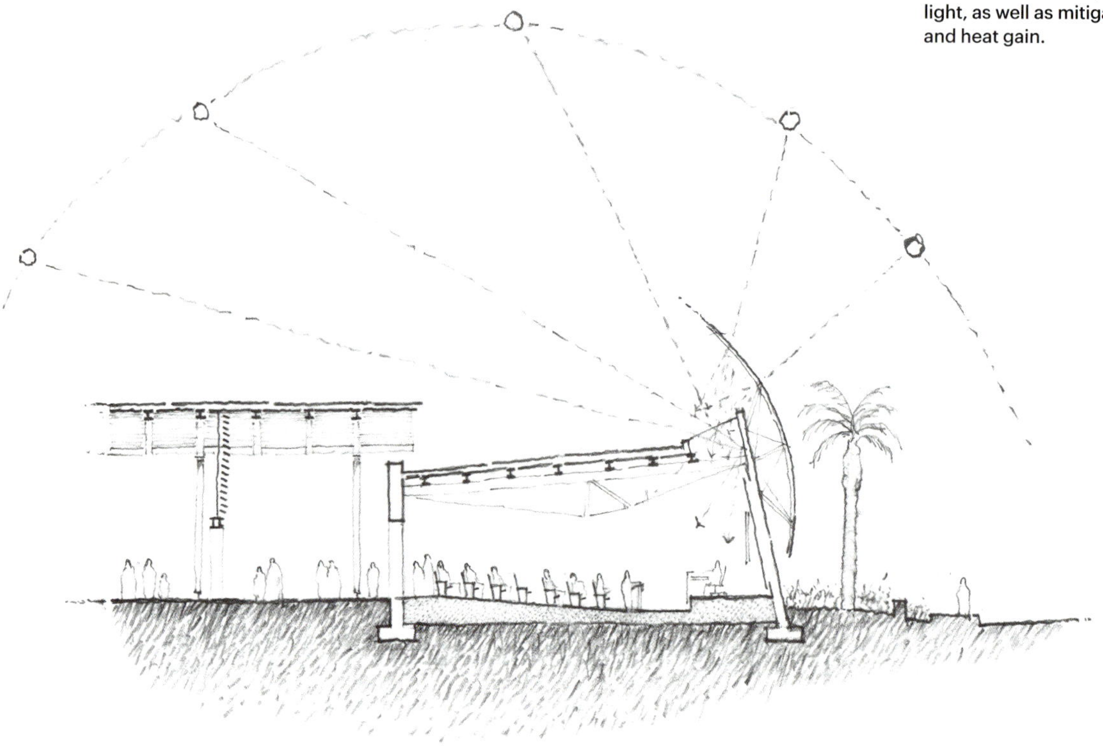

The Civic Center's community room hosts city events and is available to the public. Overhangs and generous openings connect to the outdoors and civic green.

Newport Beach Civic Center and Park

City Hall itself is a glazed bar—symbolic of increased government transparency—open to natural light and covered by a wave-like, trellised canopy inspired by the area's connection to the ocean. The raised covering pulls in natural ventilation, perfect for ocean breezes. It also creates large outdoor porches, while its lines of steel louvers protect the glassy walls from excess sun.

Open, daylit offices transform what had been a constricted, muted workplace into a light-filled model of productivity. Offices flow into one another, and interaction is facilitated by break-out rooms, connective spines, and outdoor meeting zones.

The form and expression of the City Hall, including the roof and building orientation, are directly generated from sustainable strategies.

The building is organized in sixty-foot bays, stepping down at the cores in between, in order to maximize height while accommodating the slope of the site and the city's view plane restrictions.

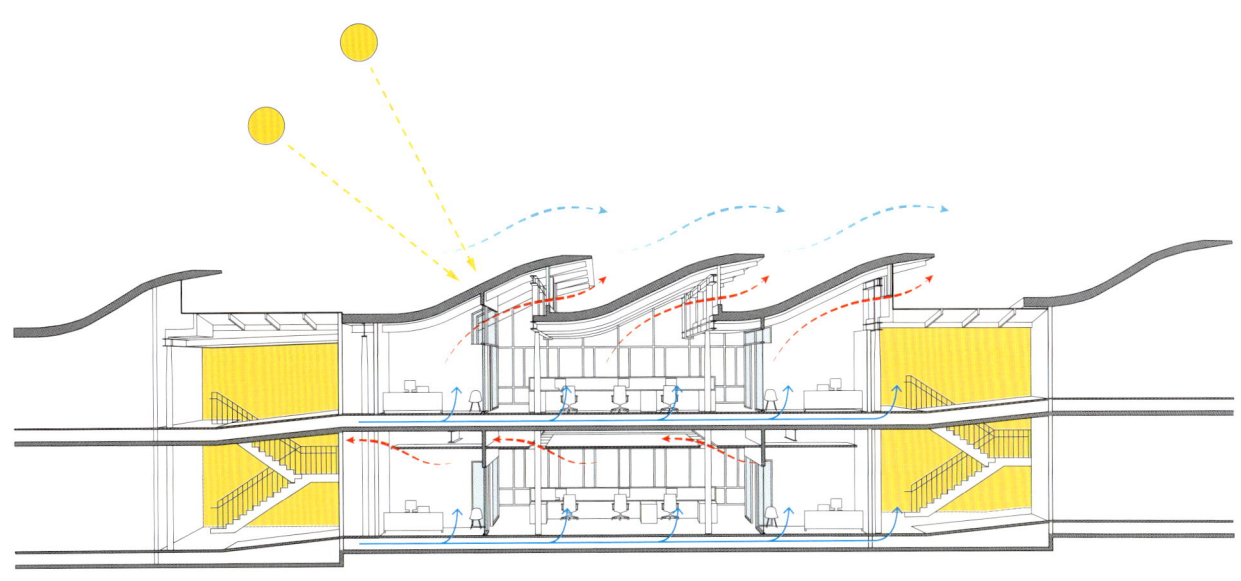

Newport Beach Civic Center and Park

"I always hear comments about how I just met someone new today. When you're working in separate buildings you never meet each other," notes Steve Badum, former Newport Beach Assistant City Manager. "The whole idea of good office design is making it so you don't think about it. It's automatic. You can just focus on the work," he adds.

Each city department has its own bay, connected on the east side of the building with clear and open public circulation. On the west side, the departments are connected with a private circulation path that unifies all departments.

0   25   50   100

The spaces fundamentally alter how citizens and city workers interact. Instead of the public coming to the city, the city comes to the public, through a series of elegant, custom designed service desks that seem more like concierges at a hotel than intimidating bureaucratic counters. Often citizens and city employees work side by side, figuring out problems together, not in opposition.

Such changes on all levels have fundamentally altered how the city operates, notes Badum, and have finally given Newport Beach the center it never had.

The library addition defines the southern end of the civic green. Outside, a new raised entrance with a cantilevered roof doubles as a stage for events.

Inside, a new stair knits the existing library to the addition and the green beyond.

Extending northeast from City Hall, the new civic park provides a loop of picnic areas, walking trails, public art, a dog park, and active spaces. Three sculptural bridges—two elevated over natural barriers, and another spanning several lanes of traffic and cantilevering bravely toward the Pacific—help unify the park.

"We're all really proud of what we created," Badum says. "It has changed the face of the city. Newport was always a place people wanted to live and work, but now it truly has a civic center where the community can come together."

The Civic Center Park features a restored wetland that includes a mixture of native and drought tolerant species that offer significant savings in water use.

Three new bridges, one designed as a bird blind, allow visitors to engage this wetland as they move through the park.

Newport Beach Civic Center and Park

Nu Skin
Innovation Center

Nu Skin Enterprises, a beauty and wellness-focused company based in Provo, Utah, found themselves at a crossroads when they hit twenty-five. Growing quickly, they wanted to expand, but hoped, more than that, to reflect their ethos of openness, collaboration, and innovation. They couldn't see themselves achieving this goal in their mirrored glass headquarters, which was relatively cloistered inside and opaque to the street outside.

After acquiring land adjacent to their building, the company engaged Bohlin Cywinski Jackson to create a luminous addition that would be a storyteller: sharing their message in physical form through contemporary, light-filled spaces, flowing organization, and a focus on accommodating large group gatherings, particularly for their network of worldwide distributors.

Location
Provo, Utah

Dates
2010–2013

Client
Nu Skin Enterprises

Size
168,000 SF

At ten stories, the existing Nu Skin building was an anomaly in the city. The addition to the campus had to skillfully expand the program while responding to the pedestrian scale and character of historic Center Street.

The existing headquarters building had several entrances and lacked a common experience for visitors and employees alike. The design team explored a variety of schemes that responded to issues of scale, security, visitor and employee experience, and flexibility for future expansion.

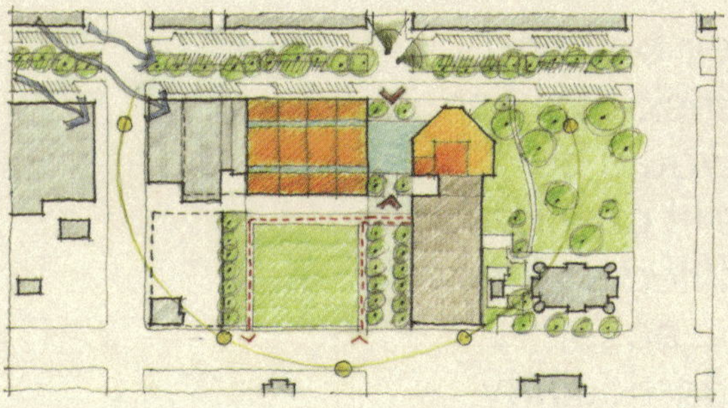

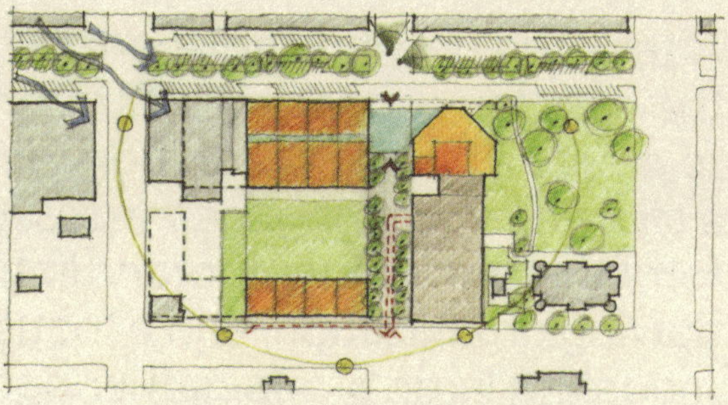

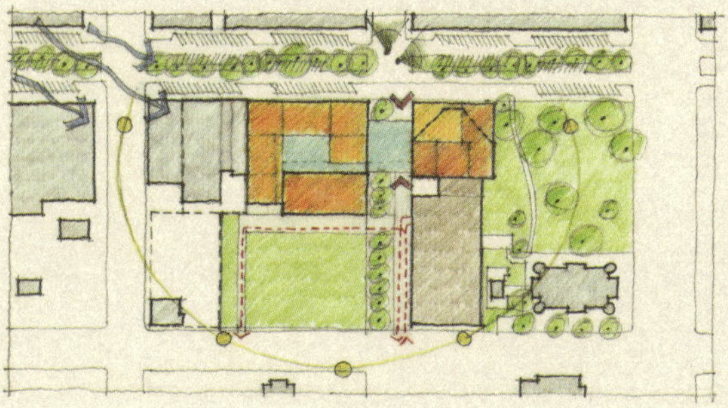

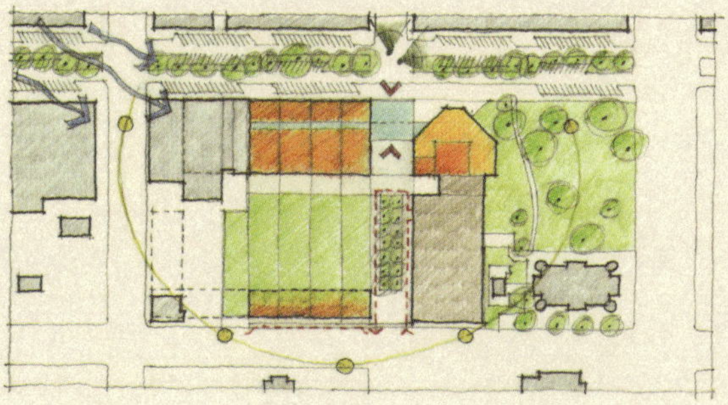

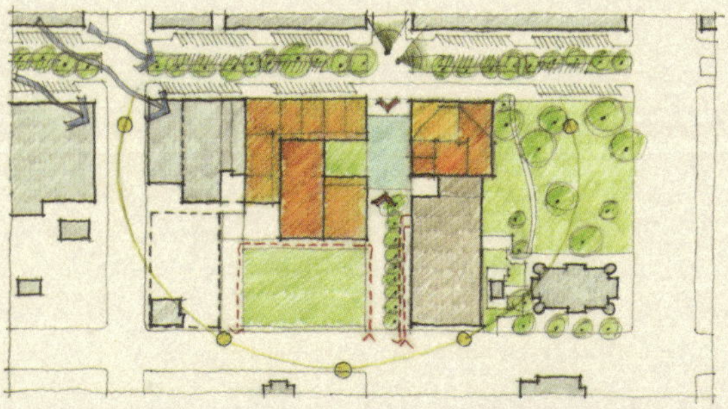

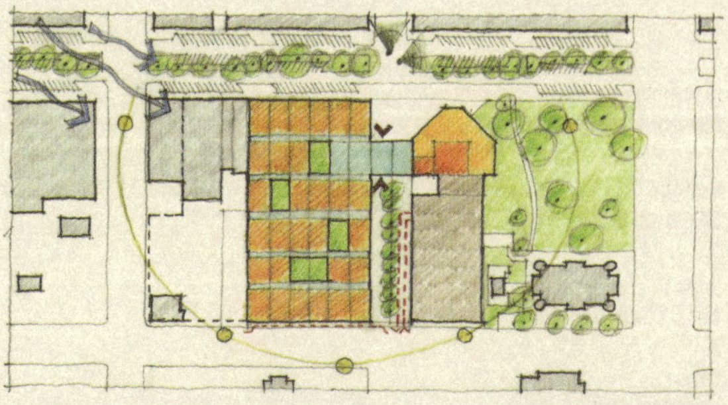

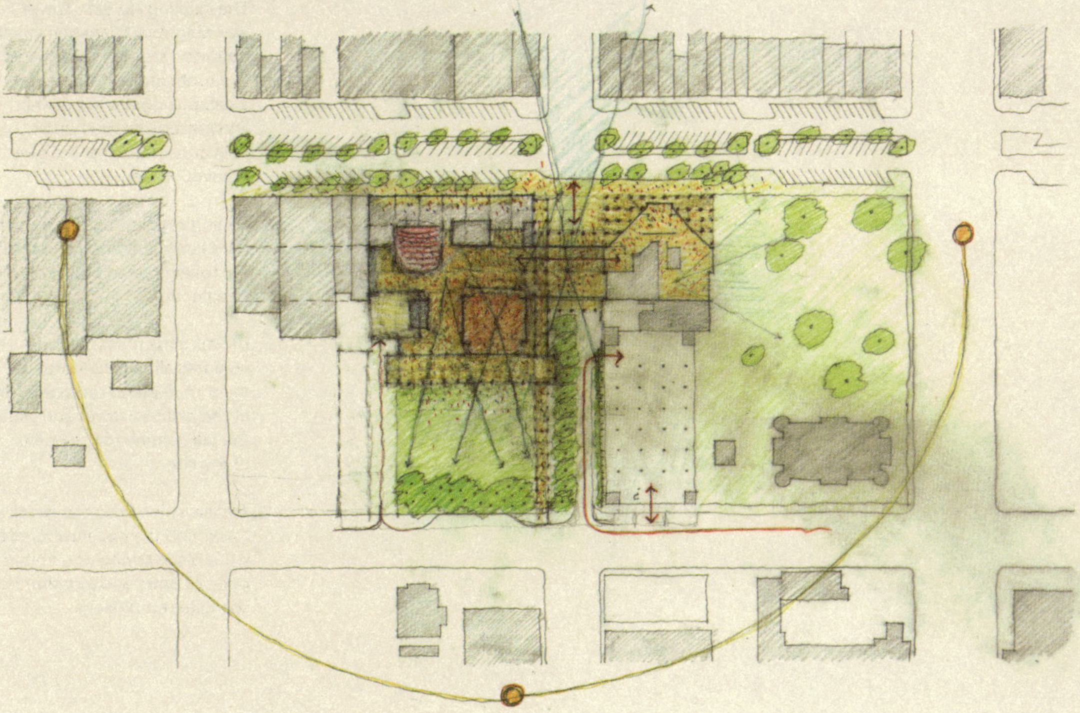

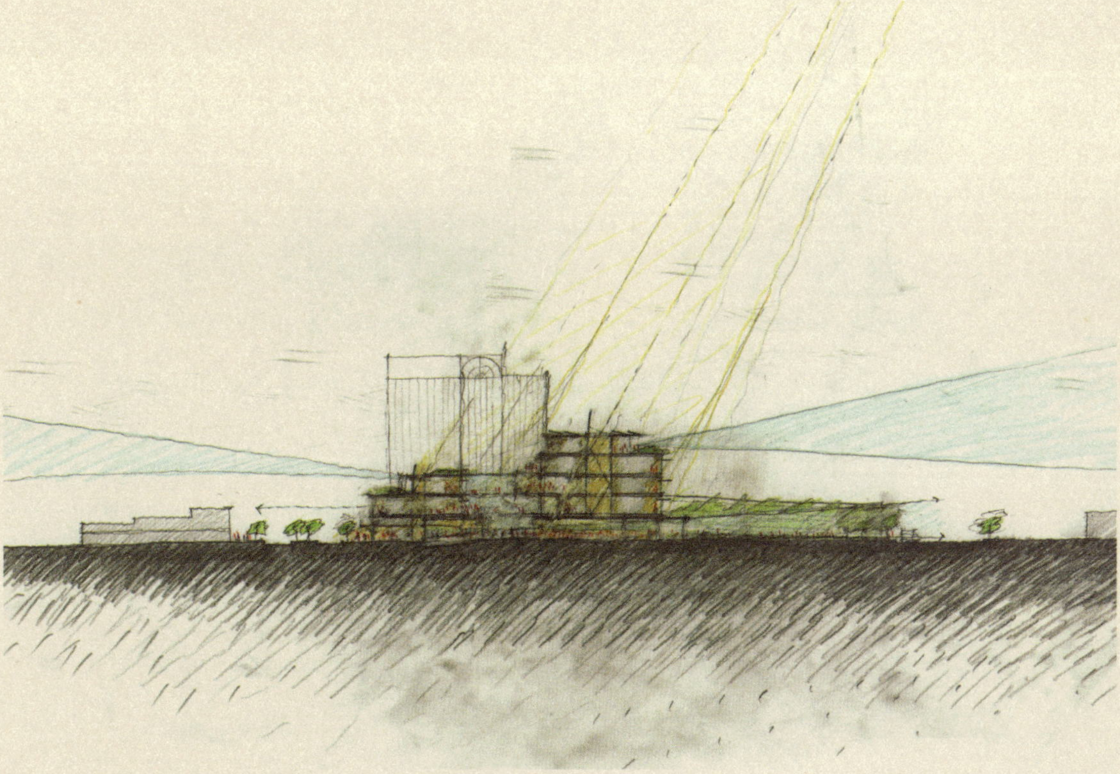

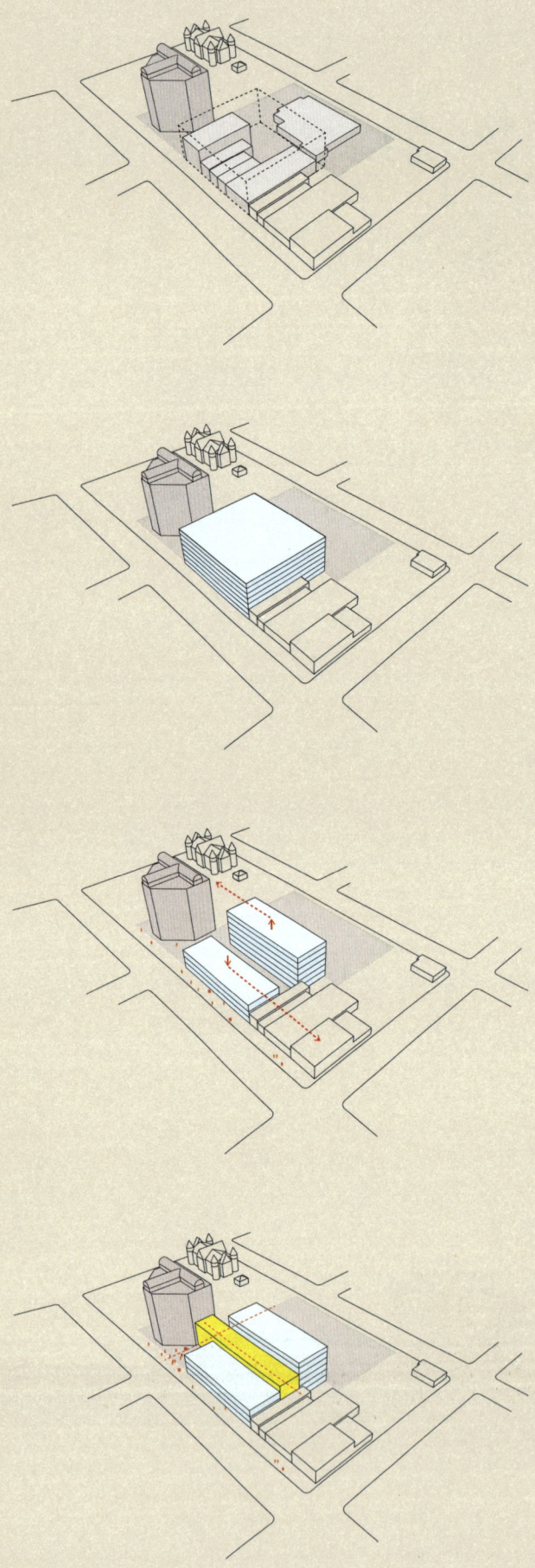

The existing Nu Skin Tower was neighbor to several smaller, outdated structures. Reserving the south area of the site for a campus green, the dashed line represents the buildable area on site for the new Innovation Center.

Zoning regulations allow for a six-story building, affecting the tower design but not the streetscape.

Dividing the mass into two volumes allows the north element to relate to the scale of the historic street and shifts the tall volume to the center of the site.

A glass spine joins the existing tower and the two new masses, while also serving as a united point of entry and a gathering space for employees.

A new campus green to the south of the Innovation Center provides employees with outdoor gathering space for everyday recreation, such as morning yoga, as well as programmed event uses.

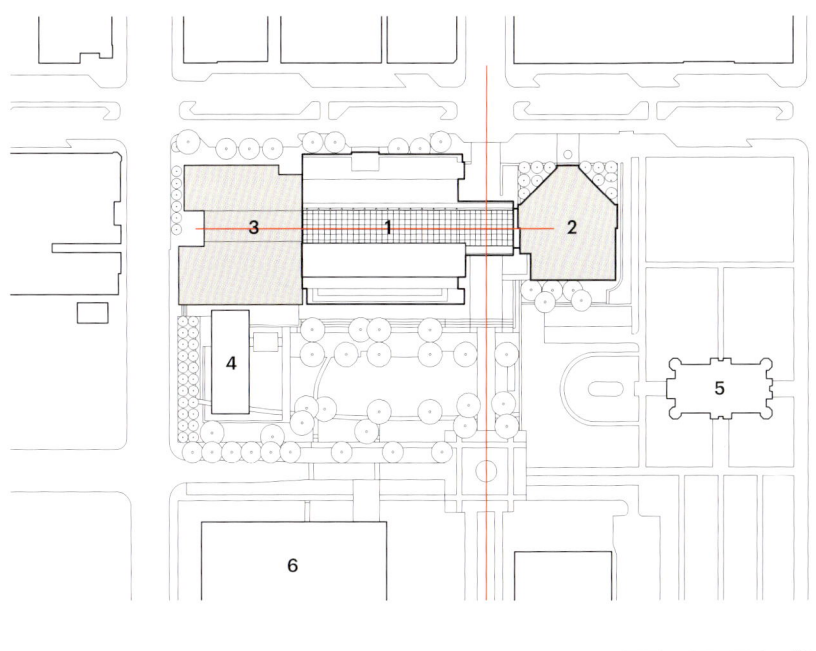

1 Innovation Center
2 Existing Nu Skin Tower
3 Future Development
4 Nu Skin Pavilion
5 Provo City Center Temple
6 Parking Structure

0 50 100   200

Nu Skin Innovation Center

The design team investigated several configurations for the addition, challenged by the idea of placing an ambitious amount of office space on Provo's historic Center Street. They chose to divide the facility in two, creating a smaller lab building on the street, fronted with shops and a café, and a larger building toward the center of the company's site hosting offices, a data center, public events, cafés, and multipurpose spaces.

First Floor Plan
1   Existing Nu Skin Tower
2   Entry/Reception
3   Retail
4   Atrium
5   500-seat Meeting Room
6   150-seat Auditorium
7   Café

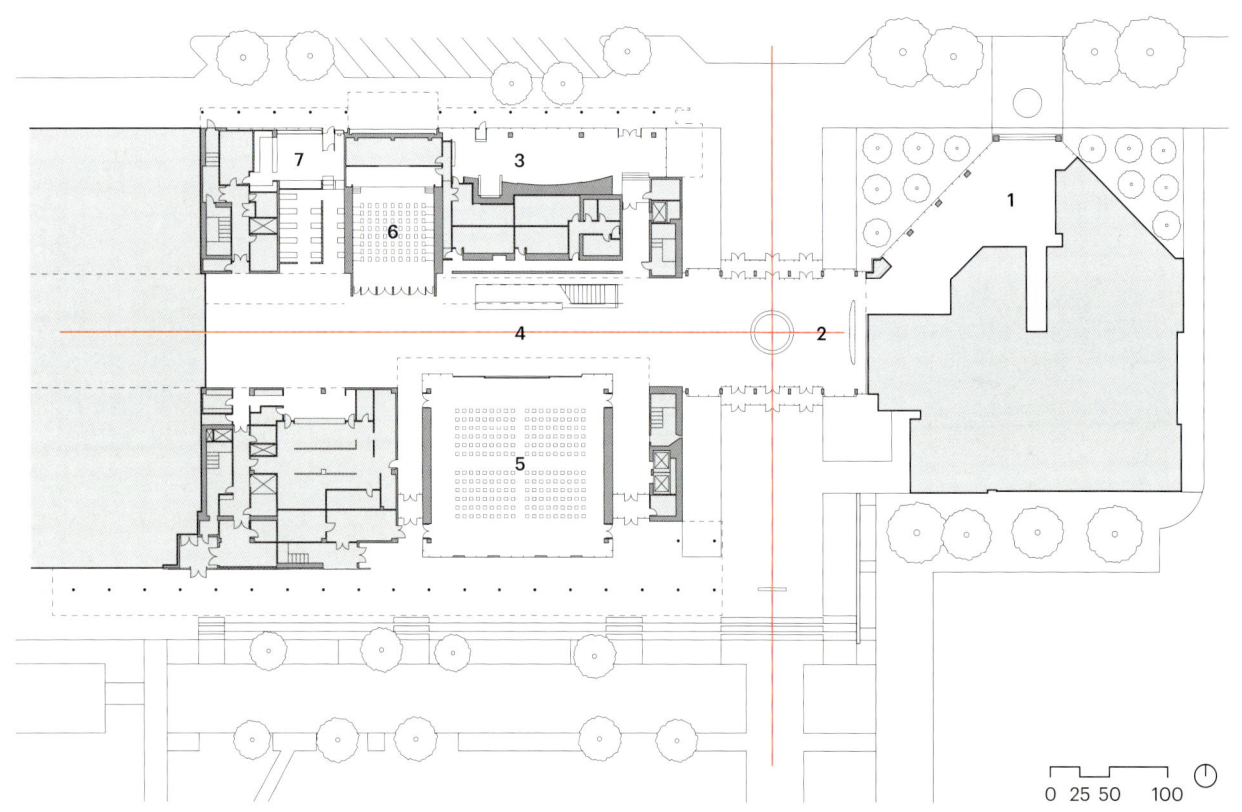

0   25 50   100

The atrium is an internal street that connects the diverse spaces of the Innovation Center. Bridges and cantilevered walkways connect the upper floors and the existing Nu Skin tower, encouraging more visible circulation.

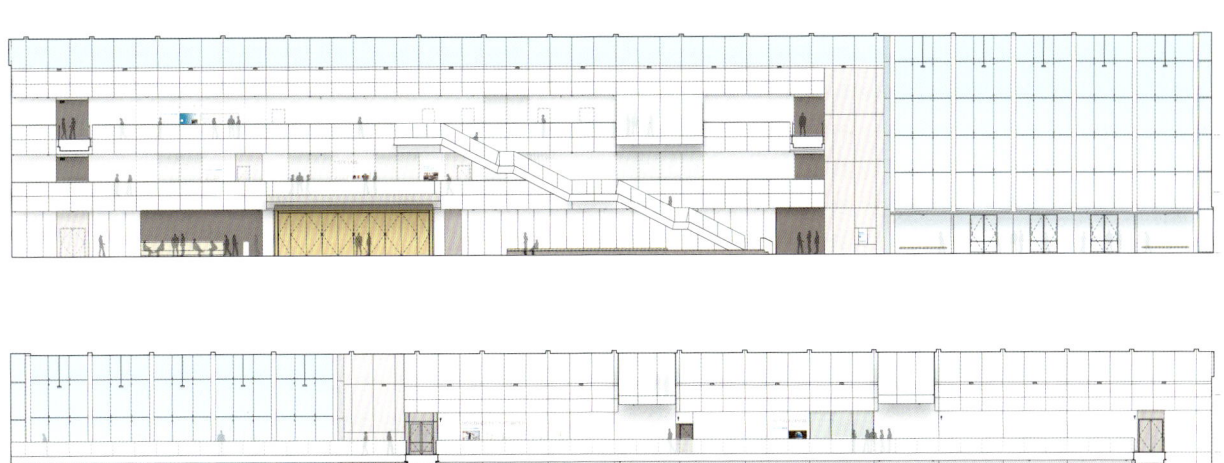

Nu Skin Innovation Center

Linked by a glazed entry hall to Nu Skin's existing structure, the Innovation Center has become the complex's new heart: a monumental, linear atrium forming a unified entry, an inspiring centerpiece and a natural congregation point. The clear glass and aluminum structure feels light, open, and buoyantly airy. Visitors' eyes immediately lift toward the barrel-shaped curve of its laminated glass panel ceiling. And its layered system of skylights and aluminum louvers modulate soft, ethereal light, which changes through the day.

The glowing glass ceiling of the atrium is achieved through a layered roof system of alternating skylights with exterior louvers and etch-matte glass panels suspended by a series of light steel trusses.

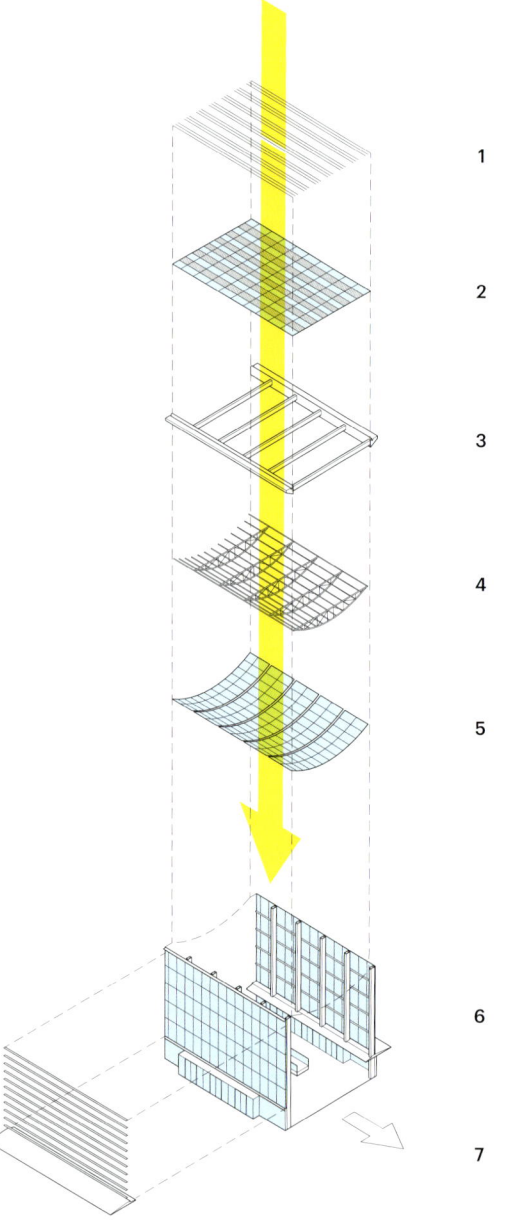

1   Roof Louvers
2   Skylights
    (vision and spandrel)
3   Structure
4   Ceiling and Structure
5   Glass "Cloud" Ceiling
6   Entry Atrium
7   To Existing Tower

The atrium connects multiple places of gathering—a ballroom, auditorium, and café—which when combined allow Nu Skin to flexibly accommodate all 1,200 employees in the same space for meetings and special events.

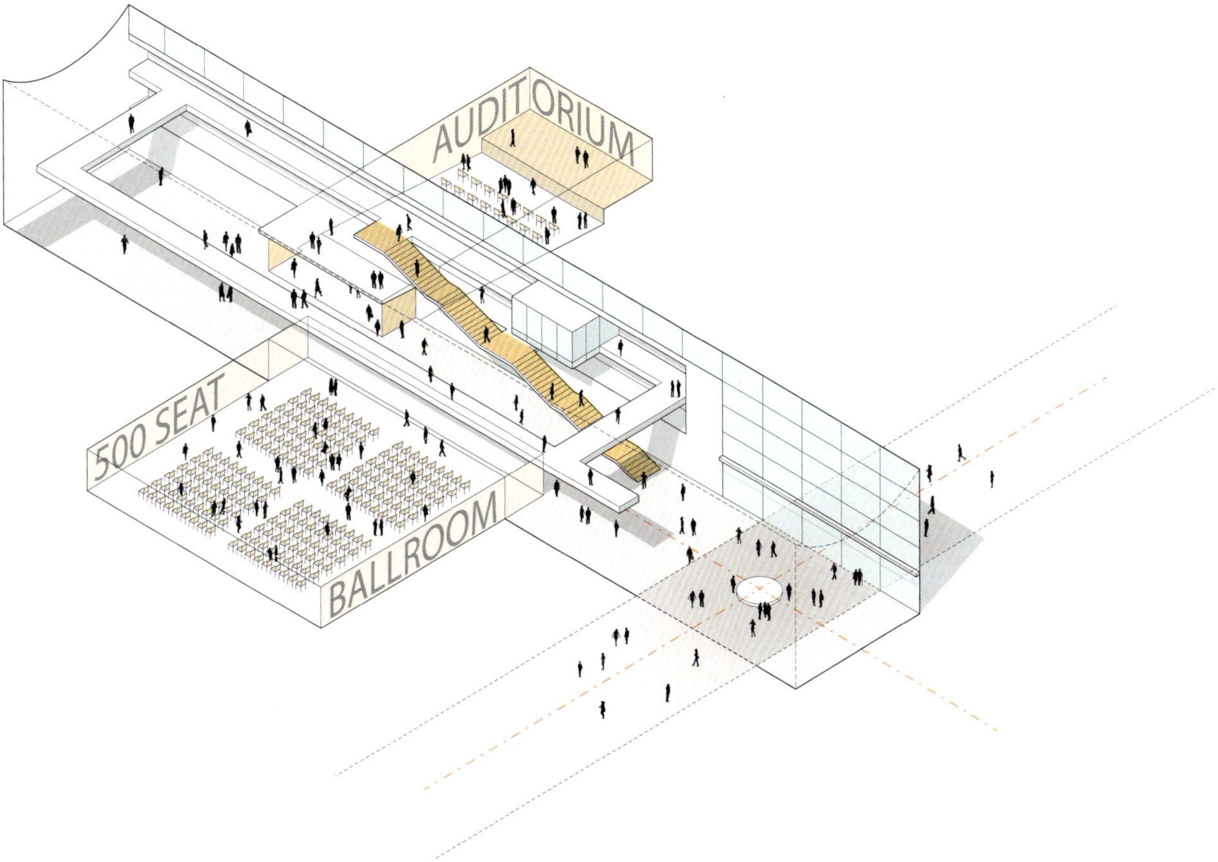

AUDITORIUM

500 SEAT

BALLROOM

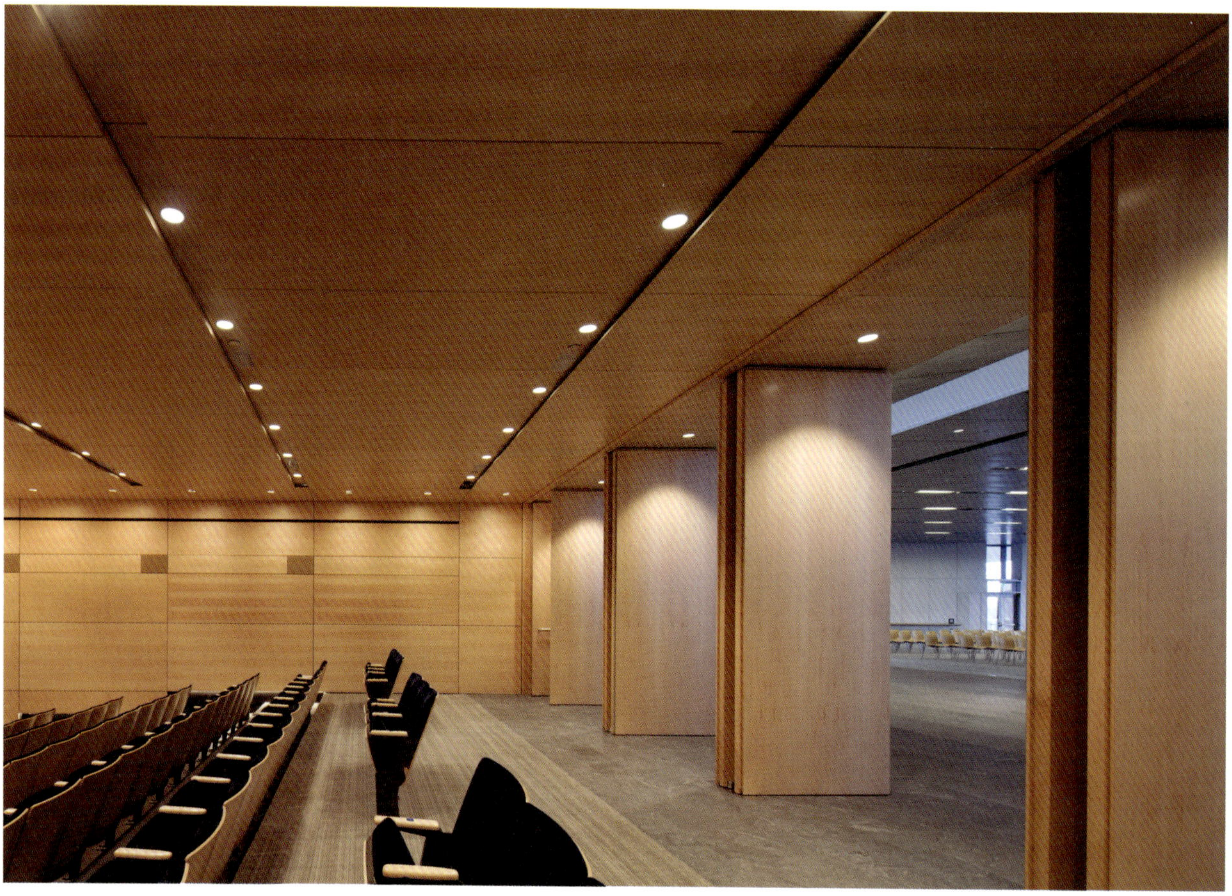

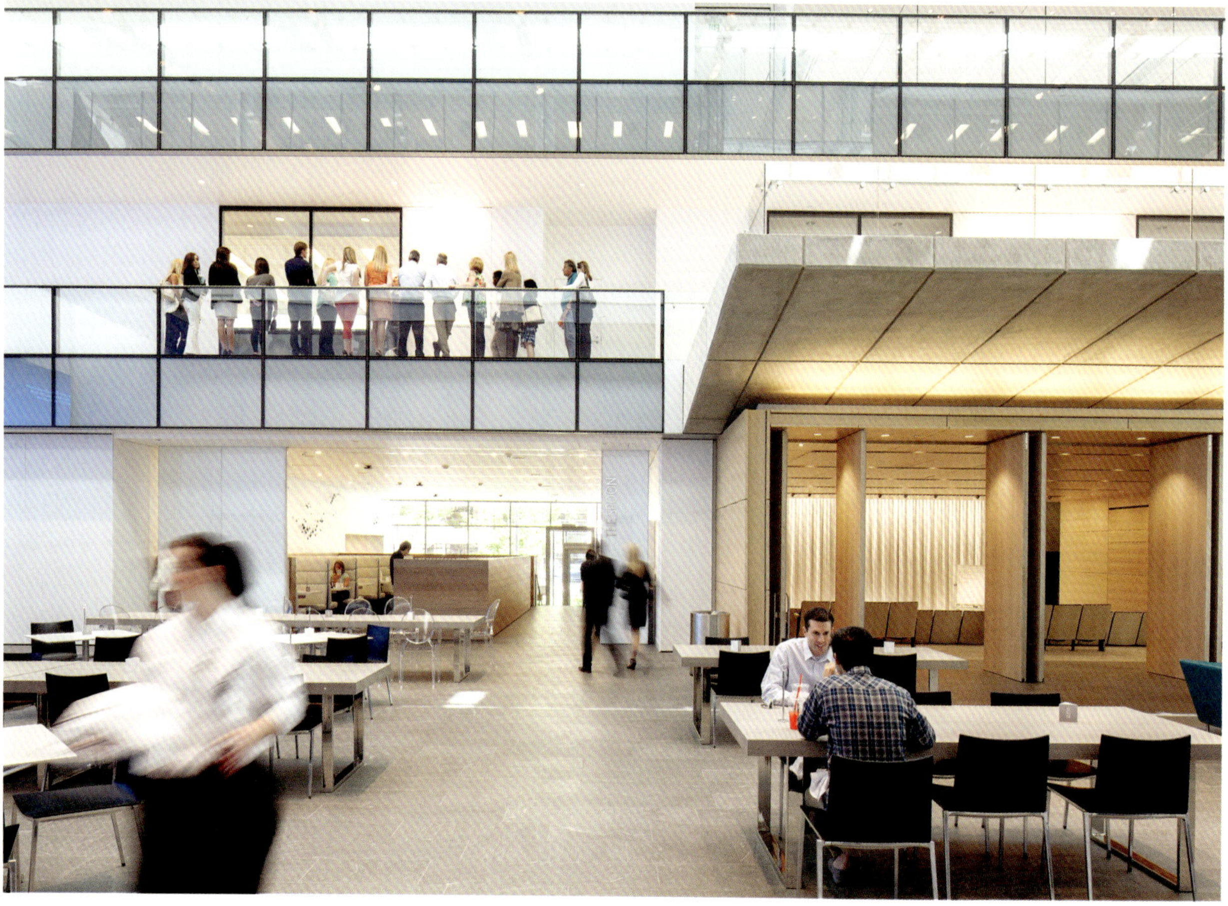

From the elegant stone floor, visitors can scan the diverse array of activities taking place inside, from retail and offices to conference rooms that literally pop out into the space. Employees seem to hover above on bridges and move between floors on the stairs. Innovative research, meetings, and administration are all clearly visible.

The atrium hosts, among many events, gatherings of Nu Skin's worldwide distributors, creating an enhanced sense of global community. Surrounding spaces—including the 500-seat ballroom, 150-seat theater and two cafés—work together as a conference center.

The arrangement of the atrium's first floor allows each of the gathering spaces to be used independently or together as a conference center.

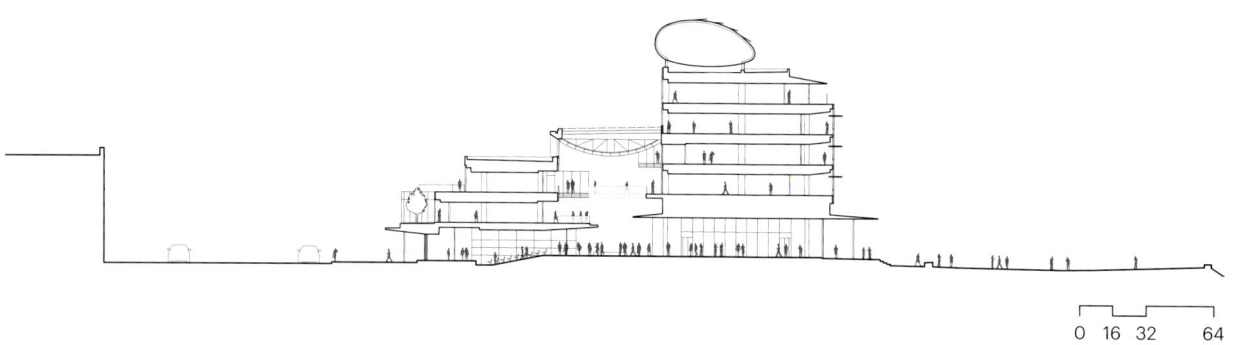

0 16 32   64

86

An airfoil-shaped, aluminum-clad form cantilevers above, enclosing mechanical systems and nodding to the barrel-shaped forms of Nu Skin's first building. The entry hall, fully glazed on its lateral sides and equipped with a curved and layered ceiling system, provides a single dramatic entry sequence and a secure checkpoint for people entering the campus.

To the south of the new buildings, the firm, along with Gustafson Guthrie Nichol (GGN) landscape architects, have created a broad green that hosts outdoor gatherings for Nu Skin and the city of Provo.

Each elevation of the Innovation Center responds to its particular solar orientation, with the south-facing offices and meeting rooms shielded by broad canopies and slender sunshades.

A suspended system of horizontal fins shades the interior of the entry atrium and provides a distinctive texture at the south entry.

Nu Skin Innovation Center

It's a lively, open, welcoming campus that has, notes Matthew Burke, former Nu Skin Director of Global Facilities, become a center of the Provo community and reinforced a tremendous change in the company's culture. "The shift has been a huge amount of pride and productivity," he says. "When you invest in great design, it's reflected in how the employees see themselves and the company."

Sawyer Library

Williams College, a private, liberal arts school nestled in the heart of the Berkshires, prides itself on its focus on student interaction and personalized learning. But its 1972 library, located on the northeast edge of Williams's eclectic, postcard-worthy campus, wasn't contributing to that mission. The cramped, bunker-like facility impeded access through campus, and did not foster a sense of forward-thinking, communal purpose.

After careful study, and several meetings with students and faculty, Bohlin Cywinski Jackson proposed to demolish the building, clearing the way for what has become a popular new quadrangle. The firm located the new Sawyer Library—filled with advanced, diverse, collaborative spaces—on the sloping site behind Stetson Hall, a red brick, Georgian Revival structure, anchoring the new quadrangle. Stetson was once Williams's main library and contains a renowned collection of rare books and artifacts.

Location
Williamstown, MA

Dates
2005–2009, 2011–2014

Client
Williams College

Size
45,500 GSF (Existing); 131,700 GSF (Addition)

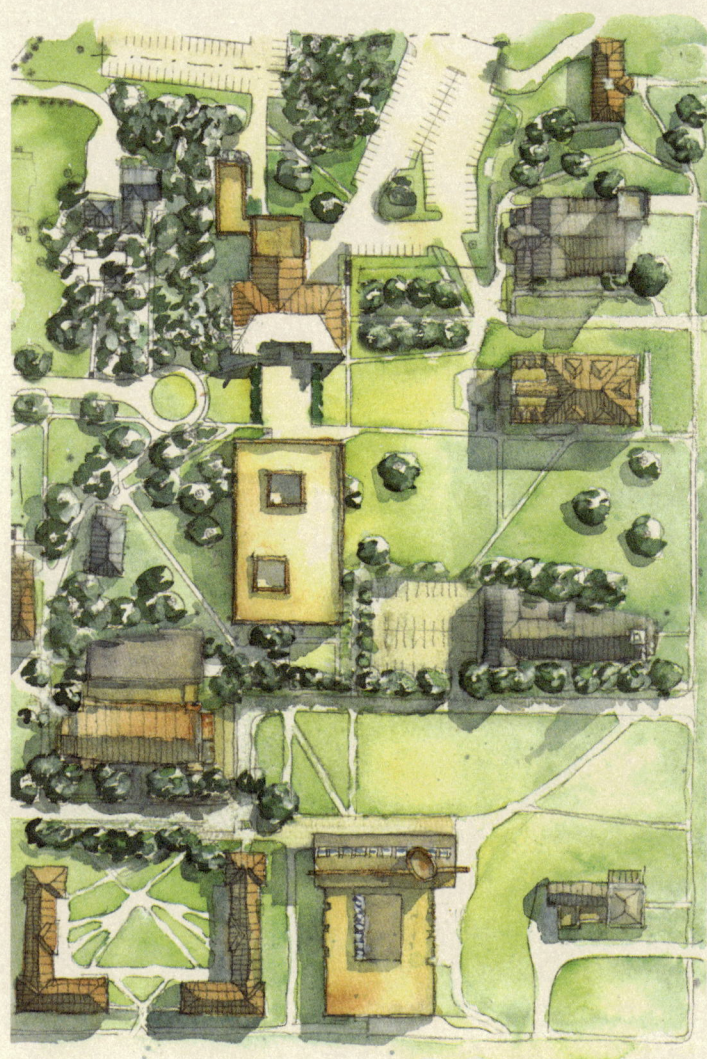

Campus sector plan "before": The large rectangular building in the center is the College's former 1970s library, surrounded on three sides by open lawn. Its east facade is aligned with Stetson Hall.

Designed by the nationally-celebrated architects, Cram and Ferguson, Stetson had been the Williams library since its construction in 1920. However, after 1975, it was downgraded to interim uses, including an awkward array of faculty offices and classrooms.

Before

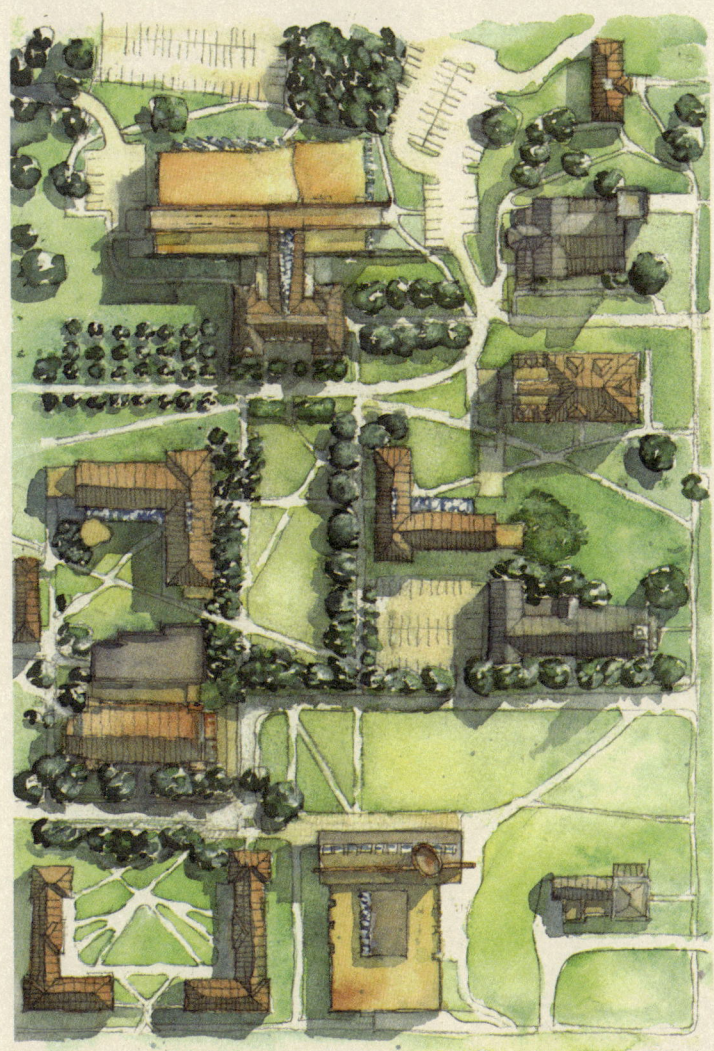

Campus sector plan "after": With the new Sawyer Library added to the east of Stetson Hall, the 1975 library was replaced by a new campus green. In an orchestrated sequence, two new Humanities and Social Sciences buildings were constructed, both designed by Bohlin Cywinski Jackson. Built first, they flank both sides of the new lawn and freed Stetson Hall for restoration and reuse. Stetson's historic facade now presides over the new quadrangle where it serves as the frontispiece for the new library. This master planning sequence allowed the existing library to remain in service until the completion of its replacement building. As a significant bonus, inverting the pattern of open and built space brought new focus to the campus landscape.

After

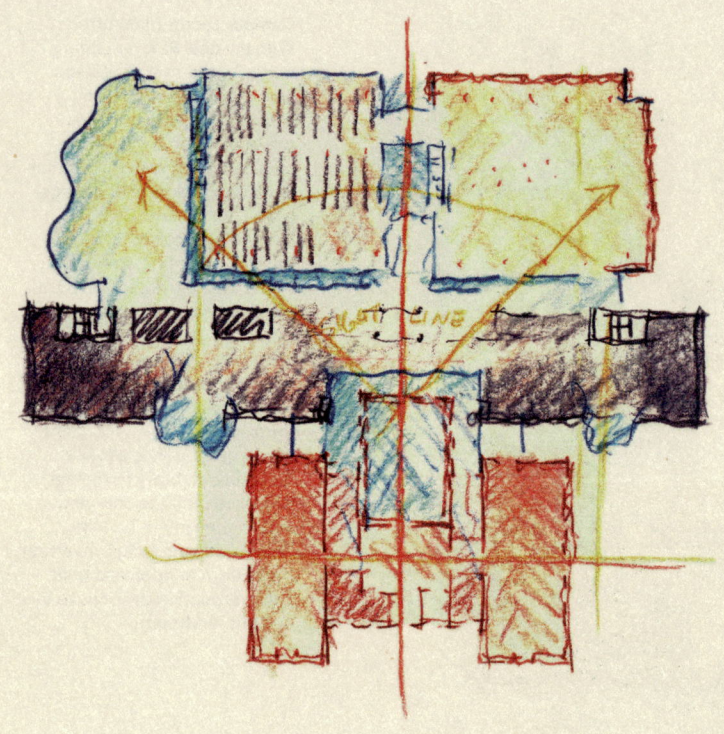

The library is an axial enfilade of formal, top-lit public spaces bisecting the building along Stetson Hall's center line. Starting at Stetson's foyer, the line progresses through the former bookstacks and the new building's services bar, before cascading into the heart of the complex. To the north, the Book Zone efficiently houses the library collections in a flexible semicompacted stack system. To the south, the People Zone provides the library's varied services—reference, information technology, and rare books—and an atmosphere of interaction and scholarly work.

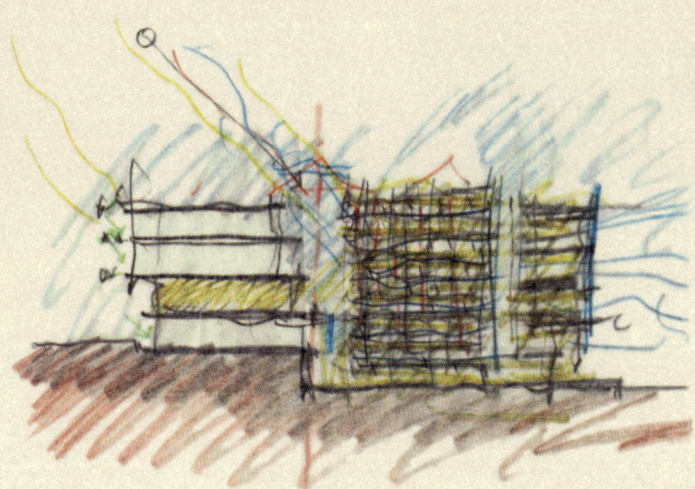

A classic 1920s library, old Stetson Hall operated on the closed stack principle, illustrated in this historic photo of the Delivery Room. Rather than browsing, the reader would select a book from the card catalogs that flank the desk and request it from the librarian. Just behind the desk, a pair of ornate doors connected to a large, vertical book vault. Here, the entire collection was housed in a nine-level matrix of cast iron shelving and marble catwalks. After retrieving a book from the vault, the librarian would deliver it to the reader at the desk.

The Delivery Room has been beautifully restored as the new library's foyer. The central desk and doors are replaced with a portal leading through the former book vault into the heart of the library.

Book Zone   People Zone

Entry Level Plan
1   Serrated Study Carrels
2   Study Area/
    Collection Expansion
3   Informal Reading
4   Reference Collection
5   Building Services
6   Reference Services
7   Library Services
8   Charge Desk
9   Teleconferencing
10 Restored Reading Room
11 Restored Seminar Room

0   15   30   60

Passing first through Stetson's softly lit, carefully restored lobby, visitors arrive at its former stacks, which have been replaced with a breathtakingly tall, glowing transitional space called the Stack Atrium. The old cast-iron and marble stacks have been repurposed into new flooring and display cases, and into the stair treads of the new library's main atrium.

That luminous, linear space, located beyond Stetson's preserved rear brick wall, is the focal point of the new complex; its angled skylights and transparent study spaces creating a distinct contrast to its historical neighbor. A steel-braced rear glass wall draws one toward its flood of light and breathtaking views of the area's wooded mountains and valleys.

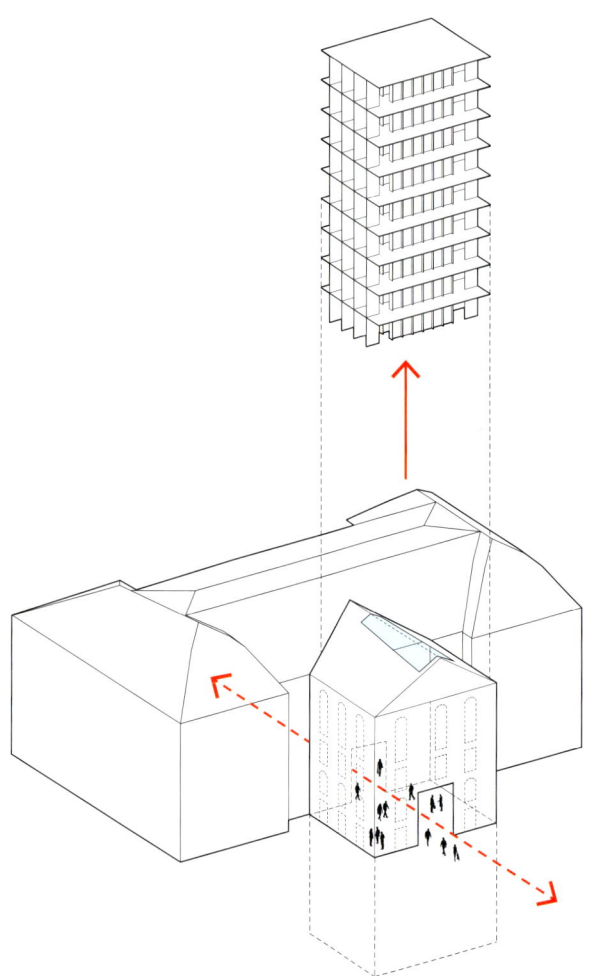

Stetson Hall's restored east facade provides a backdrop for the new library's central atrium. Its large, new portal links axially through the former book vault and delivery room back toward the main entry doors and out to the new quadrangle beyond.

A pair of glazed study balconies perch above the reference area along the building's central spine.

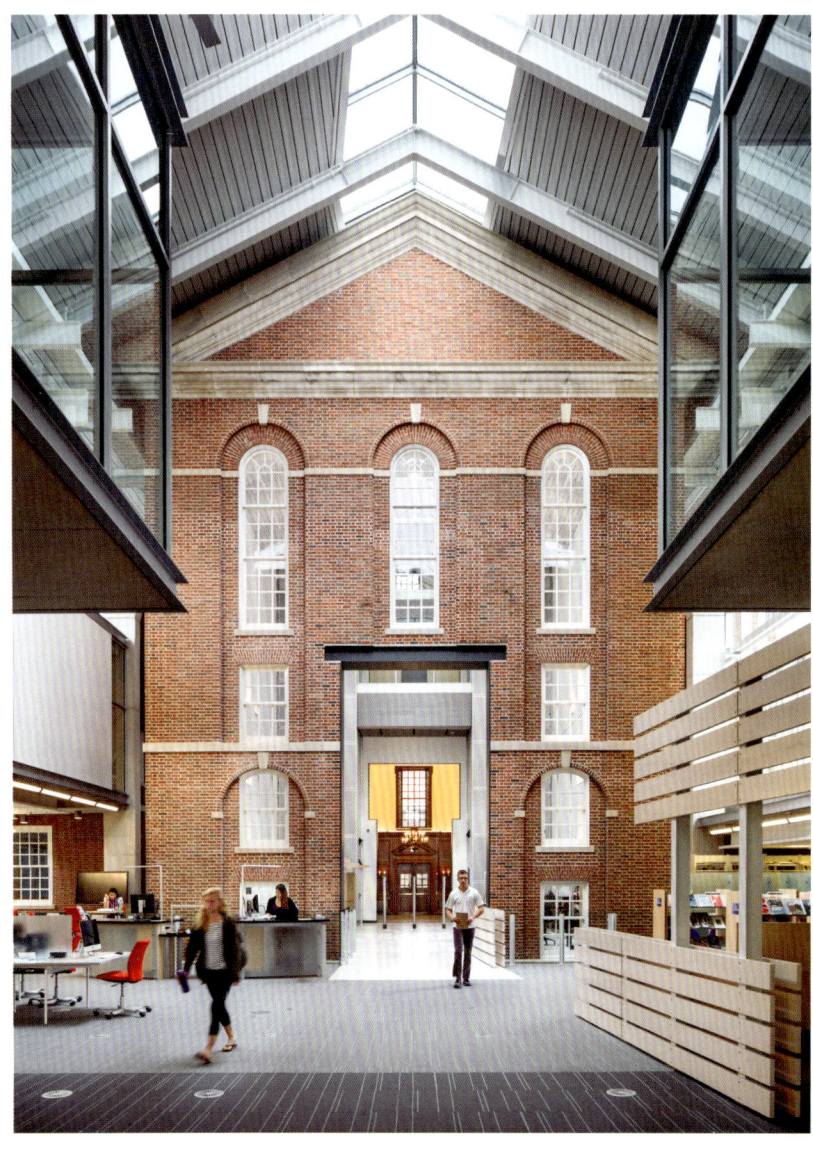

The soaring, five-level atrium is filled with warm, dappled illumination, conjuring up a feeling of liveliness. To one side of its central stair are staggered, sound-scattering baffles, to the other a snaking shell of light-reflecting boards. At most points a visitor can see through the building, getting a vivid sense of orientation and never feeling cramped or alienated. Sawyer's surrounding spaces are divided into distinct wings, connected via bridges that traverse the atrium: one for collaboration and one for collection.

Viewing east through the atrium, the Book Zone is on the left behind the curved wood light reflector. The People Zone is on the right.

Along the edges of the People Zone, a freeform wood shield houses services and study carrels while concealing the floor's thickness. An under-floor air distribution system, designed to promote comfort and flexibility, accounts for the Book Zone's more substantial floor depth.

View looking west, showing the café and green gathering space at the base of the atrium. The open bridge links the People Zone's Information Technology Center at the left with the Book Zone to the right. The central stair is cantilevered from the Book Zone's light reflector.

The upper level of the People Zone showcases Special Collections. Previously hidden within Stetson Hall, it now invites access to its contents.

Sawyer Library

A key finding of the firm's research was that students like to study in myriad ways, and in many locations. Thus Sawyer's exceptionally wide variety of volumes and experiences include enclosed conference rooms, tucked-away study edges, informal huddle areas, and wide-open lounges. Several study typologies were inspired by the most beloved aspects of the 1972 Library, including the climbable "monkey carrels," and half-buried "sunken carrels." Some zones look over the stacks themselves, while others—like the faceted wood carrels projecting toward the north—virtually leap into magical vistas.

"I think of it as building a diverse community of scholars," says David Pilachowski, Williams's former director of libraries. "Everybody finds a place where they are comfortable. Students just want to be in the building."

The building, coursing with innovative facilities like a 3D-printing makerspace, labs for creating content-rich scholarly work, and videoconferencing rooms, is also a pioneer: an early example of a university "learning commons." It's as much a focus for campus collaboration and socializing as it is for heads-down study. In fact, it's one of the liveliest places on campus.

Study opportunities are vertically stacked—mezzanine, raised booths, tables, and sunken carrels along the glass—to allow unencumbered views for all.

Cozy study nooks recall a beloved feature of the 1975 library.

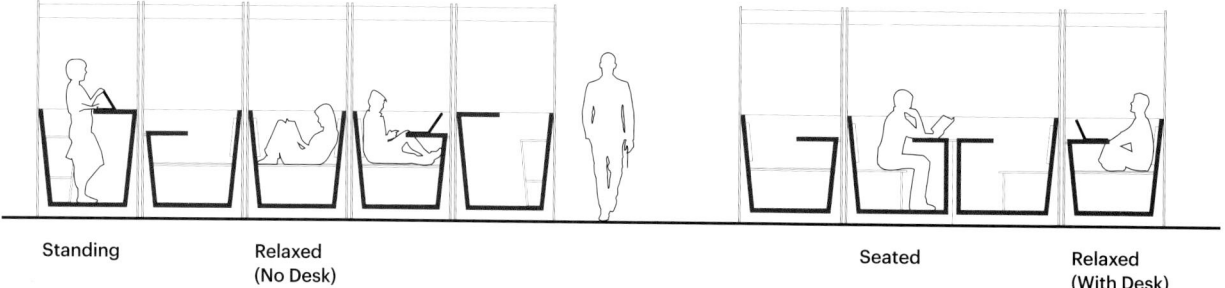

Standing
Relaxed (No Desk)
Seated
Relaxed (With Desk)

Sawyer Library

The east face of the Book Zone is an occupiable wall composed of serrated flippers. Each flipper houses a carrel, offering readers privacy, soft north light, and extraordinary views of the Berkshires. By orienting its glazing away from the east, the facade filters the morning sun, contributing to the light and thermal comfort quality of the interior.

While the west face of Sawyer showcases historic Stetson hall by tucking discretely behind it, the east facade offers an opportunity to express the library's most significant parts. Aided by the dramatic drop in grade, it creates a prominently-tall composition divided into three principle parts: the People Zone, the Book Zone, and the tall atrium marking the center line of Stetson Hall and its new quadrangle.

A detail of the facade's principle materials: glass, metal, and slate. Soft-greenish-gray slates from nearby Vermont harmonize with the green tones of the landscape.

The new facility has elevated academic scholarship on campus, enhanced collaboration, and become, without a doubt, the center of campus life. It has seen a 58 percent boost in visits (140,000 in its first year of operation) over the old facility.

"We believe that learning is more than just being in front of your computer. It's a social interaction. And for people to have a place to collaborate, to run into each other, to interact with resources, is central to what Williams is about," says Greg Avis, a Williams alumnus and former chairman of its Board of Trustees.

Square, Inc. Headquarters

By now we've all bought products with Square, a hardware and software suite that helps entrepreneurs easily process credit card payments. Bohlin Cywinski Jackson's design of the company's new San Francisco offices—necessitated by exponential growth—is as intuitive, clear, and usable as Square's products.

Located in what was previously a Bank of America data center, the 300,000-square-foot, four-floor office has been transformed into just the opposite: an open, light-filled, and flexible workspace whose massive floorplates are organized by patterns of circulation and connection inspired by some of the world's great urban spaces.

The firm bisected the structure's asymmetrical floorplans with central "boulevards," dotted with varied collaboration zones, like a library, galleries, cabanas, and a café. Edges are lined with diverse working spaces, including bench-style work desks, tables, conference rooms, and private and semiprivate cubbies. New windows were added along the perimeter, drawing much-needed natural light into the deep floor plates.

Location
San Francisco, CA

Dates
2012–2015

Client
Square, Inc.

Size
295,000 SF

The design ambitions were set against the backdrop of the project's challenging context: the modest budget of a startup company in the business of financial transactions, and a vast building within a converted Bank of America data center riddled with complex building infrastructure that needed to remain in place for the bank's dwindling, but continued, operations.

Square's primary office floors were originally windowless spaces designed for data processing supercomputers and check-sorting devices.

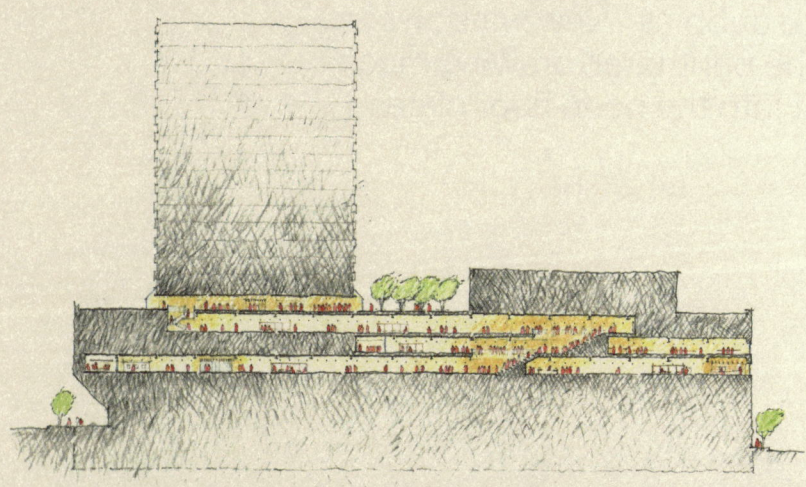

In order to break down the scale of the 100,000-square-foot floorplate, the design team looked for organizational strategies at an urban scale. Examples like the boulevard of Placa Street in Dubrovnik, the neighborhood parks of the Oglethorpe Plan in Savannah, and the circulation patterns of Louis Kahn's Traffic Study in Philadelphia, were particularly informative in creating definition between spaces and a clear hierarchy of circulation.

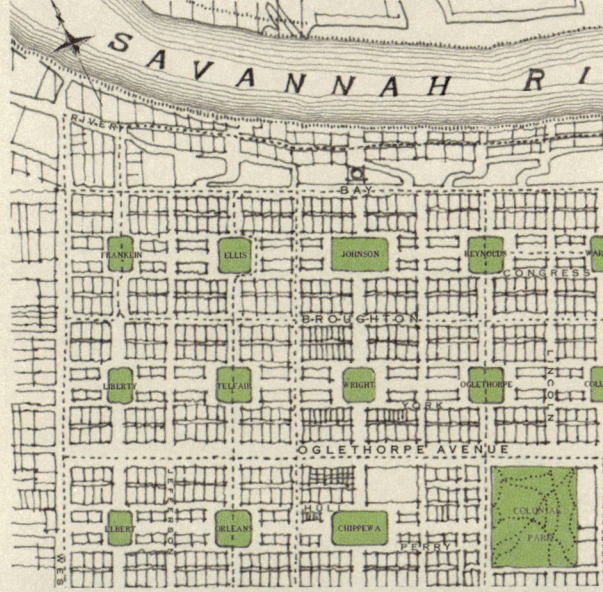

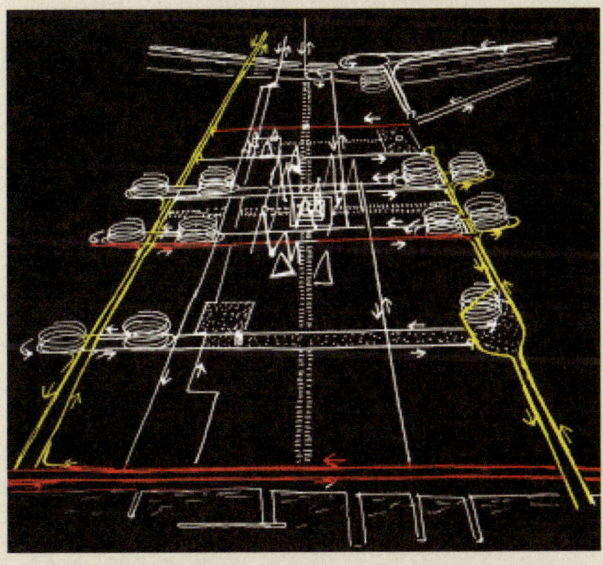

Square, Inc. Headquarters

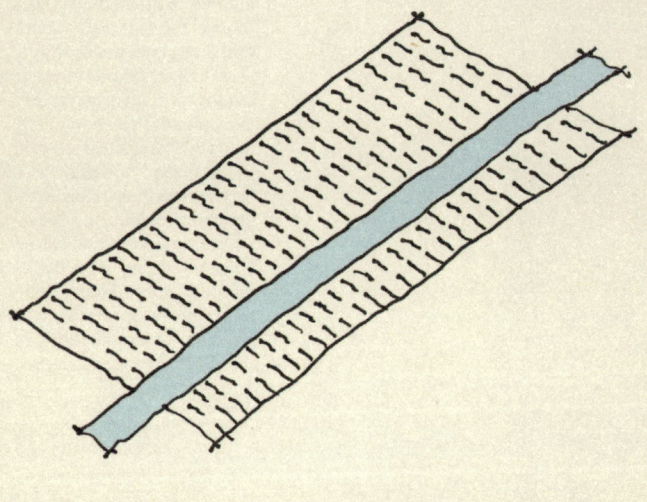

The boulevard is a dynamic thoroughfare punctuated with common amenities.

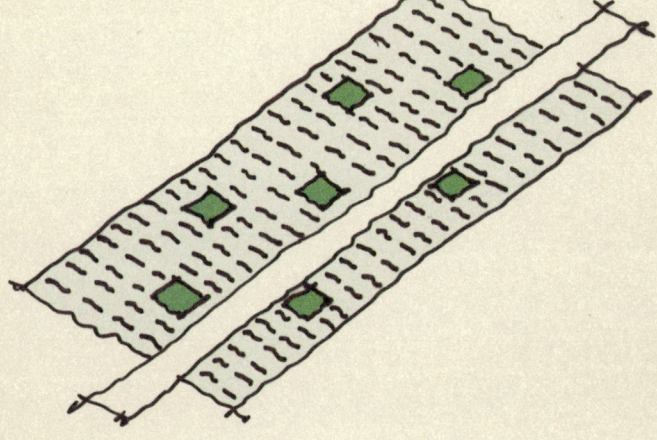

Team rooms break down the scale of the floor plate and define "neighborhoods."

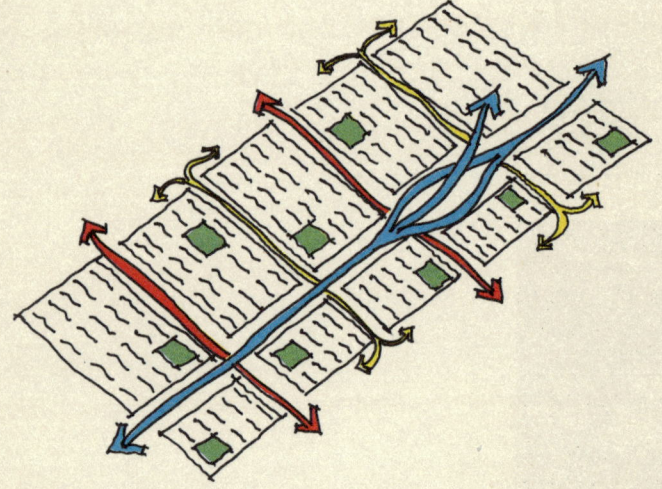

A hierarchy of circulation creates clear paths through the floor plates.

Unifying the office floors is a sizable amphitheater stair, providing a perfect setting for group meetings and large presentations. Connecting three floors, the wood-clad flights, fitted with thin, lightweight tables, step their way down to create informal environments for work and relaxation. Employees regularly crowd the amphitheater, their legs dangling happily while they work away. Another office anchor is the Square Stair, a floating wood and glass switchback, adding warmth and texture to the office's white and gray palette while connecting the office floors to the main dining level.

Clean lines, simple materials, and pale hues reflect the brand's identity and lighten the mood, while felt surfaces, salvaged wood, and the occasional splash of intense color add variety, demarcate spaces, and reflect the locale. Bright orange, for instance, recalls the Golden Gate Bridge, while blue shades evoke the San Francisco Bay. They added to the sense of eclectic spontaneity by employing a variety of lighting techniques, including sharp recessed lines, glowing coves, simple spots, and sculptural accent pendants.

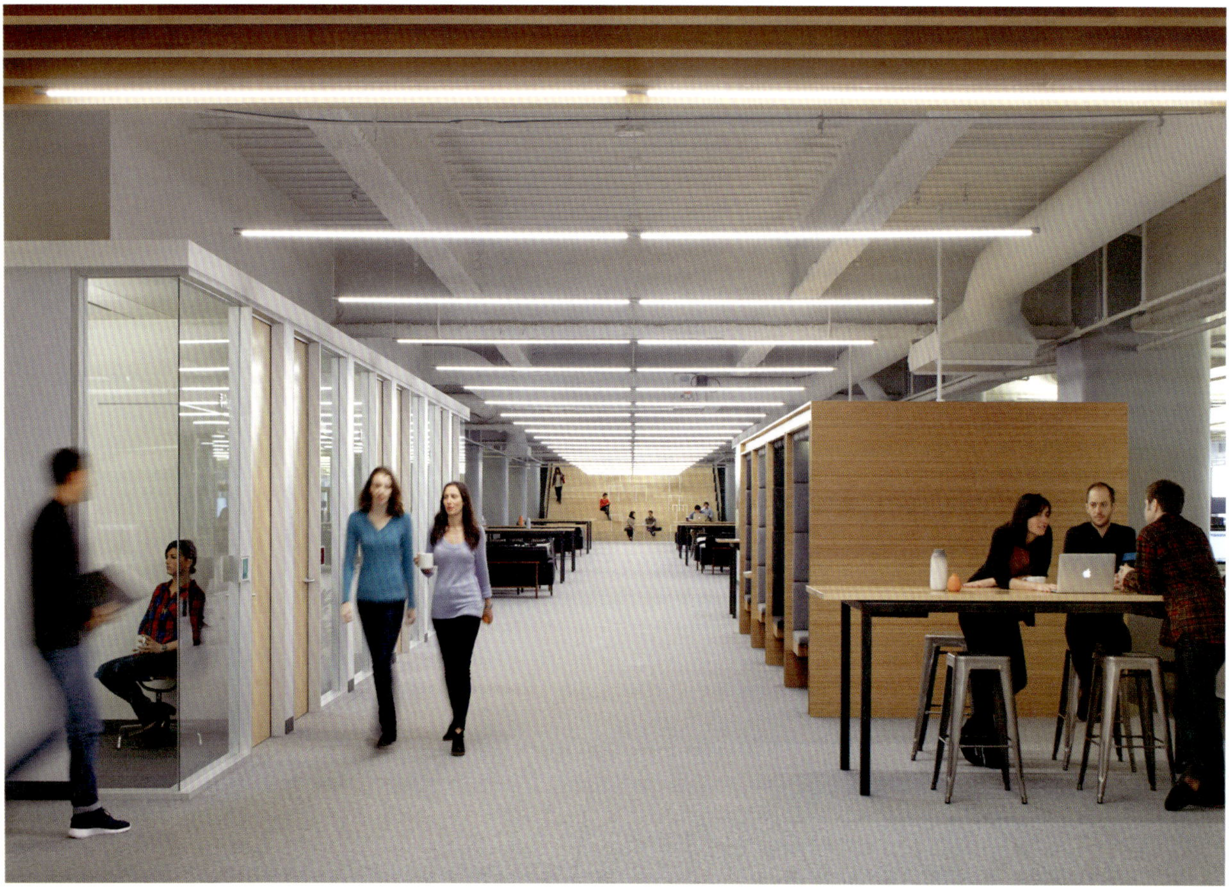

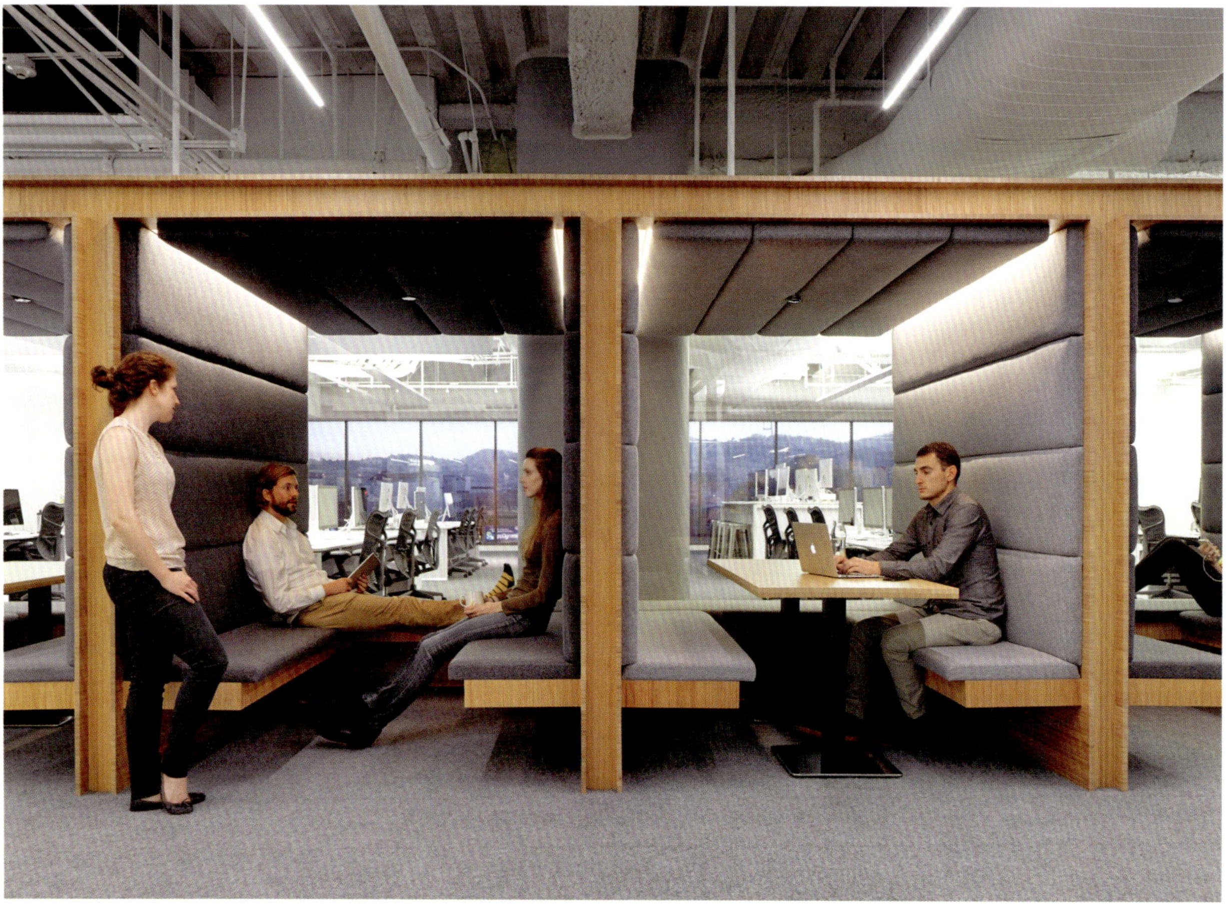

Sixth-Floor Plan
1   Reception
2   Boardroom
3   Gallery
4   Boulevard
5   Amphitheater Stair
6   Coffee Bar
7   Library
8   Team Room
9   Conference Room Bar

0   20   50   100

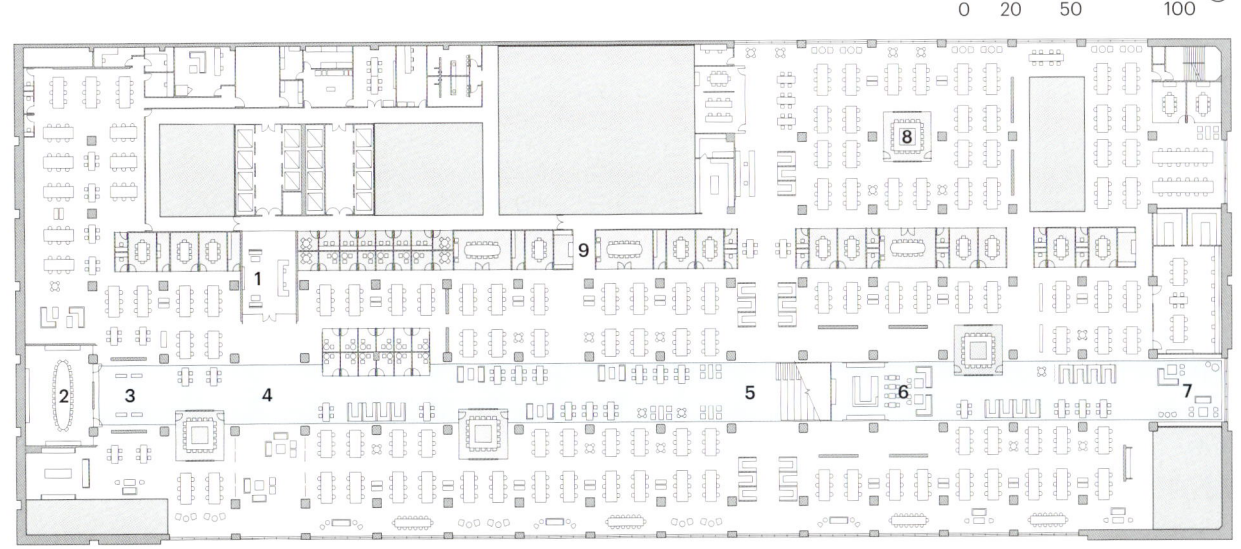

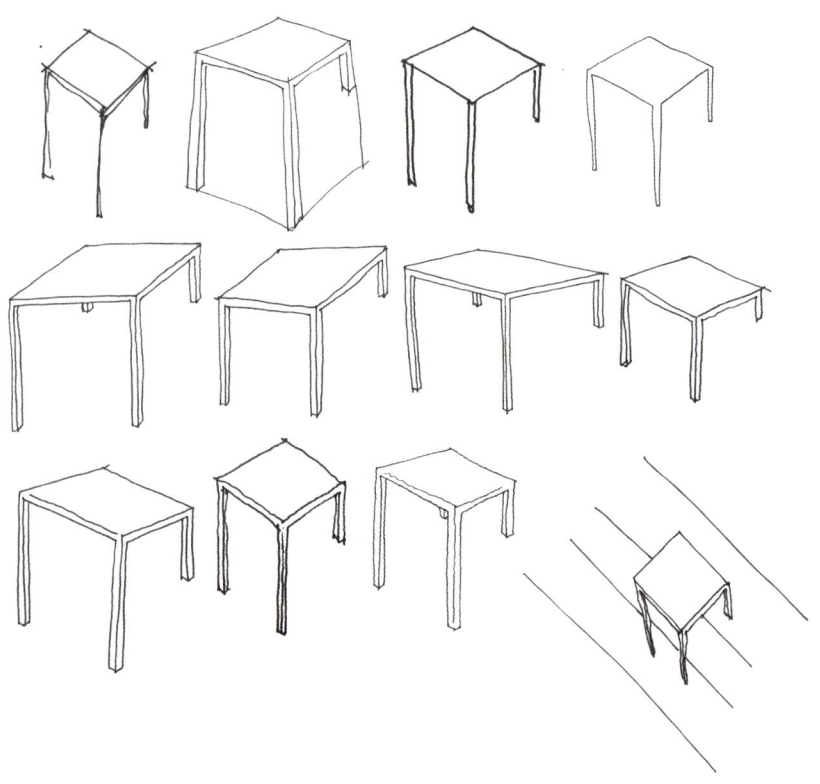

The Gazelle Table was cus-
tom-designed to support
a range of activities while also
providing a delicate sculptural
counterpoint to the grand gesture of the stair.

As Square continues to grow, the airy, collaborative, and flexible spaces will allow the company to expand and shift over time. Almost every move came from the team's steady tinkering and tweaking, adapting to challenges to make the space better.

Square, Inc. Headquarters

"Architects should make spaces where people can be themselves—to gather, to trade stories, and to create," says Square, Inc. Founder Jack Dorsey. "Bohlin Cywinski Jackson has been responsible for some of the best manifestations of that in the world, and we've been fortunate to feel it every day at Square."

The dining floor is connected to the office floors by an interior staircase anchored below an existing skylight. The seating area converts into the All-Hands space seating 1,400 employees.

Cherie Flores Garden Pavilion

Like so many public spaces in the United States, the northeast edge of Houston's Hermann Park had long been a victim of ad hoc, automobile-centered design. Dominated by an aging, Colonial-style garden club and a semicircular asphalt parking lot, the complex needed restoration and rethinking.

The Hermann Park Conservancy—set to celebrate the park's centennial and upgrade its last untouched parcel—commissioned Bohlin Cywinski Jackson to create the new Cherie Flores Garden Pavilion and McGovern Centennial Gardens. In the process, the firm crafted not just a daring new entryway filled with meeting and support spaces, but also a memorable new visitor experience, building on a master plan by Olin Partnership and a new landscape by Hoerr Schaudt.

Location
Houston, TX

Dates
2012–2014

Client
Hermann Park Conservancy

Size
7,000 SF

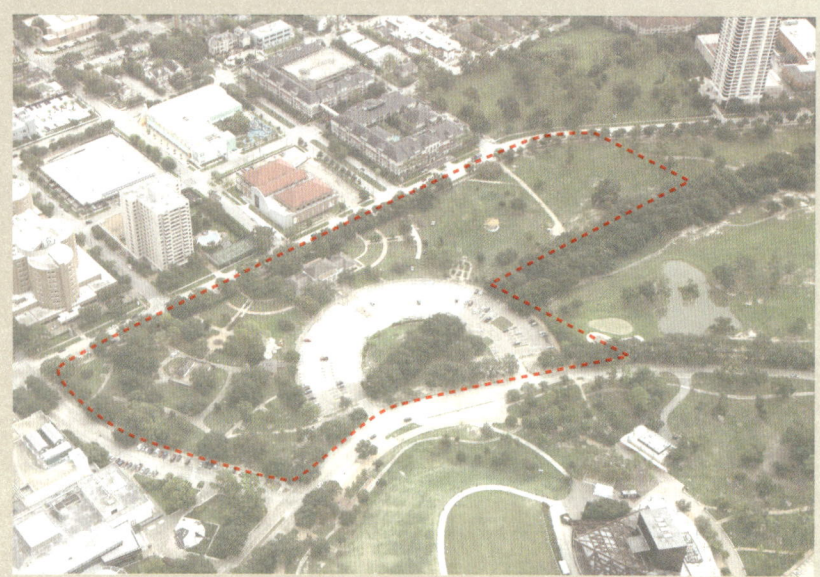

The fifteen-acre site dedicated to the new Garden and Pavilion is bordered by the Museum of Natural Science, Miller Outdoor Theater, and a public golf course. The existing entry to this portion of the Park created a bottleneck due to the layout of the parking lot, specifically in regard to pick-up/drop-off.

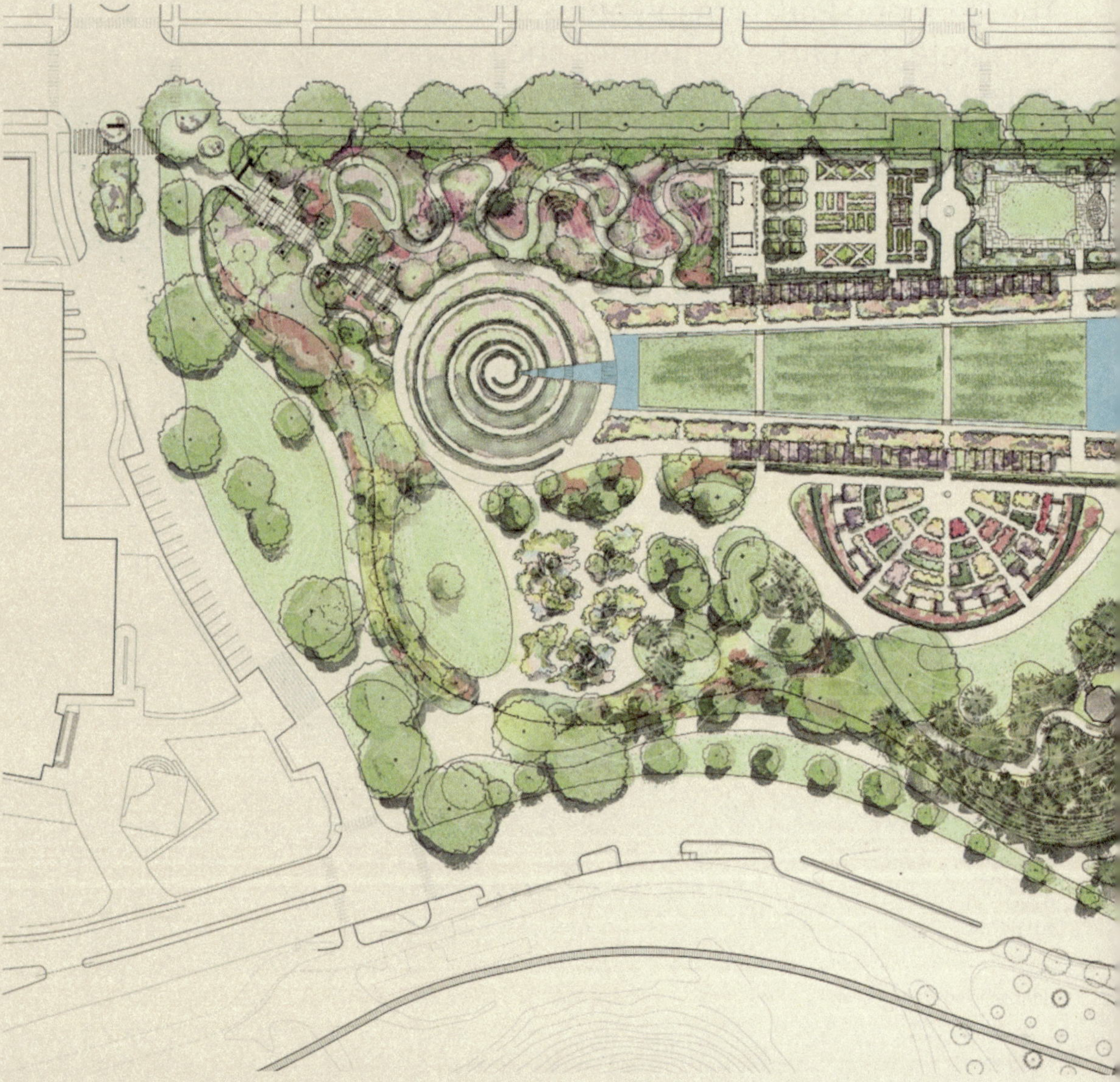

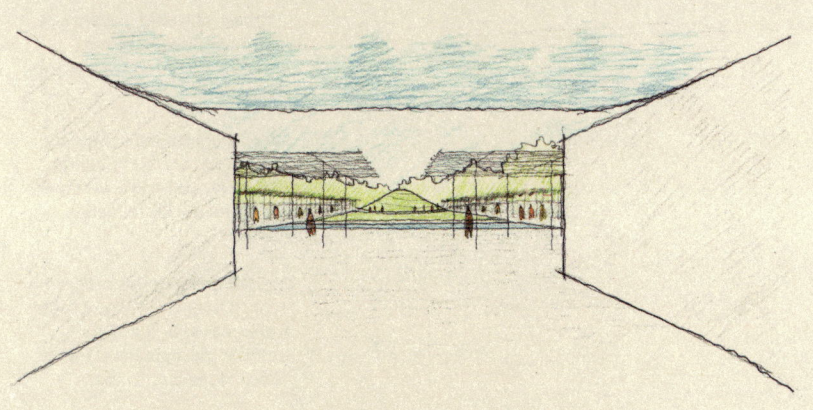

Initial concepts studied
the arrival experience from
urban to garden.

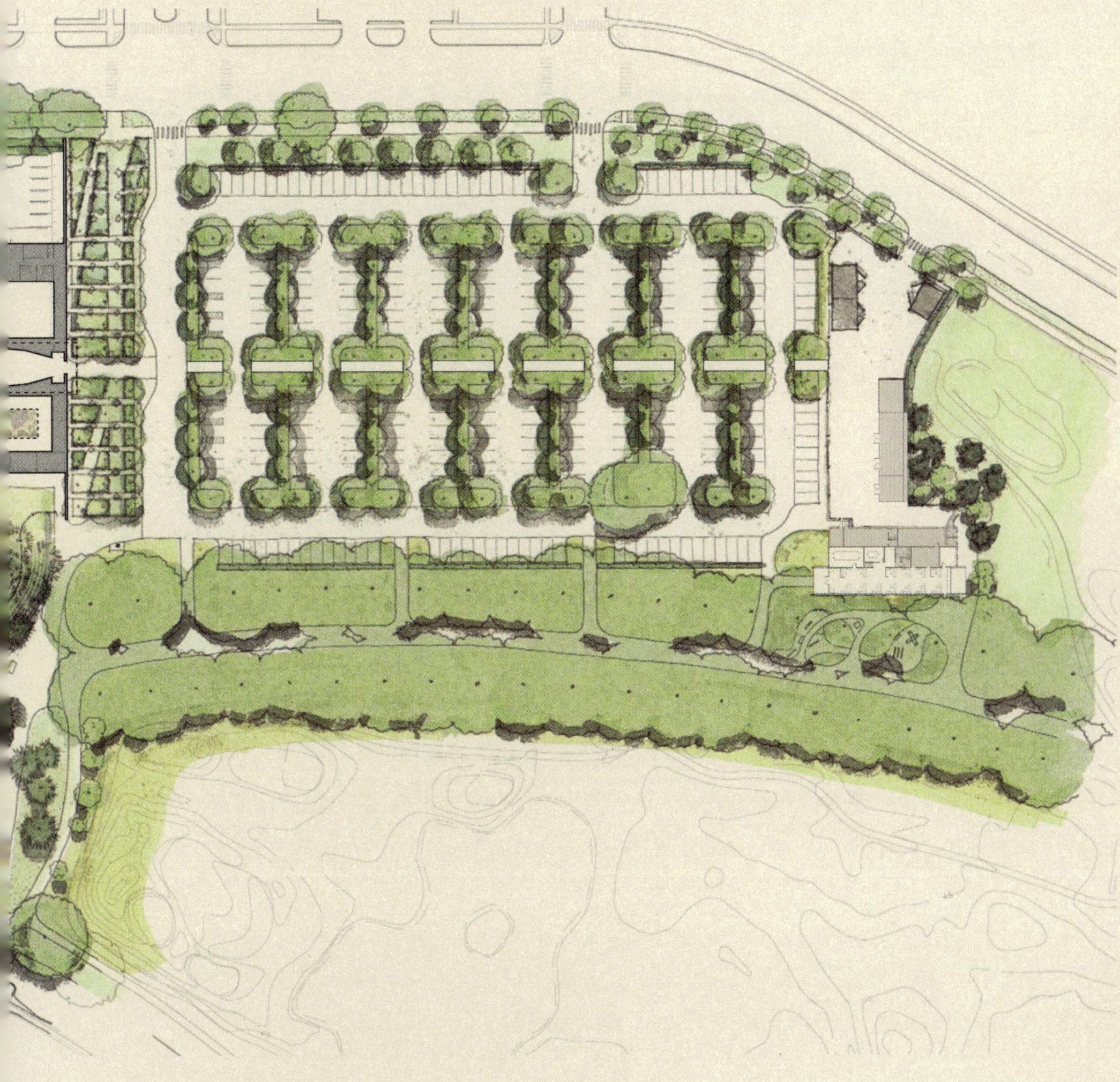

Cherie Flores Garden Pavilion

A broad, chiseled granite site wall and a grove of trees separate the new Garden from the parking.

An entry gateway, comprised of a human scaled opening in the site wall and a shimmering metal portal, reveals the Garden.

Interior and exterior program spaces flank the entry. A metal trellis provides shade for outdoor gathering and frames views of the landscape.

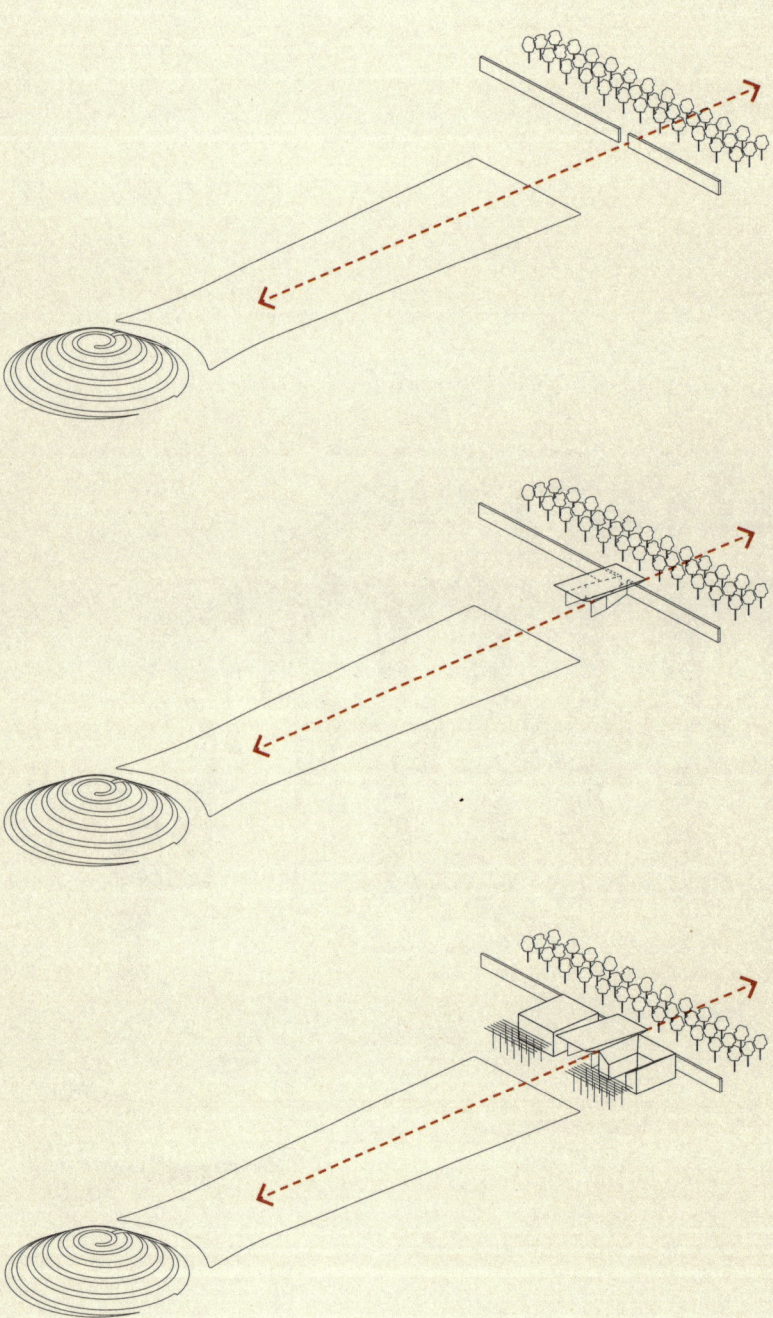

The centerpiece of the team's strategy—which became clear after careful design study and charrettes with Conservancy members—would be to create a dramatic new axis, stretching from a new landscaped parking lot to the east, through the shimmering new building, to the gardens to the west. The pavilion, therefore, would not be just an object, but a magnetic entry threshold, ushering visitors from the outside world into a new, richly layered series of spaces, whose visual focus is a remarkable thirty-foot-tall spiral mount at its rear.

Cherie Flores Garden Pavilion

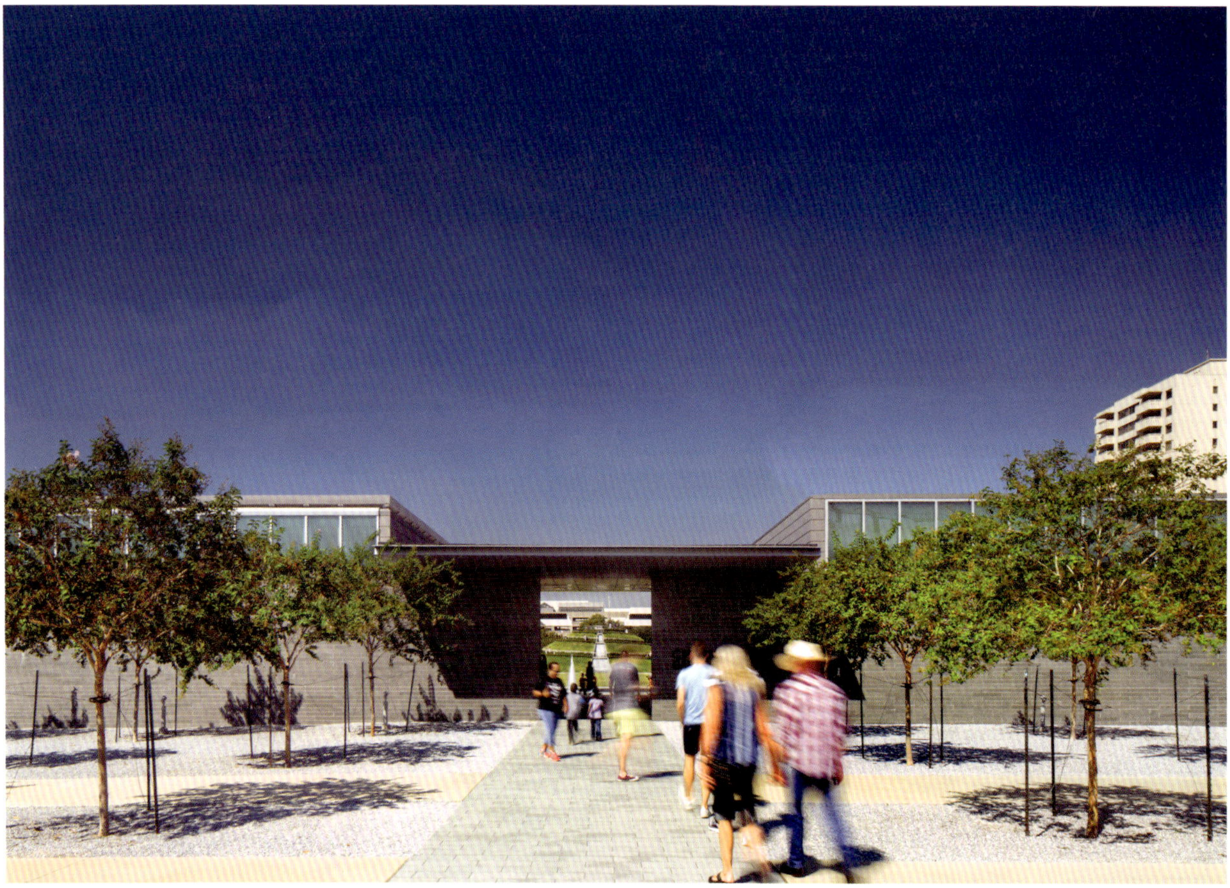

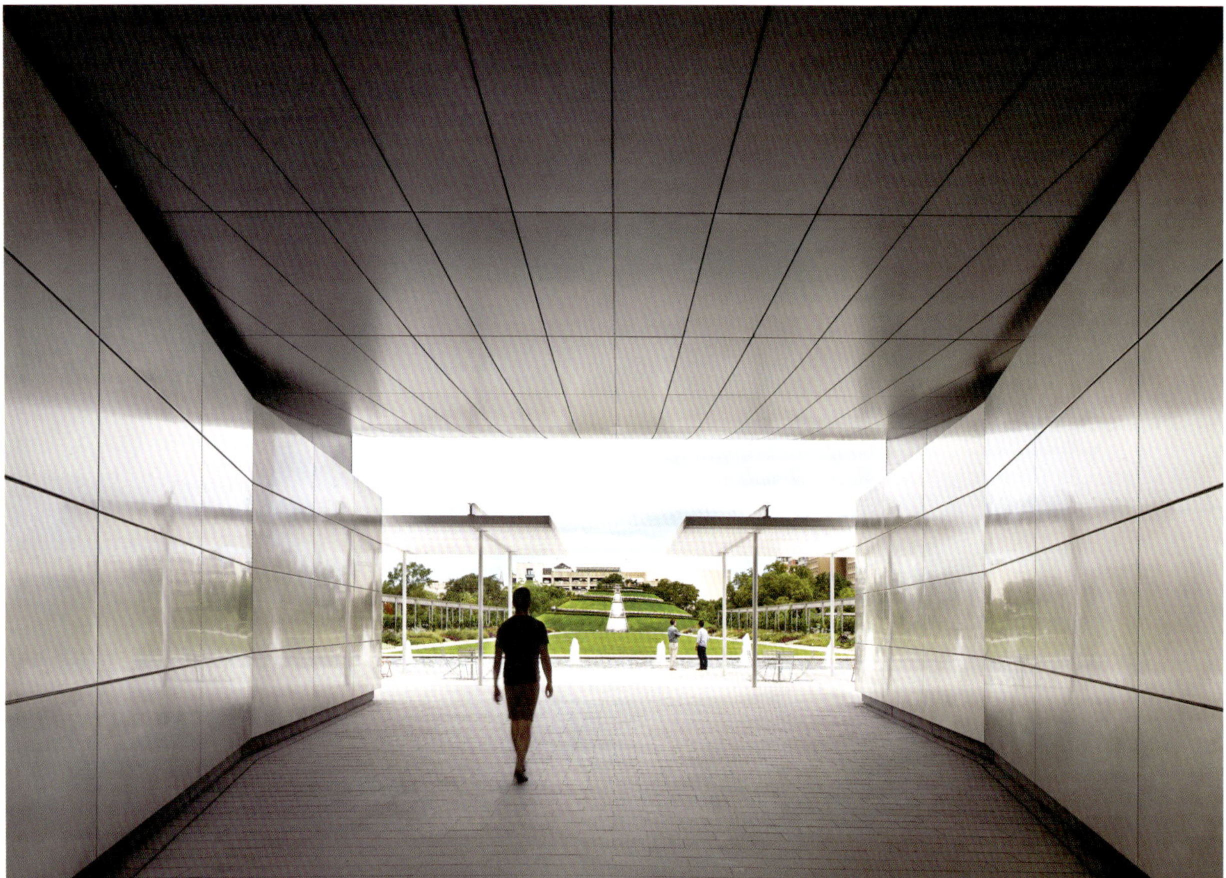

Visitors approach the double-winged pavilion through a grove of crepe myrtles, moving past its imposing, charcoal-hued granite wall into a measured gateway of shimmering stainless steel surfaces, which angle up toward and reflect the gardens.

"As you progress inside, the walls keep getting wider, and the roof keeps lifting. The view is literally expanding around you, which is pretty magical," explains Doreen Stoller, president of the Hermann Park Conservancy.

The pavilion's entrance is flanked by a zinc-clad, glass-walled meeting room to the north and a small contemplative courtyard to the south. Both spaces provide indoor and outdoor amenities for gatherings—from weddings to office retreats—and reinforce the connection to the landscape with clear views of the garden.

The opening in the site wall creates an experience of compression.

Cherie Flores Garden Pavilion

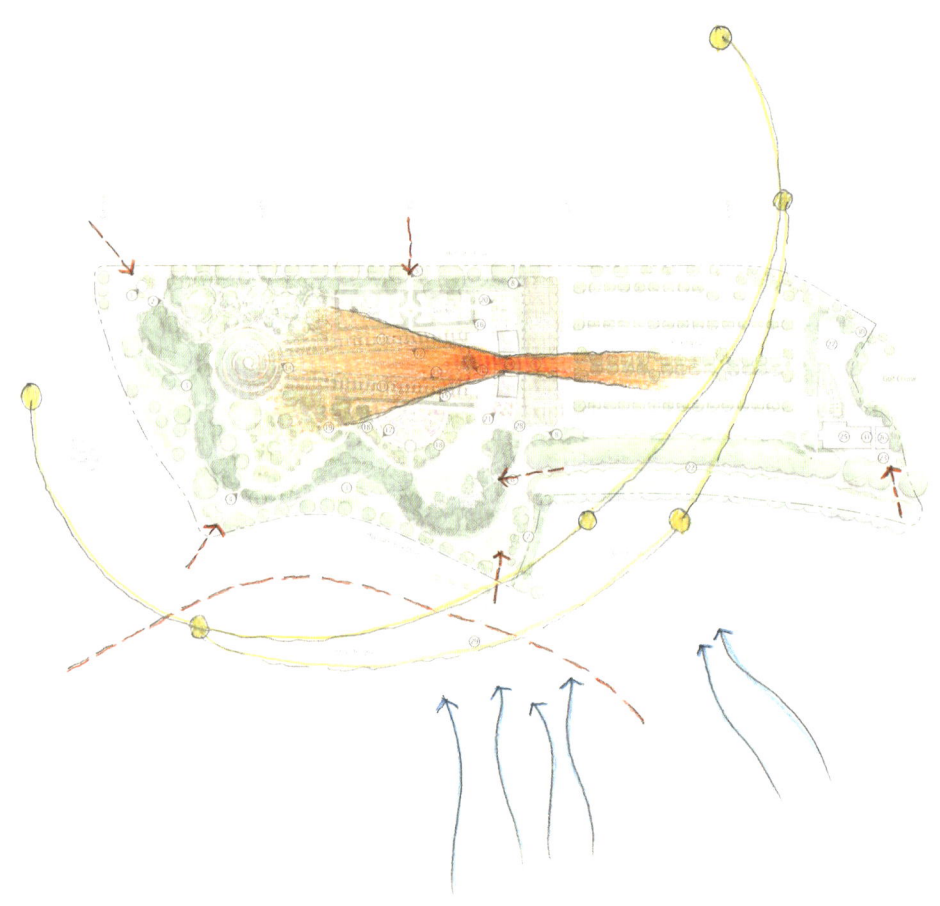

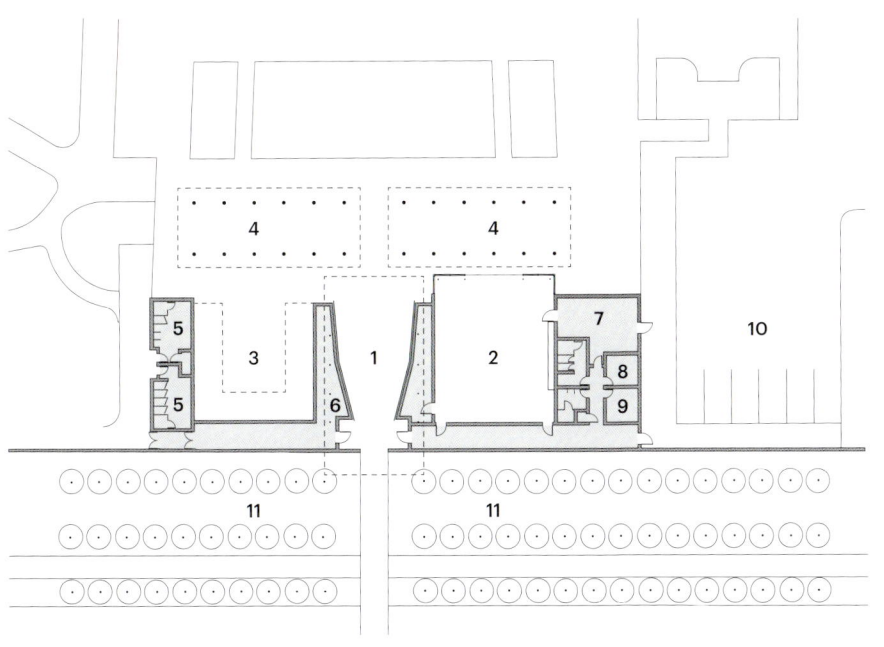

1   Entry
2   Meeting Room
3   Courtyard
4   Porch
5   Restrooms
6   Storage
7   Catering Prep
8   Office
9   Green Room
10 Service Court
11 Grove

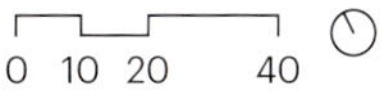

0 10 20   40

Cherie Flores Garden Pavilion   153

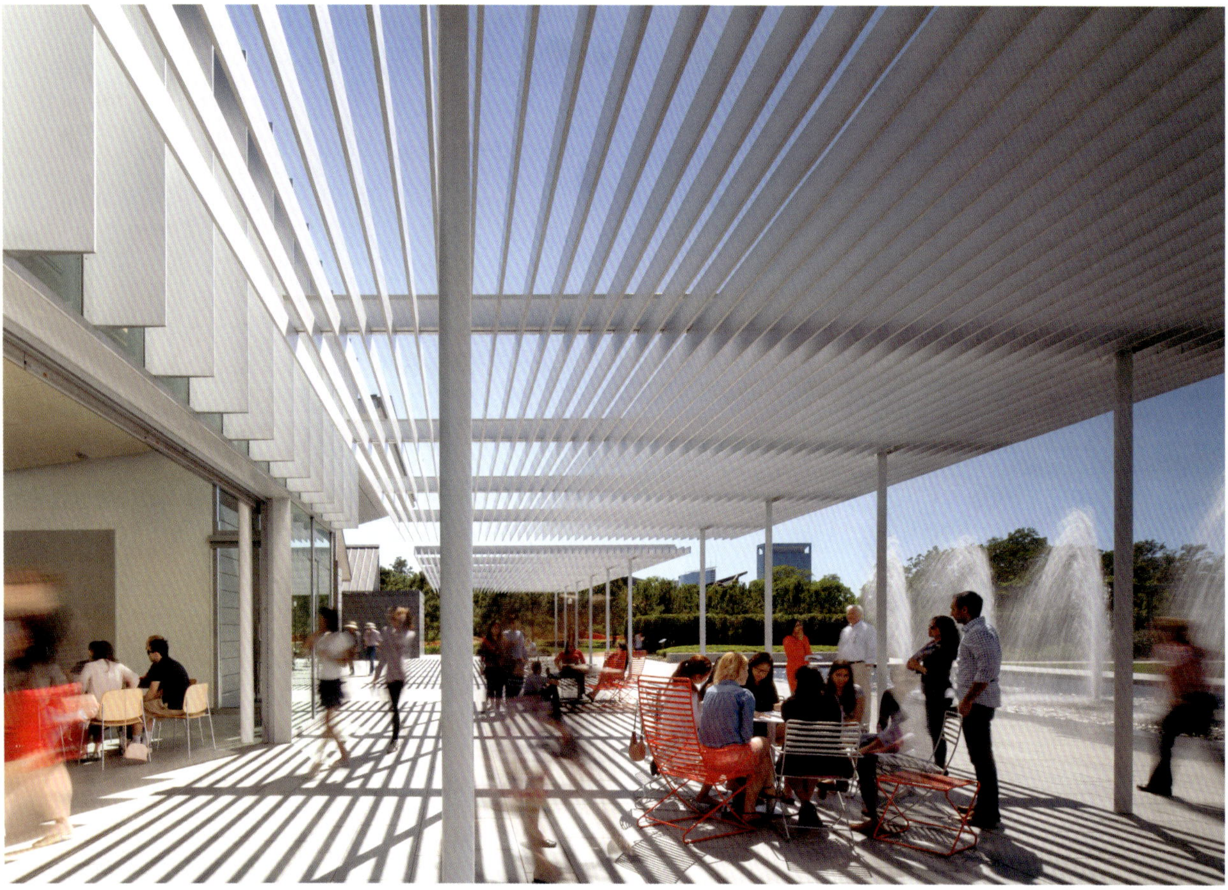

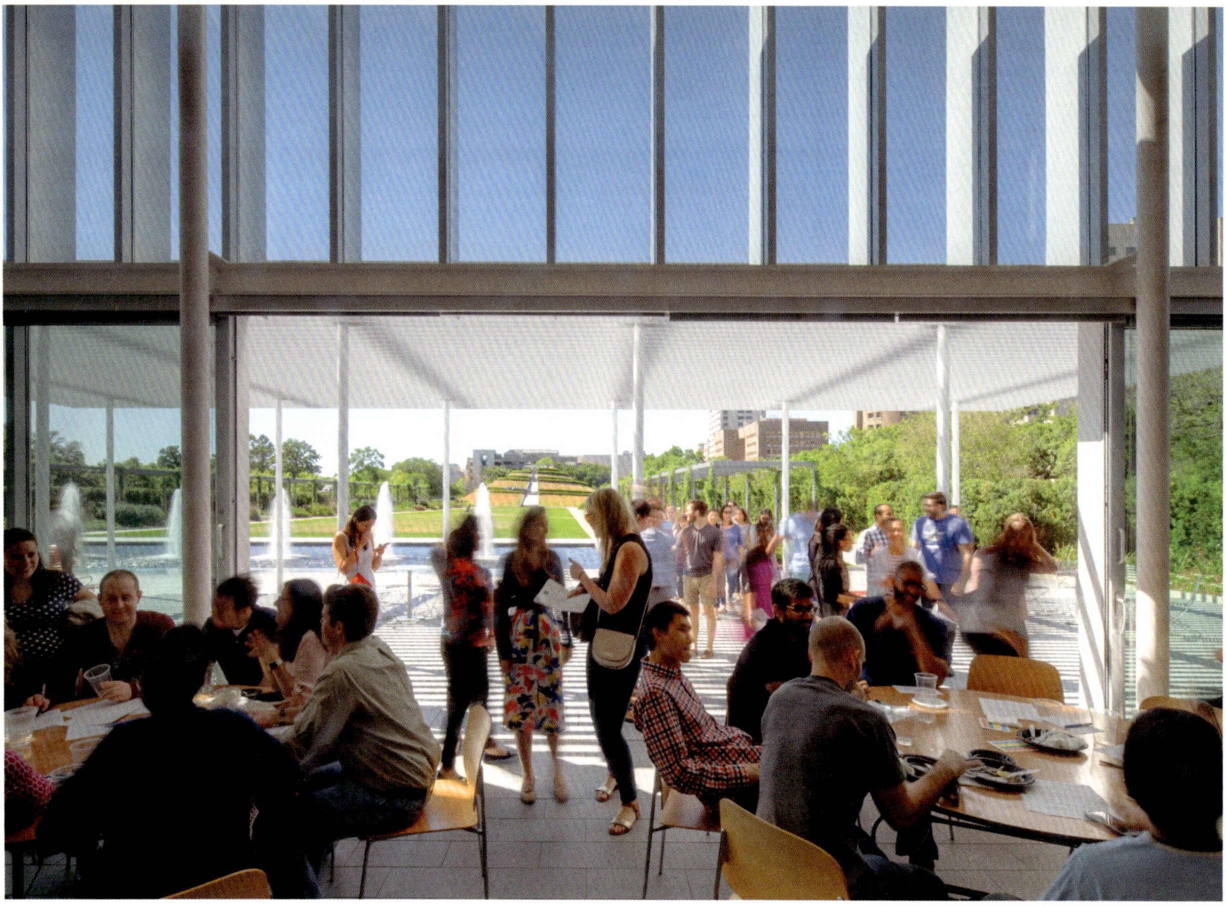

The meeting room's granite pavers extend into the garden, where a broad, white, metal trellis serves as a front porch and provides much-needed shade. This transition zone has become a popular spot for sitting and picnicking, with Houstonians enjoying views of the garden's central green.

The entry sequence and the new garden have rejuvenated the area, drawing thousands to the site and creating steady revenue for the non-profit Hermann Park Conservancy to help with upkeep for the entire park.

Cherie Flores Garden Pavilion

The Conservancy needed a building with durable, low-maintenance but aspirational materials. Zinc, granite, maple, and light-colored metal were selected to act as a neutral canvas to the vibrant flora in the gardens.

Cherie Flores Garden Pavilion

"We get so many compliments," said Stoller, emphasizing that the process and end results far exceeded what they expected. "We had been focusing on the practical and programmatic elements. Bohlin Cywinksi Jackson solved those issues, but they took us well out of the realm of functionality into visitor experience and spatial progression. They convinced us of the power of experience. It was just a lovely and original thought."

Cherie Flores Garden Pavilion

Apple Stores Worldwide

Perhaps no series of projects has showcased Bohlin Cywinski Jackson's approach as prominently as the dozens of worldwide stores it designed for Apple. The stores, which became international icons and played a major role in establishing the brand as a financial, technological, and cultural power, fused the firm's values with Apple's own to create projects that equally balanced technology and humanity.

Apple Founder, Steve Jobs and Head of Retail, Ron Johnson, invited the firm early on to hone its original store template, embodying the brand by merging sleek, futuristic materials with tactile, timeless ones, and creating bright, inviting community hubs that could provide tech support, educational programs, and personalized service.

Location
Worldwide

Dates
2000–2018

Client
Apple Inc.

Number of Stores
75

From pragmatic needs to
symbolic opportunity, the forms
of the glass enclosure and
stair were explored through
a series of sketches and models.
Ultimately, the simplicity of
a cube and the elegance of a
generous spiral stair emerged.

A pure form and a single point of entry became the means of introducing the hidden store and the decent into a unique shopping experience.

Initially immersive and insular, the Apple Stores progressively became more welcoming and transparent, encouraging more engagement with visitors and community. The Stanford Shopping Center store placed product display in a three-sided glazed room with accessories, and training and technical service in a day-lit, stone-enclosed room.

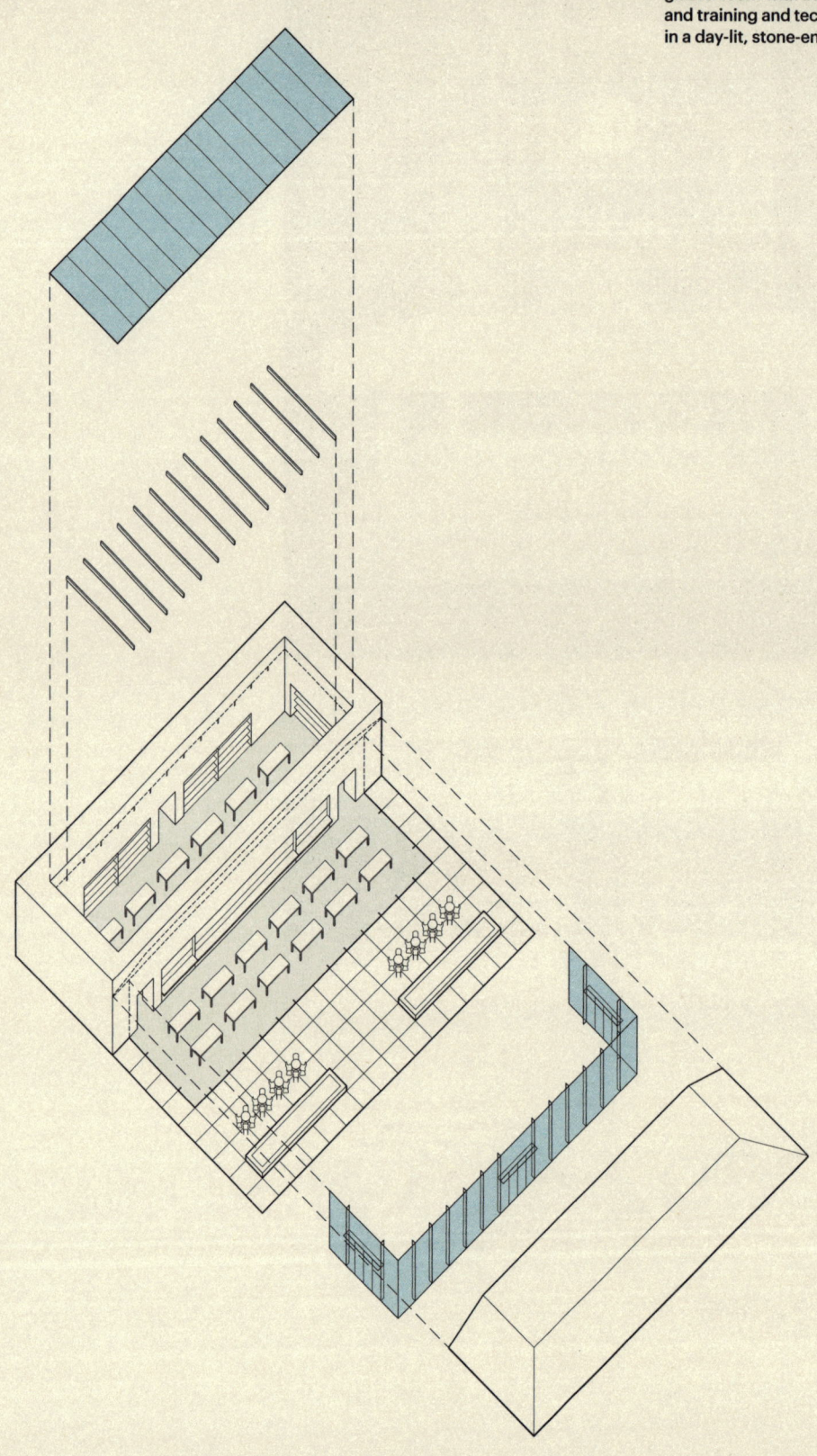

Their first major collaboration was Apple's Soho store, which relied heavily on the firm's thoughtful approach to people, place, and materials. The design team transformed a neo-classical post office into a luminous, vibrant brand showcase with a local civic focus. They clearly organized the open space, dividing it between product display downstairs and personalized product support (including the game-changing genius bar tech support stations) and group-focused learning upstairs. Rectangular maple tables and limestone floors dialogue with plate glass and stainless steel to create a feeling that is both "high tech and high touch," points out Johnson. As its visual centerpiece they installed a dramatic structural, laminated glass stair, above which floats a glowing skylight.

Earliest Apple Store designs were based on axial progression, from entryway to a presentation theater with a product display and service area flanking the central space. In SoHo, the first two-story Apple Store introduced the specialized glass assemblies to the retail program, adding visual and technical energy to the space.

"Everything was stunning, but not showy," noted Johnson, capturing the essence of why Apple and Bohlin Cywinski Jackson work so well together.

The glass staircase attracts visitors upstairs by enticing one's tactile curiosity to experience the feeling of *walking on air*. The top surface of the treads is diamond-plate patterned for safety and etched for modesty.

Working with structural engineer James O'Callaghan and his teams, and fabrication specialists at Seele and Tri-Pyramid, the adventurous glass assemblies were meticulously detailed and engineered.

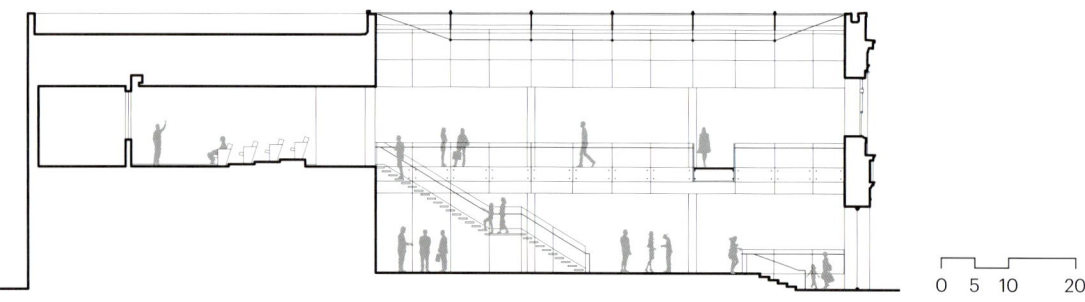

0   5   10   20

From here, the team built on the strategies employed at the Soho store to create stunning, multiple-floor facilities around the world, evolving their designs to Apple's changing brand strategies and to the needs of each location.

The next major touchstone was also in New York: Apple Fifth Avenue, highlighted by a thirty-two-foot-tall glass cube, made of extra-large self-supporting sheets of glass and interconnected glass fins and beams, which became the focus of the once-forgotten General Motors Plaza. Visitors descend via a glass spiral stair or a glass cylindrical elevator—both glowing from below—into bustling, elegant spaces meticulously detailed with similar maple tables and gray limestone floors, along with bead-blasted stainless-steel wall panels.

The General Motors Plaza was conceived in 1968 when the corporation agreed to provide an open public area in exchange for increased allowable height for their office tower. The plaza area directly in front of the office tower took on many forms, but never fulfilled its potential. It was once a sunken forecourt of retail stores that were difficult to access and experience.

The project presented the opportunity to recapture the space below street level, transforming it into a viable and engaging retail environment, and to reestablish the plaza as an exceptional urban place.

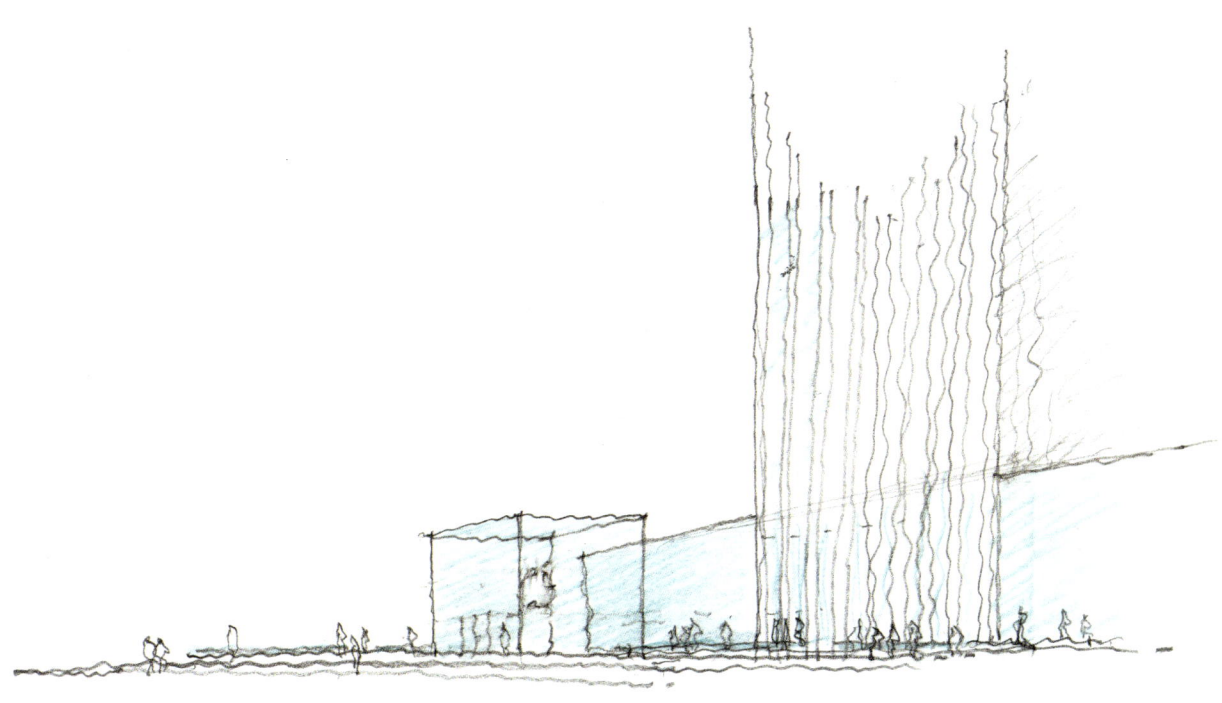

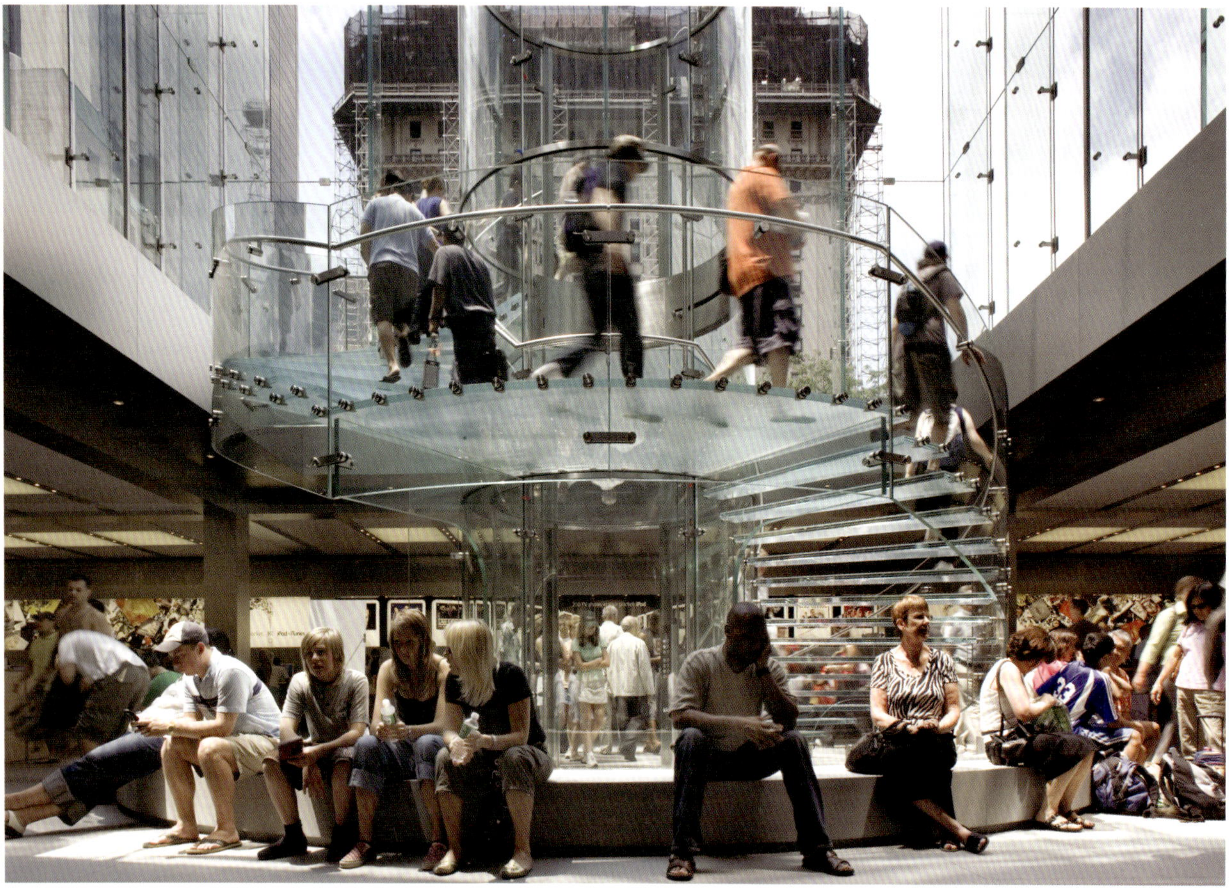

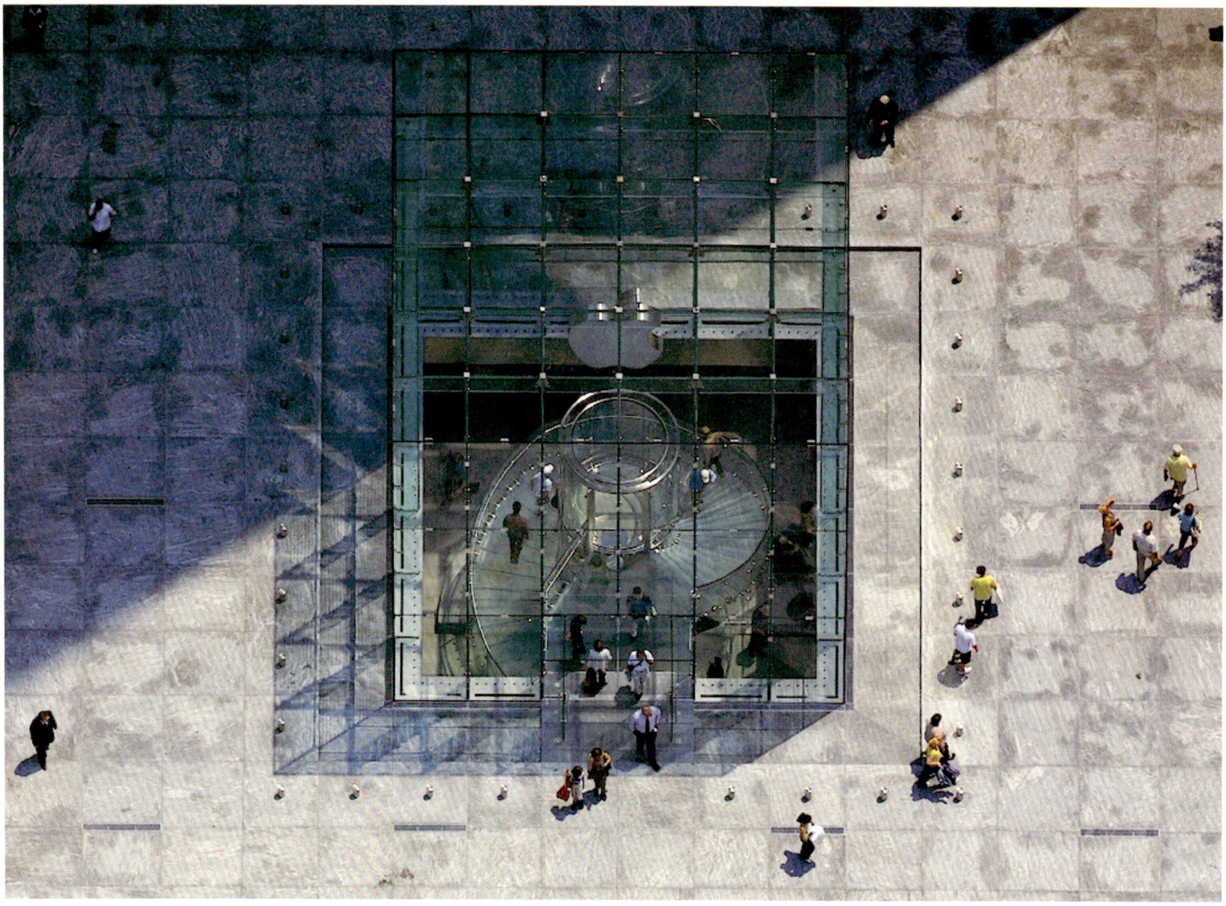

The project accomplished first-of-its-kind technical innovations. Entirely free of structural steel, the glass cube is self-supporting through the seamless integration of large laminated glass panels, multi-layered vertical glass fins, and horizontal glass beams. Stainless steel fittings are used to interlock all glass components into one assembly, which floats on the plaza with the glow of the store emanating from below.

The team's technological developments continued to push the stores' evolution. A cylindrical glass entry for a location in Shanghai's Pudong district—also highlighting a plaza and sitting atop a spiral glazed stair—employed even taller glass panels and further encouraged fabricators to hone curved glass technology.

While in conceptual design, the project team was familiarized with the Shanghai government's plans for constructing a large, elevated circular walkway to transform the pedestrian experience for the 2010 Shanghai Exposition. The team modified the plaza's design to create a civic landmark connected both thematically and experientially to the larger regional context.

On New York's Upper West Side, the team created a forty-foot-tall, transparent market hall, whose angled glass facade is supported by wide glazed panels and thin glazed fins. Its gently arcing glass roof is supported in turn by thin steel trusses spanning sixty feet between heavy stone walls. Other stores pushed technologies in exposed tectonics, metalwork, digital fabrication, and the tricky merger of futuristic and historic.

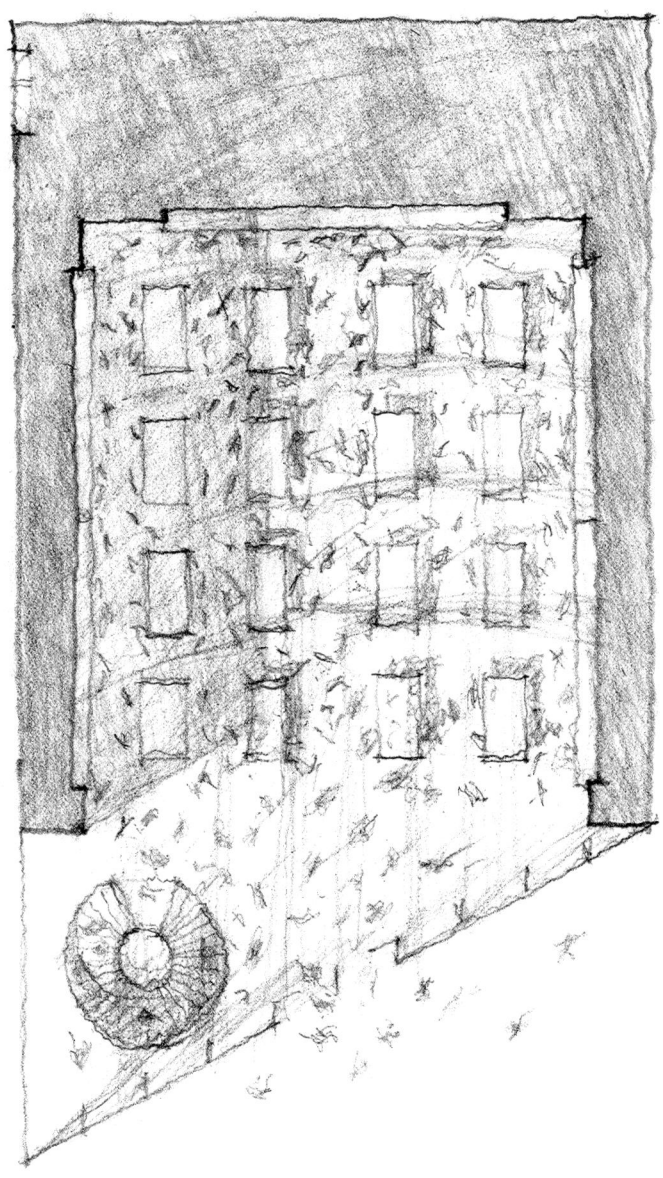

Each new location became another urban locus, another tool for civic revitalization. Apple made a focused effort to purchase sites in the centers of major cities, from Tokyo to Madrid, and each store would both fit seamlessly into the existing context and stand out—a balance that the firm has always specialized in.

"They really are superb at honoring the rhythm of things," added Johnson. "It's all about fitting in while doing magical things." As a result, each store became a sensation, a buzzing place to be.

Working in city centers pushed the team to interact more actively with history and context. At London's Covent Garden, where a store occupies the first three levels of a nineteenth century hotel and adjacent warehouse, the firm's strategic alterations provide clarity and openness, while bold technological and graphical insertions interact with painstakingly preserved historic details. At the building's entry portico, the team installed eight glazed storefronts opening to a lively public square, and they transformed several windows and doors into portals looking upward into a central atrium. Inside, they covered a central courtyard with a stainless-steel glazed roof, and a linear glass stair and elevator, all serving as visual anchors and organizers. Custom LED light boxes, known as "clouds," hover above each display table, while graphic display panels float in front of unfinished and reclaimed brick walls and under exposed ducts and pipes. The team simultaneously restored and revealed key markers of the building's past, including wrought-iron beams and concrete decking.

Through careful stripping and cleaning of interior wall surfaces, order was brought to the previously unconsidered arrangement of plastered, painted, and unfinished brick surfaces. Where walls were patched and repaired, bricks were carefully selected from reclaimed brick "libraries" for both their historic appropriateness and color range. The resulting material palate brought continuity to the medley of interlocking retail spaces and activities.

On New York's Upper East Side, a store occupying a 1922 neoclassical bank building by Henry Otis Chapman utilizes carefully reconstructed ceiling ornaments, ornamental lighting, recovered historic details, and reconstructed stone detailing to reestablish the splendor of a once-tired edifice. All is infused with contemporary luminance and efficiency through LED fixtures, temperature stratification, and other sustainable interventions.

Wherever possible, interior historic finishes were carefully restored. However, since many of the historic elements were completely missing or unsalvageable, a considerable amount of reconstruction was necessary. In many cases, the historic record was of limited detail or determined to be unreliable, thus the design of missing elements required interpolation, and reliance on other historic precedents.

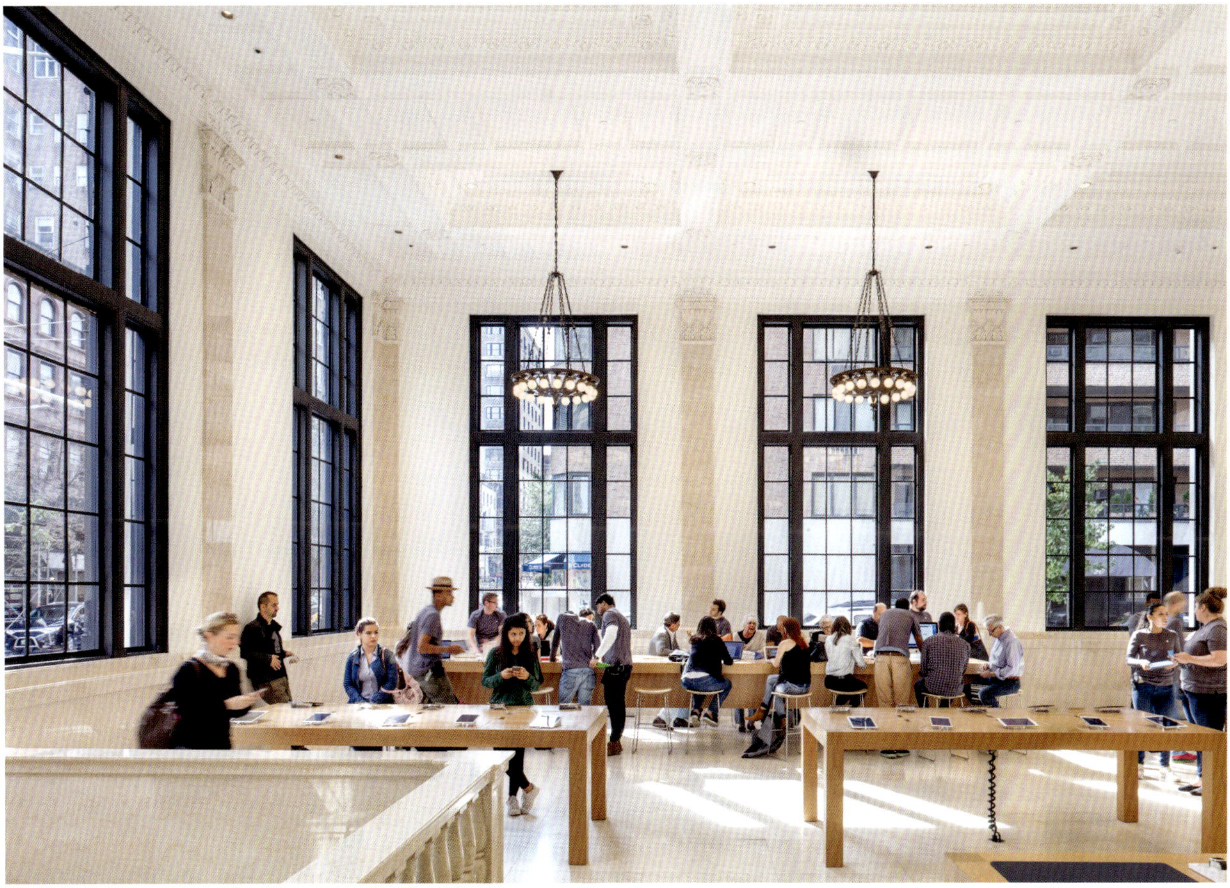

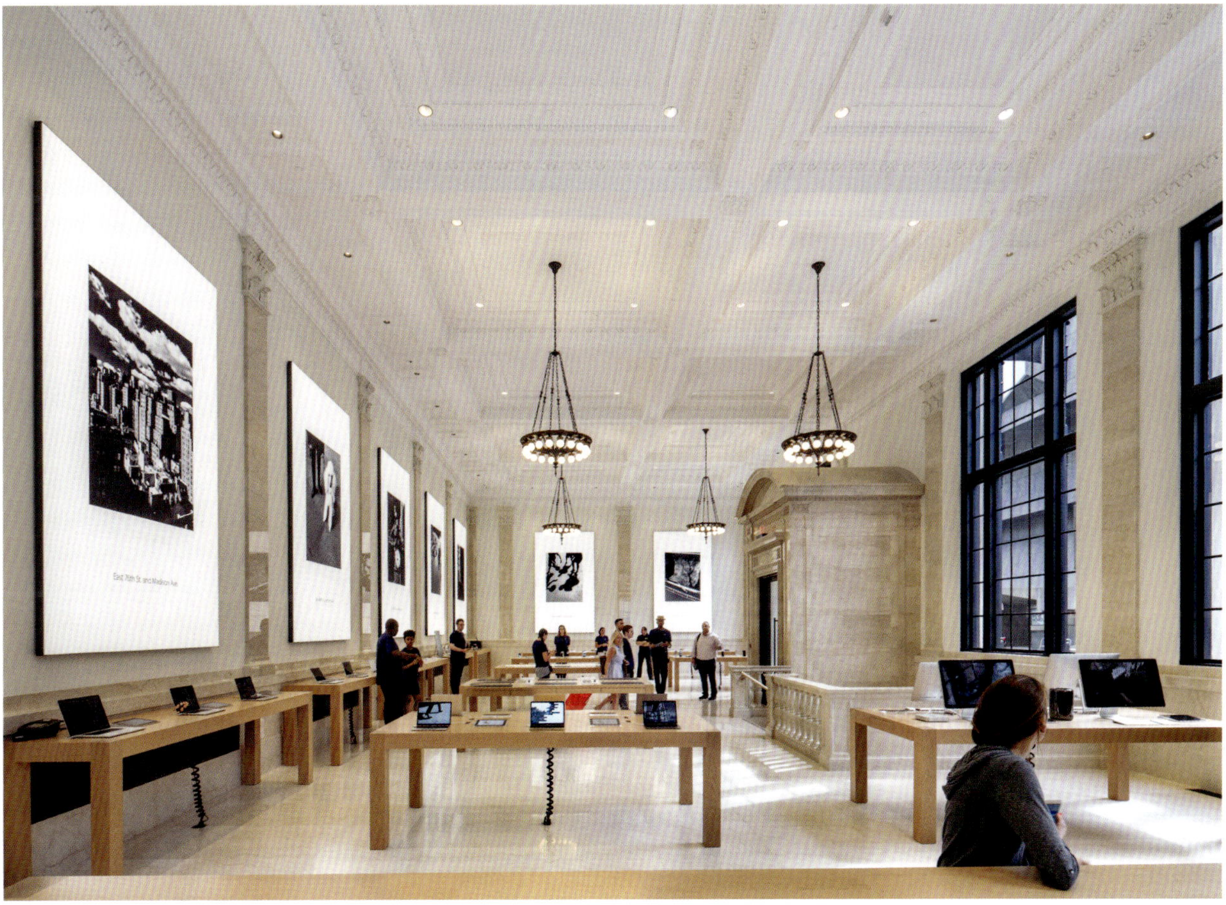

In less-historic contexts, the firm has created more futuristic insertions, offset by recognizable stone floors, walls, and wood tables. Their new Palo Alto store features 140 linear feet of storefront glass, blending outdoor public and indoor retail spaces. Slender glass fins along the facade support a column-free front room for browsing, while a bowed glass roof—supported by delicate stainless steel beams—streams sunlight into a quieter, stone-enclosed rear space.

While each location has added something new, each, like the evolving Apple products inside, still maintains the familiar magic.

"It evolved like Apple's products evolved," says Johnson. "You're constantly looking at what you can improve. You don't want to start over. But if it's good you want to make it better."

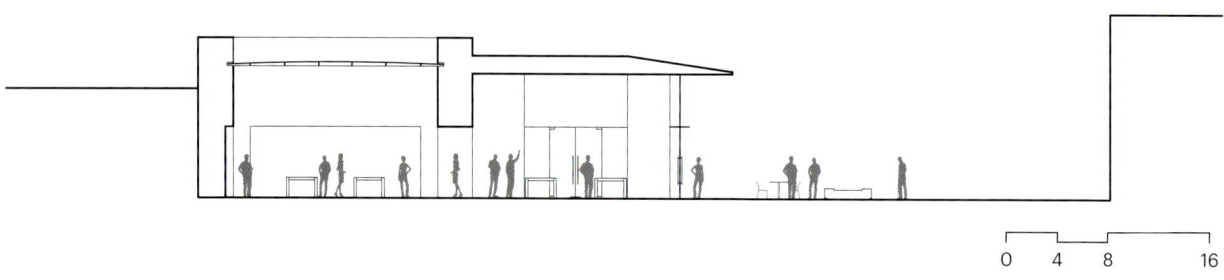

0   4   8   16

Delicate stainless steel beams support the gently arching glass roof of Apple Stanford, which provides integrated light illuminating the customer service area below. A careful balance of tint, dot patterned frit, and high-performance coatings allow modulated daylight to fill the space while maintaining thermal comfort year-round.

A major part of that improvement has been continual refinement. The design team was just as serious as Jobs at paying attention to the smallest details, from half-inch timber joints to tight window seams. Johnson lauds the firm's meticulous attention to detail. "Peter used to tell me if you think about a problem hard enough we would all come down to the inevitable answer. It just belongs."

Johnson argues that their stores played as large a role as the iPod in changing what was a niche computer company into a multi-faceted tech giant. They welcomed people into the company, and famously hosted long lines for products.

"Apple went from a tech company to a beloved community for humankind. You couldn't have done that without the stores," says Johnson.

As for his partnership with Bohlin Cywinski Jackson, Johnson lauds firm members as more than designers. "They're all thinkers. They think through a space; they don't imagine their way through a space. It's not about being flashy; it's about being functional. Authentic. Genuine. Honest. It's about being true to Apple."

For the firm, the lessons learned at the stores have filtered through to countless other projects—elements like glass detailing and space layout, and perhaps more than anything, an appreciation of elegant restraint and minimalism.

Located in the cultural center of Madrid and facing the vibrant Puerta del Sol plaza, this project is an extensive rehabilitation of a classic 1850s mid-rise hotel, with the parallel goals of restoring the cast-iron structure to its former beauty, and reconnecting the building to the public life of the plaza.

At the ground and first floors, the granite facade has been carefully restored to its original character and geometry, while on the interior the granite piers have been exposed and left rough-hewn, highlighting the robust nature of the building's facade.

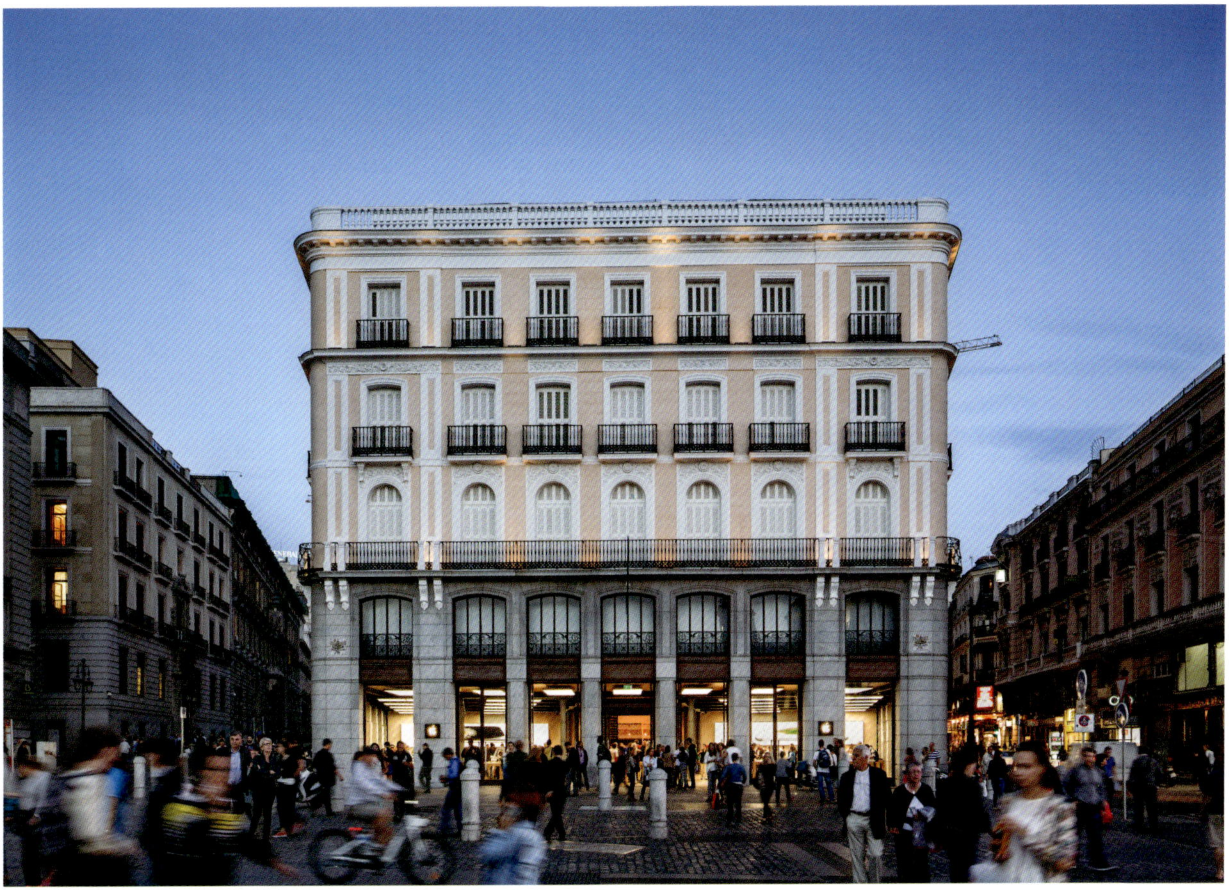

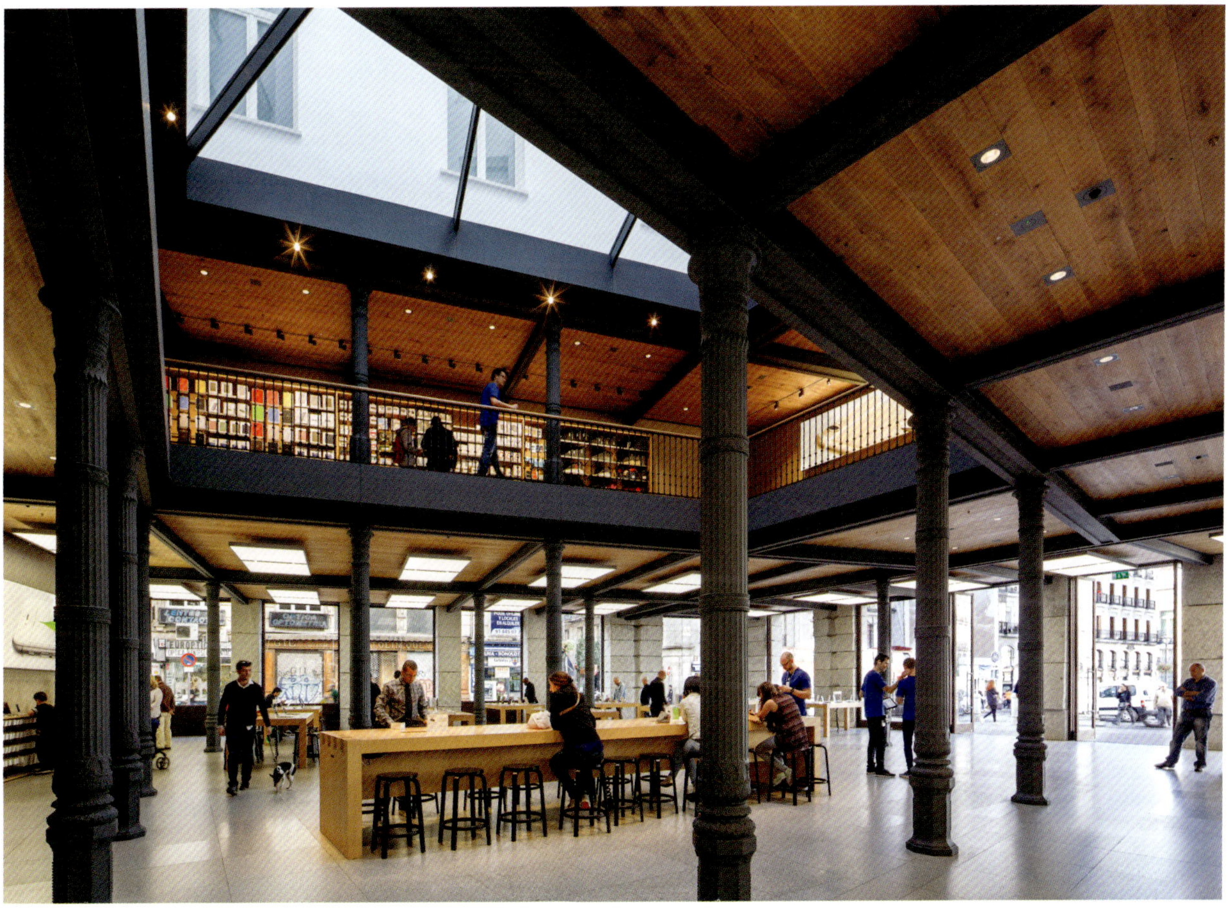

Manetti Shrem
Museum of Art

Located in the heart of California's Central Valley, the University of California, Davis, has a storied history of artistic scholarship and achievement. But for years it lacked a world-class art venue.

The new Jan Shrem and Maria Manetti Shrem Museum of Art, occupying the southern site of the Vanderhoef Quad in the University Gateway District, dramatically fills that void while projecting a spirit of informal experimentation and openness that is perfect for an art department that prides itself on irreverence.

Chosen in an international design-build competition, the team of Bohlin Cywinski Jackson, SO – IL, and Whiting-Turner conducted workshops with museum staff and university personnel throughout the design process, while simultaneously sharing ideas and staff between their offices.

In association with
SO – IL; Whiting–Turner

Location
Davis, CA

Dates
2012–2016

Client
University of California, Davis

Size
30,000 SF

The competition entry proposed a single-level design that seamlessly integrates the museum into the campus setting, while accommodating a broad range of exhibition opportunities and educational experiences.

Referencing the quilted agrarian landscape that stretches beyond the site and throughout California's central valley, the Manetti Shrem Museum is inspired by its diverse and interwoven patterns, forms, textures, and colors.

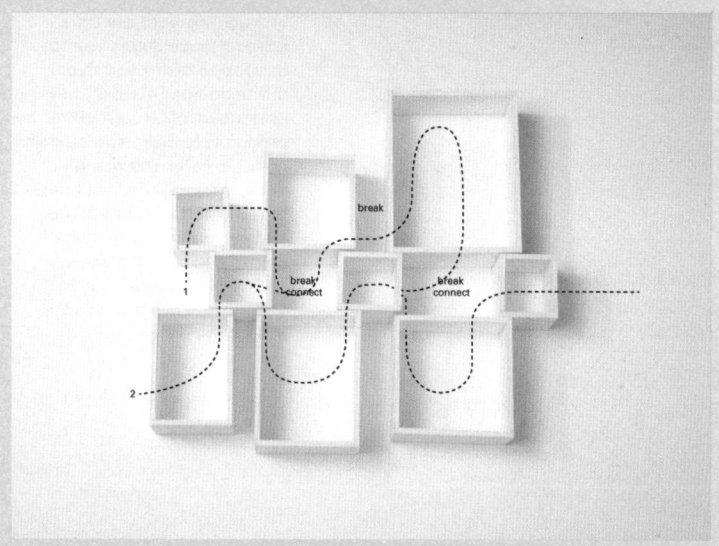

To maximize programming possibilities, the galleries consist of a portfolio of exhibition rooms with distinct spatial qualities. Diverse gallery configurations were explored to provide a wide range of spaces for exhibiting artworks and to study various options of visitor circulation patterns.

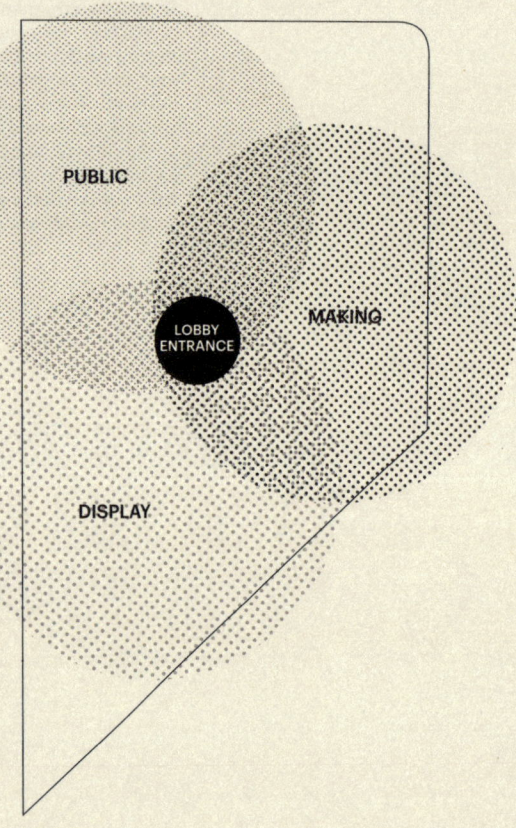

PUBLIC

MAKING

LOBBY ENTRANCE

DISPLAY

In order to create a nonhier-archical museum experience, the design team conceived of a building with a centrally positioned lobby surrounded by program elements strategically oriented to nearby site influences. This approach supported the idea of open-endedness and exploration, with multiple inward and outward views, and created an opportunity to visit a broad range of spaces, exhibits, and events.

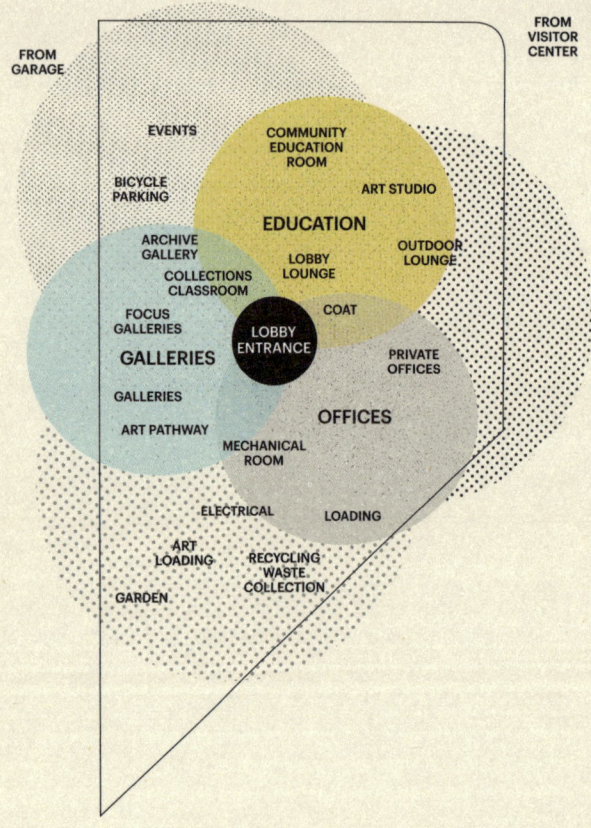

FROM GARAGE

FROM VISITOR CENTER

EVENTS

COMMUNITY EDUCATION ROOM

ART STUDIO

BICYCLE PARKING

EDUCATION

OUTDOOR LOUNGE

ARCHIVE GALLERY

COLLECTIONS CLASSROOM

LOBBY LOUNGE

FOCUS GALLERIES

COAT

LOBBY ENTRANCE

GALLERIES

PRIVATE OFFICES

GALLERIES

OFFICES

ART PATHWAY

MECHANICAL ROOM

ELECTRICAL

LOADING

ART LOADING

RECYCLING WASTE COLLECTION

GARDEN

The team's scheme unites the building's three distinct volumes—for education and events, offices and back of house, and art display—with a striking, undulating white canopy composed of 952 prefabricated, perforated aluminum beams. The covering doesn't just provide valuable, shaded outdoor space. It creates a visual buffer from the nearby highway and train tracks, unites the facility's three distinct spaces (while still letting them stand on their own), and reflects the patterned topology of the agrarian region.

Just as important, it is an iconic artwork in its own right, its varied sizes and orientations creating a mesmerizing, sculptural play of dappled light and shadow. Visitors discover these extraordinary effects immediately upon approach, progressing along varied sinuous pathways to the curved glass entry.

Situated in a highly visible location, adjacent to an active Amtrak line and Interstate 80 between Sacramento and San Francisco, the museum serves as an icon for the university from a variety of vantage points and speeds—pedestrian, bicyclist, automobile, and train.

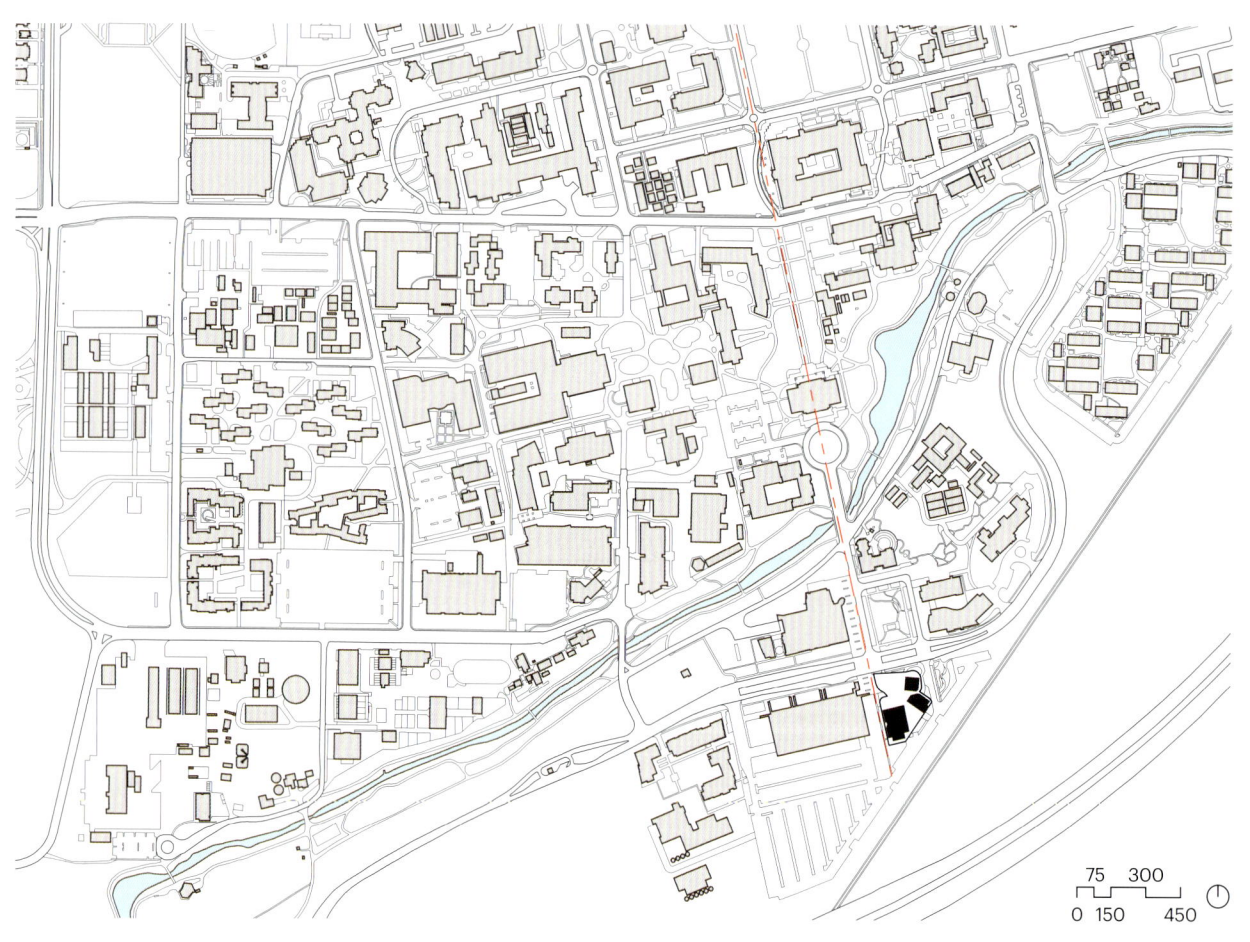

75 300
0 150   450

Manetti Shrem Museum of Art

This sense of fluid exploration continues throughout the textured, precast concrete-clad building. Proceeding past the boldly curved glazed entry, you come upon a radiant, smooth-floored lobby that provides clear views into all three wings. You can also see into the amorphous central courtyard, containing relaxation spaces and artwork, and funneling more natural light into the building's depths. The LEED Platinum museum—a rarity in the cultural world—incorporates locally sourced materials and ties into the university's centralized photovoltaic farm.

The canopy is lowest around the perimeter, creating a distinct sense of entry upon walking underneath. During the day, the variable density and orientation of the canopy shading create rooms of shade to various degrees, increasing one's awareness of the dynamic quality of the sun.

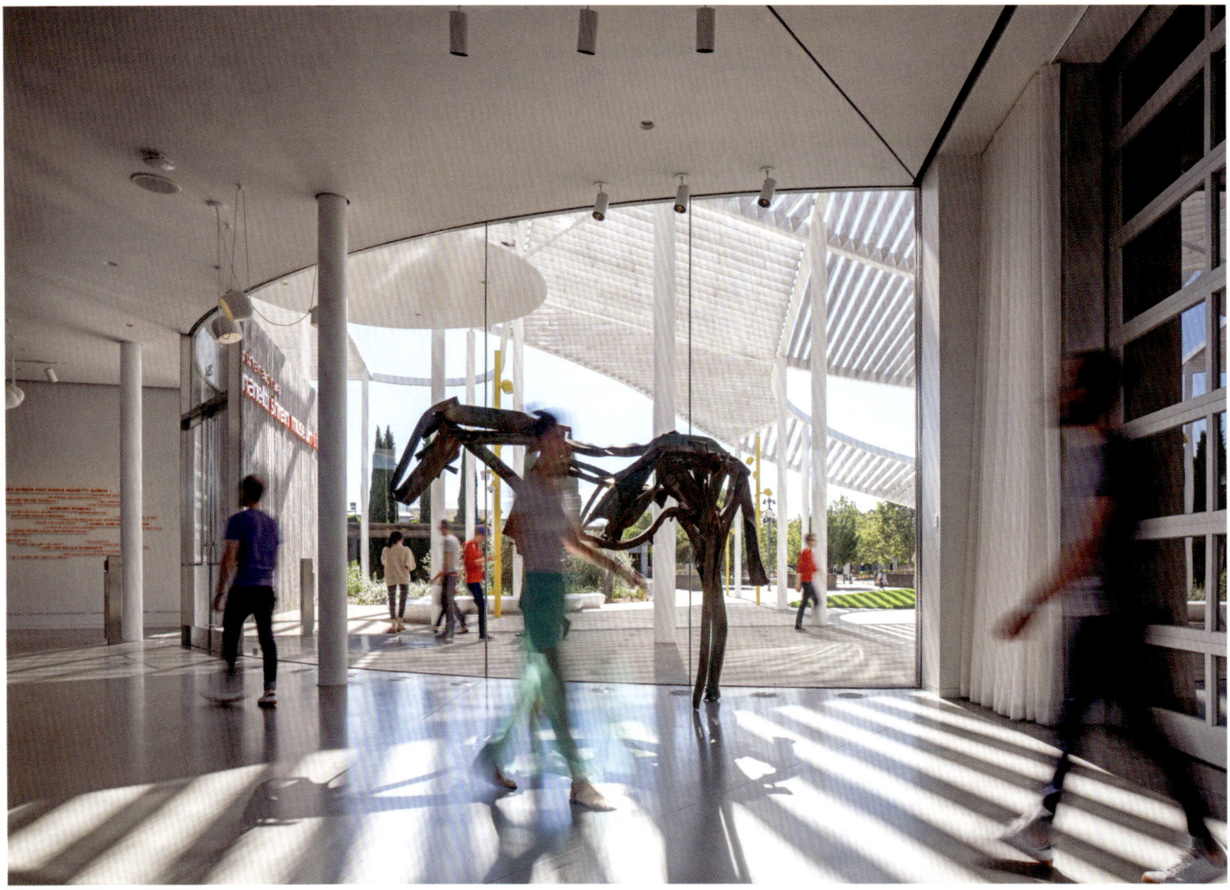

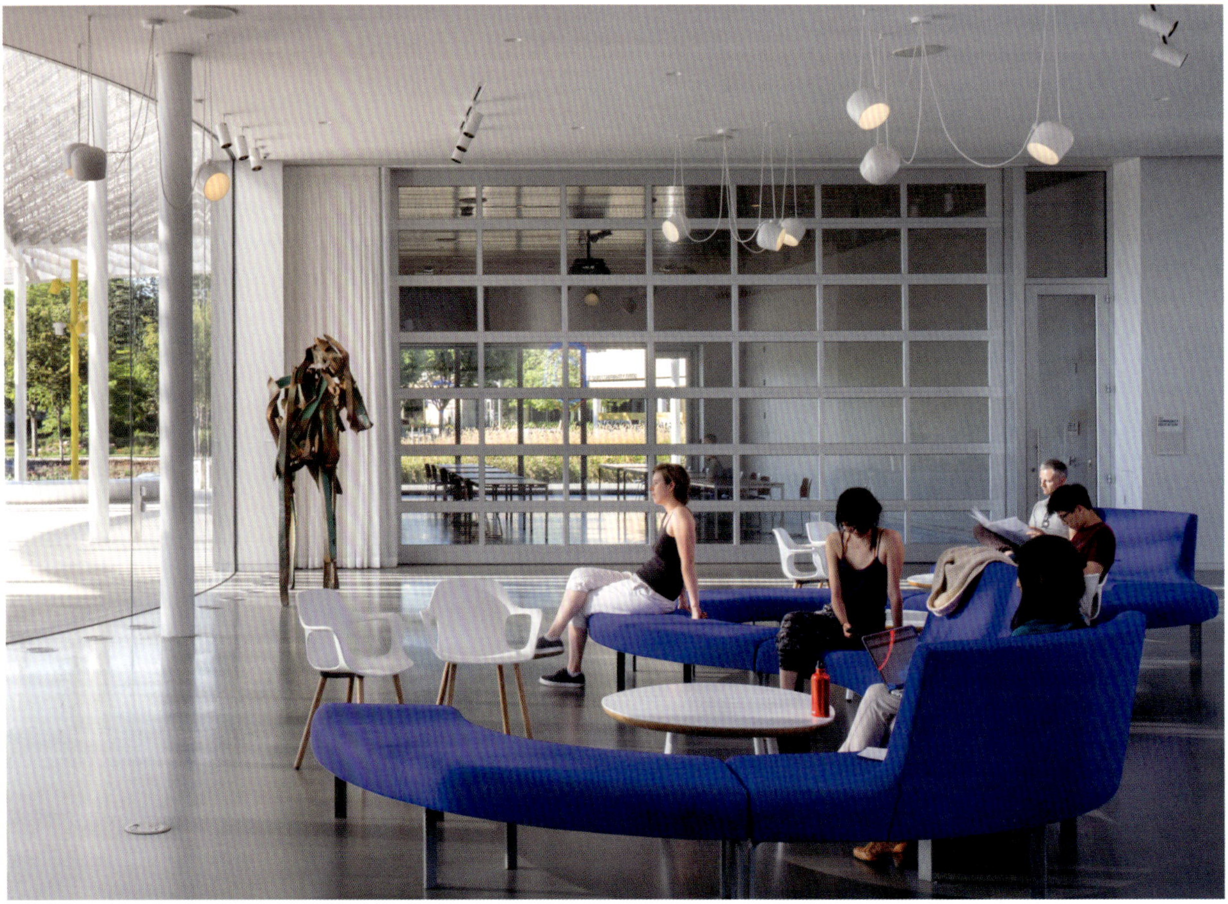

Floor Plan
1   Events Plaza
2   Lobby Lounge
3   Education Pavilion
4   Art Making Yard
5   Administration Pavilion
6   Courtyard
7   Gallery Pavilion

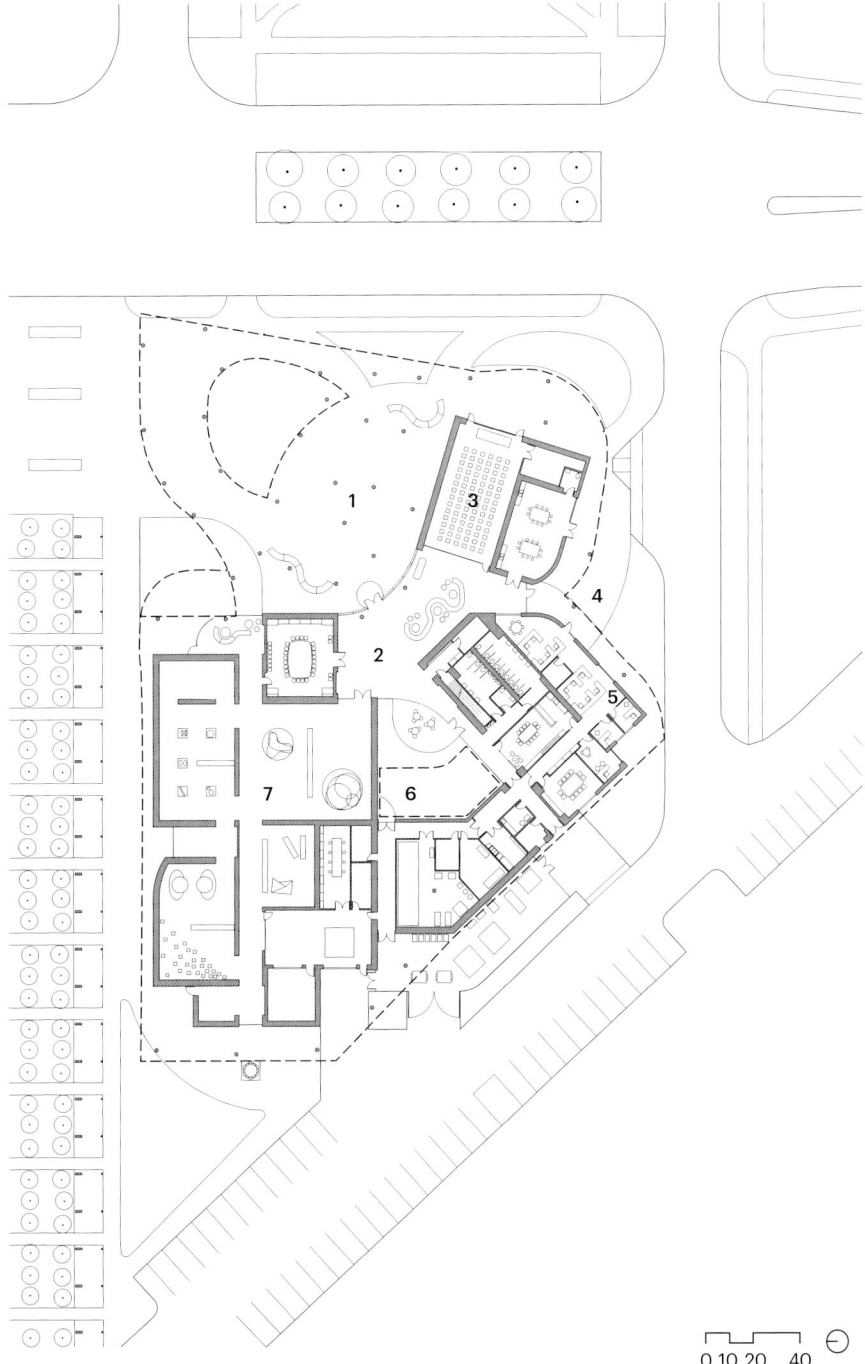

0 10 20   40

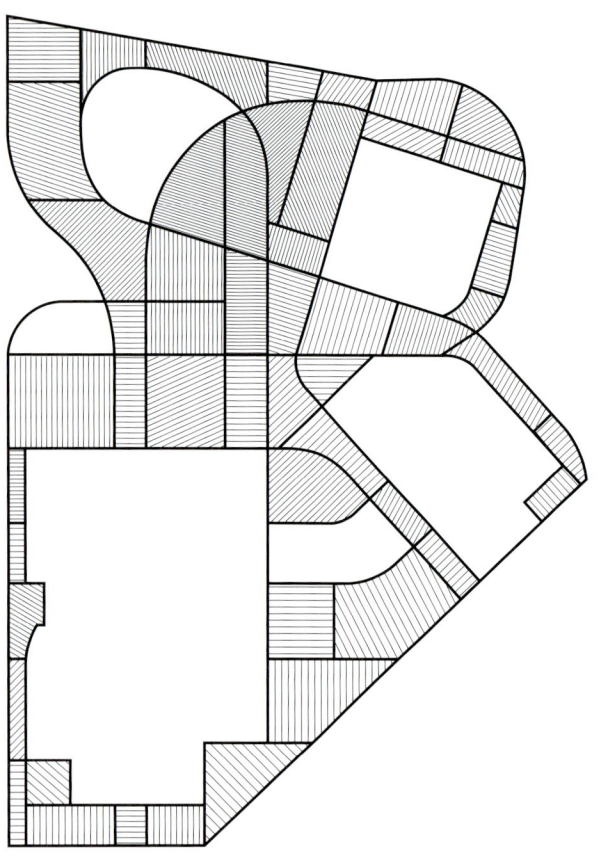

Designing a secluded but connected outdoor room for immersive art experiences and socialization, was a key programmatic objective. This courtyard provides views to the open sky, the daylight filtering through the canopy and back to the interior space of the museum.

Visitors make their way into each wing, almost constantly connected to the outdoors. The classroom wing, including facilities for studios, lectures, seminars, and collecting, features glass doors that open onto shaded outdoor spaces, providing indoor or outdoor learning environments. The facilities and staff wing open to the public through glass walls and take advantage of the central courtyard's light and space. In the gallery wing, which hosts curated, traveling, and student art exhibitions, one gets more strategic glimpses of the outdoors, often shaded by soft scrims that flow subtly through interconnected rooms, whose temporary walls allow for myriad configurations and spatial progressions. Spaces are interspersed with lounges and varying ceiling heights, allowing for large-scale works, and giving visitors a sense of freedom and rawness.

Creating art and open dialogue is essential to the educational mission of the museum. Each of these rooms are strategically positioned for access and views to the surrounding spaces.

Manetti Shrem Museum of Art

The building's sense of informality and porosity helps the museum maintain a welcoming, unpretentious presence, points out Manetti Shrem Museum Founding Director, Rachel Teagle. "The canopy, the modulation of light. The comfortable, open feel. There are a lot of ways that this building shrugs off the stiff formality of a traditional art museum experience. We're very sophisticated but we really welcome the student body."

The museum also welcomes the campus, literally bowing down to meet it, with its circulation spine connecting to a walkway guiding visitors to the rest of campus. And it clearly accentuates learning, as studios and classrooms dominate one's first impression.

"Usually education is hidden in the basement, or in the back," says Teagle. "We wanted to wear it on our sleeve." And what better firm to reinforce this, she adds, than Bohlin Cywinski Jackson, with its attention to detail, its constant testing of solutions and materials, and its unique ability to create a visceral, utterly relatable experience.

Utilizing adaptable linear track lighting and porous ceiling grid systems, temporary exhibition walls can be easily erected and configured based on the specific needs of an exhibit. The galleries can be arranged as a traditional linear route or can encourage alternate paths while supporting multiple concurrent exhibitions.

New College House

At the turn of the millennium, the University of Pennsylvania instituted its College House System, lodging students, faculty, and staff together in residential halls to enhance community and nurture constant learning. But until New College House opened, there had never been a building purposely created for the College House System. The complex, forming a new gateway to Penn at the eastern edge of its West Philadelphia Campus, vigorously embraces that role, facilitating common activity and study while helping knit the urban campus together.

Location
Philadelphia, PA

Dates
2011–2016

Client
University of Pennsylvania

Size
198,000 SF

New College House forms the gateway to Penn from Center City Philadelphia. With the site banked for half a century as a playing field, the design strives to preserve open green spaces with a generous sloping lawn and cascading green roofs (left).

Open and inviting, New College House encourages its residents to take on the dual responsibility of looking inward to build relationships on campus and outward to embrace the vibrancy of the city and the world beyond. Shared two-story Commons build community among groups of suites and provide views to the campus and city.

The facade responds to Philadelphia's masonry tradition and to Penn's historic and modernist architectural legacy, including the iconic 1960 Hill College House by Eero Saarinen (left).

A staggered pattern of custom-shaped bricks was developed for the angled and flat portions of the walls. Traditional brick and limestone materials are used to harmonize with the building's hefty masonry neighbors.

A design phase mock-up tested and refined preliminary assumptions about brick coursing, flashing, joint tooling, and constructability, and initiated a fruitful collaboration.

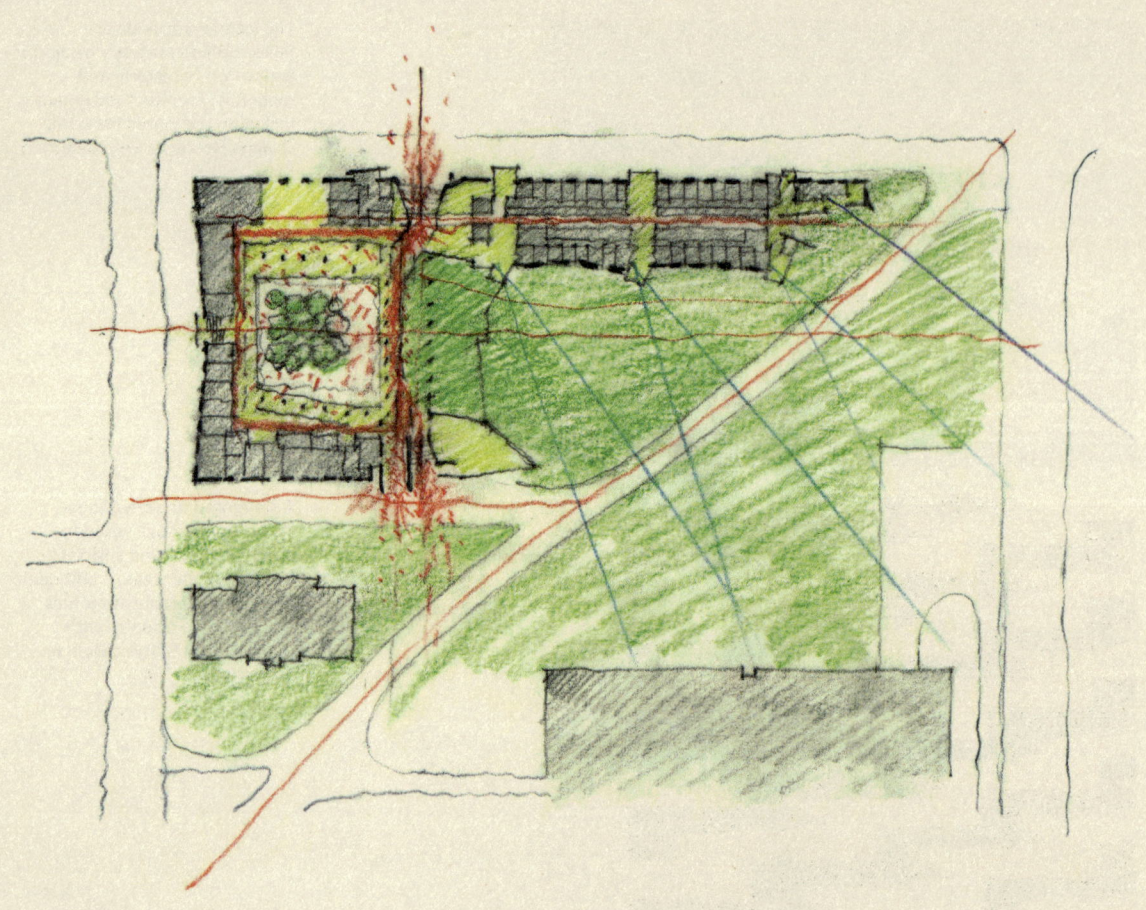

After conducting conversations with students and faculty, and undertaking studies of size, orientation, solar gain, constructability, and material palette, the design team chose to break down the sizeable building's mass through faceted, shadow-manipulating bricks, limestone accents, multi-level glass bays, and highly varied masses. As a result, New College House doesn't read like a building at all, but rather like a village shaped around its sloping landscape.

New College House redefines the boundary between Penn's campus and its immediate neighbor, Drexel University, by formalizing a proper campus gateway. The site's diagonal walk is a 2003 commemorative artwork by Jenny Holtzer honoring "125 Years of Women at Penn."

Green roofs crown the building to maximize vegetation as part of a zero-impact storm-water management strategy.

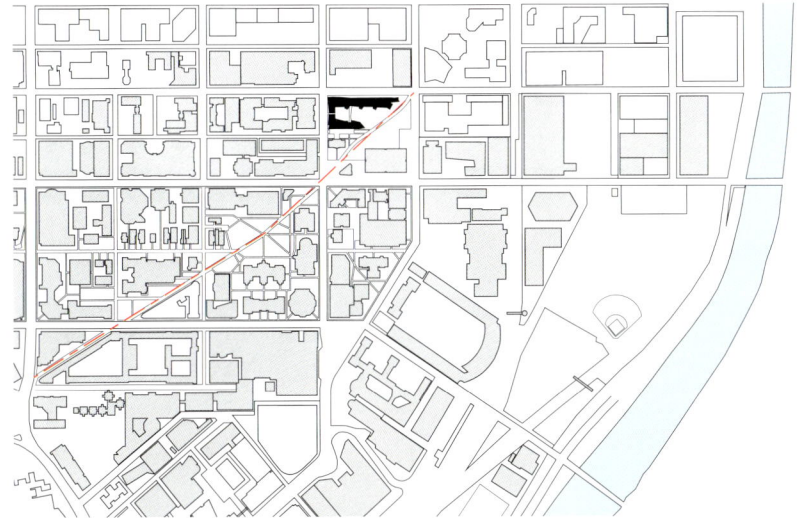

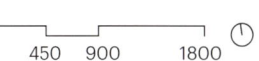

0   450   900   1800

Floor Plan
1 Entry
2 Dining Pavilion
3 Dining
4 Courtyard
5 Lobby
6 Living Room
7 Media Room
8 Seminar
9 Group Study
10 Music Practice Room

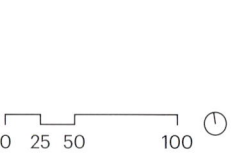

0   25 50   100

This sweeping central ground plane, known as the Lifted Lawn, rises above Woodland Walk, a key path through campus. It provides valuable public space while creating a secure zone for students and a single point of entry. Beyond this forecourt rises a series of brick, limestone, wood, and glass structures that maintain a sense of intimacy and complexity despite their large scale.

This ensemble, whose eastern edge extends like the prow of a boat, wraps around a cloister-like internal courtyard, its edges lined with structures of changing heights and opacities. From here one approaches diverse interior spaces: a triple-height entrance lobby, a cozy living room, a dining hall with a dramatic double-height pavilion, group study rooms, classrooms, and music practice spaces. Site lines prevail through most of these expanses, giving visitors a continual sense of orientation and connection.

The undulating brick building embraces two outdoor places: the private Heyman Courtyard (below) and the public Lifted Lawn (above), separated from each other by a level change. This device solved the fundamental urban design challenge of the project: how to make a building permitted with only one public entry appear open and inviting on all faces.

New College House

A publicly accessible, open-air walkway cuts through the building, drawing pedestrians upward to the Lifted Lawn and downward to Chestnut Street. This pedestrian link maintains the public site connections, despite the building length, while keeping the courtyard secure for students and visible for everyone.

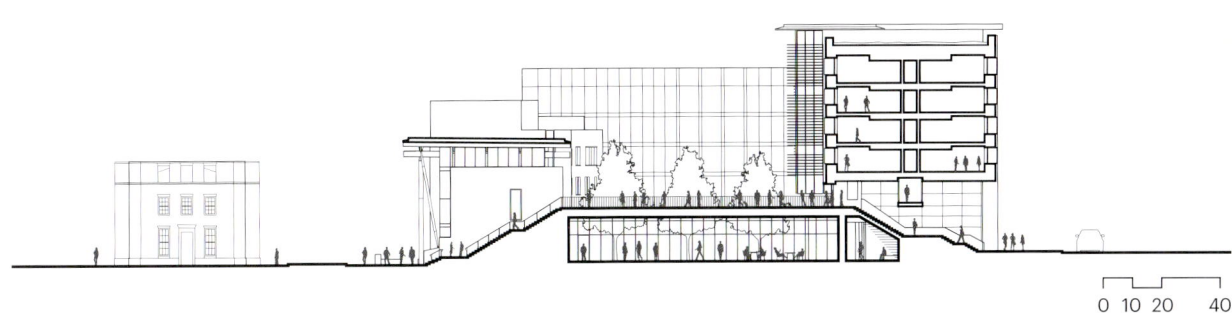

0 10 20   40

Wood-slat walls mark the exterior public passageway stair that cuts through the building, crossing over the ground-floor lobby and under the upper-level residential bridge. The wood-slat "wedge" transforms the interior underside of the passageway stair into a sculptural element that marks the intersecting paths and courtyard.

New College House

On the upper floors, "neighborhoods" of suites cluster around hallways, common areas, and sunny, double-height wood and glass towers that provide lofty gathering points and help break down the building's scale.

The vibrant mix of spaces and uses have created what New College House Faculty Director Cam Grey calls a "learning lab," which "allows our students and residents to come to the realization that life isn't bifurcated between intellectual pursuits and living."

More than anything, points out University of Pennsylvania architect David Hollenberg, the focus of New College House is community, and the building provides it at all scales. Students have their own spaces but constantly feel part of a larger body, from shared amenities and spaces to the many carefully framed views of both the Penn Campus and the city at large.

The building is an engine for promoting spontaneous and programmed human connections. Suites are collected around a Commons, offering community gathering spaces. Organized as glass towers, they punctuate the facade with lanterns of activity.

A wood-lined reading room overlooks a pair of splaying board-formed concrete columns and the campus gateway.

"The building delights on so many levels—
its marvelous integration of public and private
open space, its sophisticated approach to
fostering communities at multiple levels, its
integration with the urban fabric, its deft
use of materials, its craftsmanship, and, in particular, its assured manipulation of scale,"
notes Hollenberg. "New College House will,
we believe, instantly become an integral
part of the landscape of residential living
at Penn, a fitting partner to the beloved Quad
at the opposite end of the campus."

Soma Towers

Rising from a multilayered podium of tiered public plazas, the eighteen- and twenty-one-story SOMA towers are modern, imaginative additions to the emerging downtown of Bellevue, Washington.

Bohlin Cywinski Jackson partnered on the mixed-use buildings with John Su, a trained civil engineer, turned developer and general contractor, who wanted to make a mark on the city's skyline, keep local businesses on the site, and create a vibrant cultural space, offering retail, food, art and varied events.

"We feel the engagement with the community is a benefit for everyone, including our business," said Su, whose company, Su Development, has been working in Bellevue for almost forty years.

Location
Bellevue, WA

Dates
2010–2016

Client
Su Development

Size
416,000 SF

Early sketch discussions studied how to activate the site through circulation patterns, environmental conditions, and architectural form.

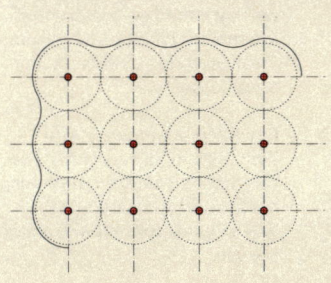

1

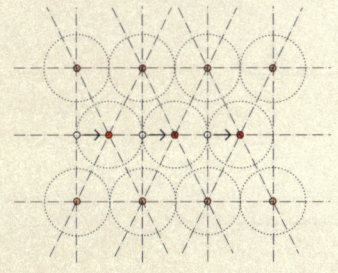

2

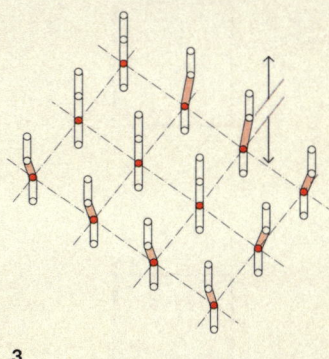

3

1 Typical Slab Shaping
2 SOMA Shifted Grid Design
3 SOMA Shifted Grid with
   Angled Columns

The design process included
a conceptual search for the
most efficient structural proper-
ties of a liquid material such
as concrete.

Sloping columns shift gravity
loads to grid patterns appropri-
ate to uses at each level, elim-
inating costly transfer beams,
and informing subtle shaping
of the towers directly related to
the forces within the structure.

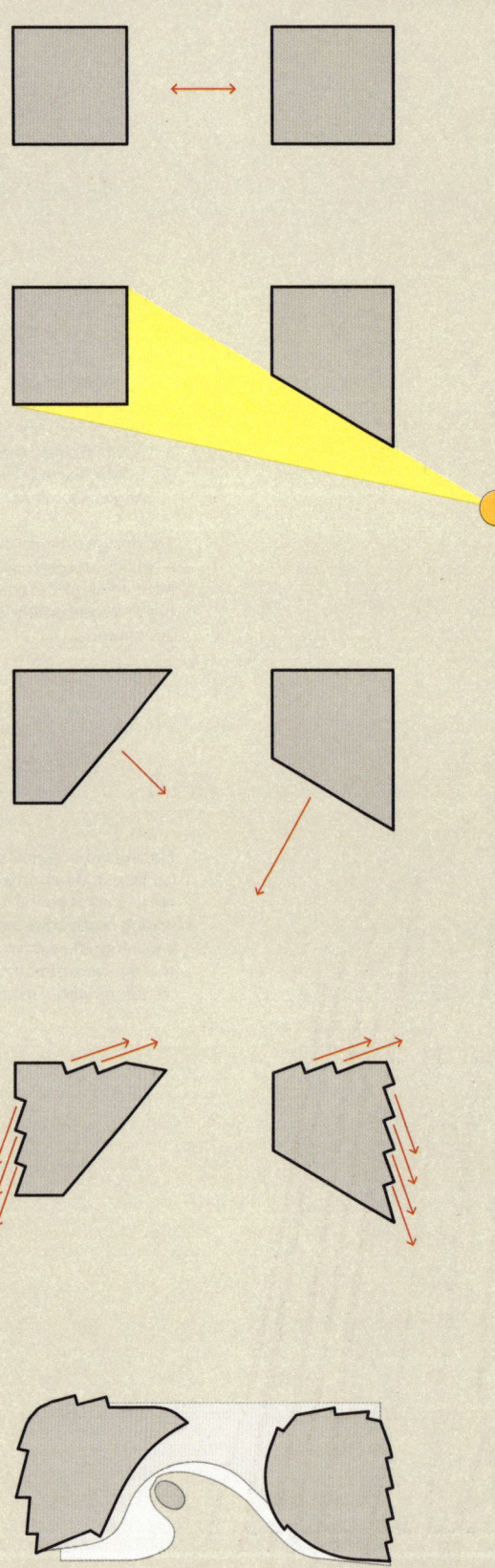

The client wanted to maximize the site by developing two towers that would be constructed in separate phases. The towers are placed side by side, facing one another.

Providing both towers with natural daylight was one of the first considerations determining the form. The square mass is carved in response to the arc of the sun.

Given the close proximity of the towers, the form is twisted to address privacy concerns and access to daylight.

Taking advantage of its setting in the Pacific Northwest, views of the Cascade Mountain Range to the east and Lake Washington and the Seattle skyline to the west are achieved through subtle shifts in the form.

The towers are further refined in their shape to encourage pedestrian traffic into the heart of the site.

The design team had never before worked on a high-rise but were intrigued by the opportunity to employ their human-centered philosophy at a larger scale. The firm's ability to approach the project with fresh eyes meant reimagining what has become a fairly predictable building type. Su, for his part, would suggest ambitious ideas and, on the flip side, keep the designers thinking pragmatically, from repeatable window wall systems to space-maximizing floor plans.

Visitors are pulled toward the graceful, modern towers at street level by a seventy-foot-tall cone of backlit fluted metal fins, from which is suspended an eighty-foot-long glass, aluminum, and steel leaf canopy. Around these focal points, operable retail storefronts open to extend, and in some cases shade, the adjacent street-level plaza, which hosts farmers markets, bazaars, and popular events.

The towers are located at the southwest edge of the high-rise zoning.

Site Plan
1   SOMA Towers
2   Downtown Bellevue Park
3   Retail District
4   Residential District

0   250   500   1000

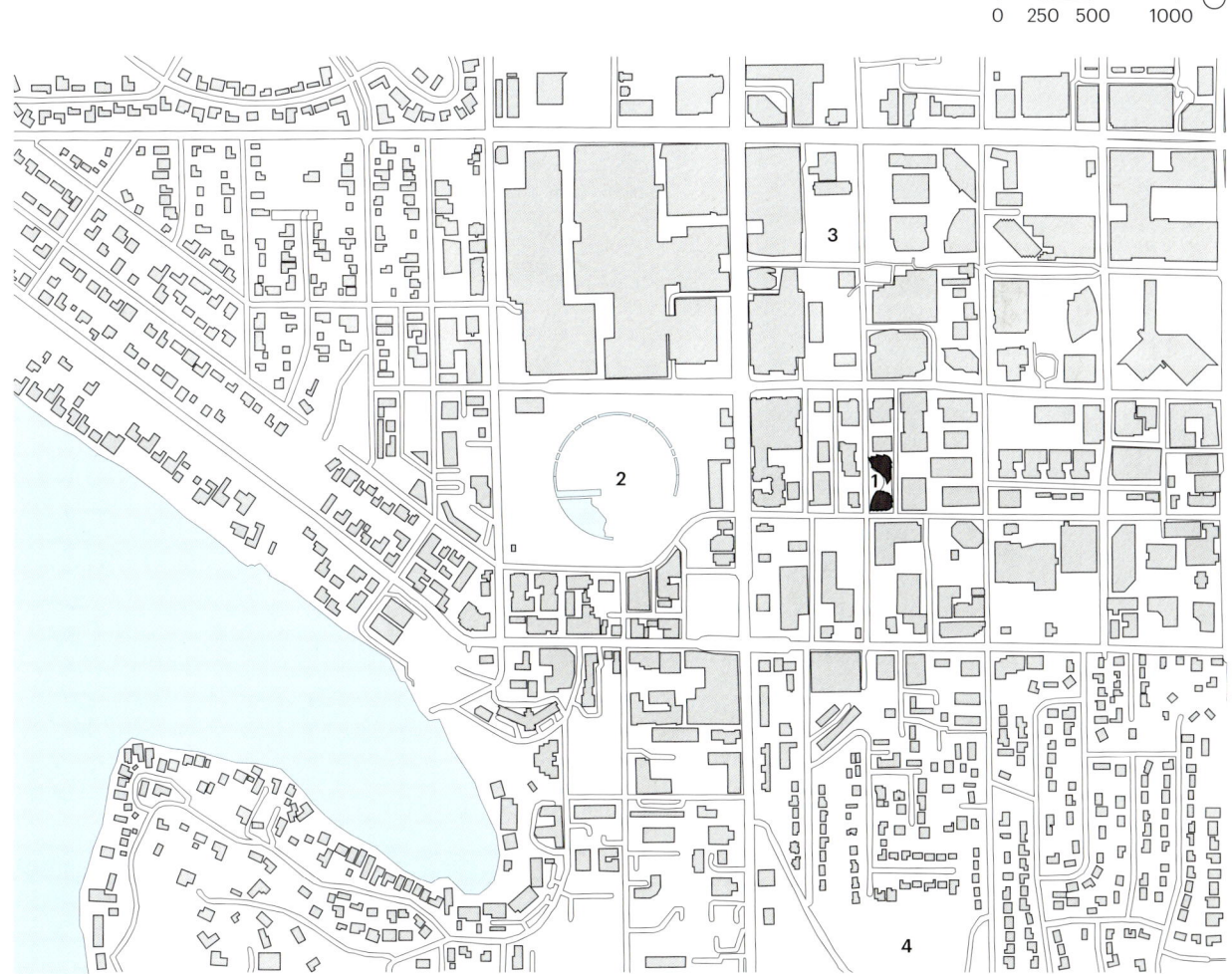

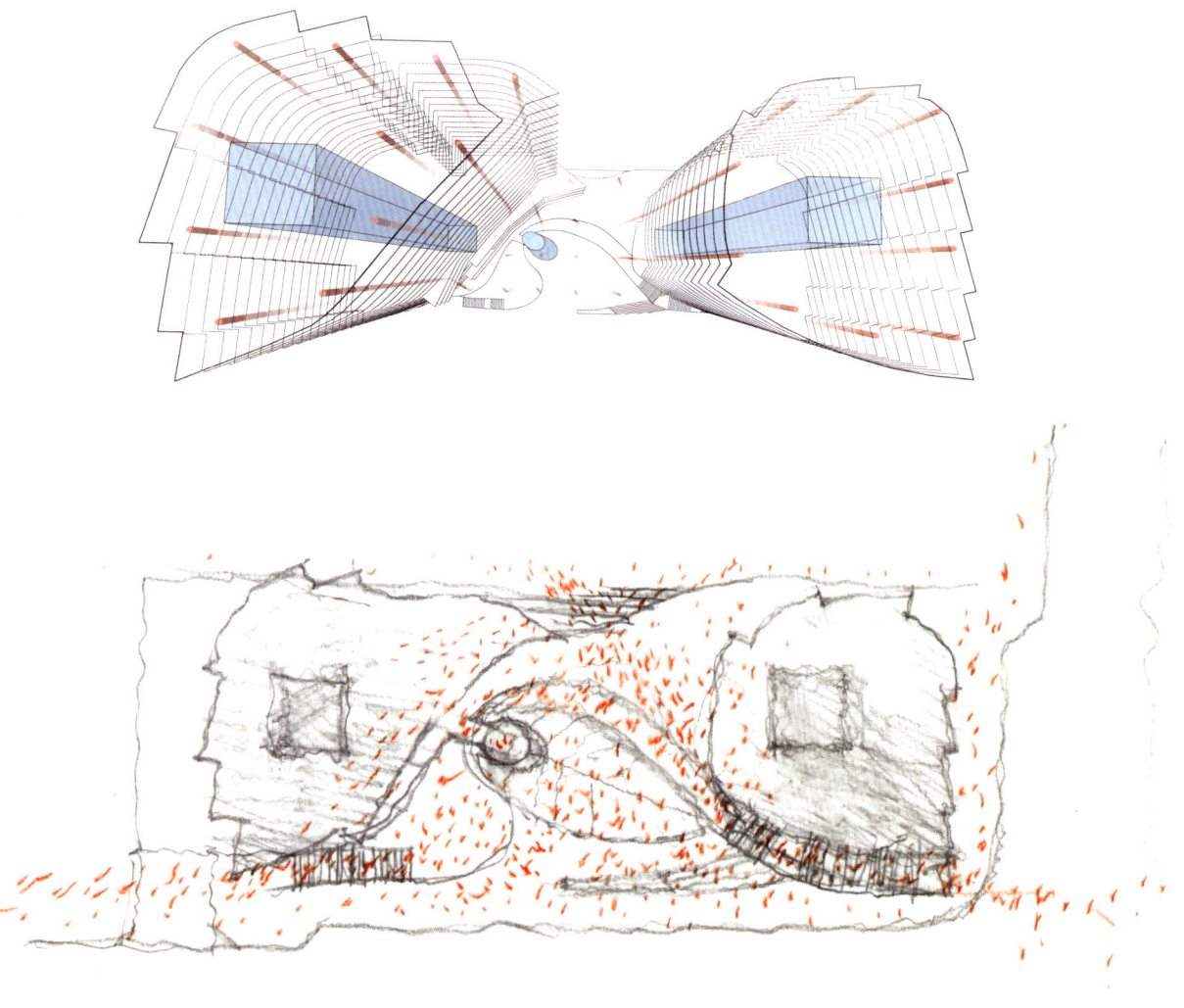

Sculptural elements in the project's center provide clear wayfinding and allow daylight deep into the below-grade garage marking the vertical circulation leading to retail, the leasing office, and public restaurants. The Cone and Leaf were designed to be shop-fabricated in Taiwan and shipped to the site in segments assuring efficient assembly.

Soma Towers

Outdoor stairs enable a natural flow to the podium floors, containing restaurants, cafés, and outdoor perches. The east edge of this level intentionally relates to a new hotel across the way, while the northwest corner houses Resonance, a double-height concert and gallery space opening to its west to bring music to the city.

Above this bustling public face, the buildings contain a linked third-floor amenity level containing a luminous lap pool and a media room, fitness studio, and sweeping public terrace for gardening and grilling. This level is topped by hundreds of one- and two-bedroom residential units.

The operable facade of Resonance, a music venue and community amenity, projects over the garage entry as a welcoming marker.

Between the towers, circulation paths, on multiple levels, orbit around the Cone and Leaf and add layers of visible activity to the plaza.

Their glass skin is a mosaic of clear, transparent, and opaque, selected to reflect the region's continually shifting skies, and ranging from clear vision glazing to matte gray and bright white. Overcast evenings and soft winter mornings render the towers in subtle, pearlescent gray tones, while bright summer afternoons bring a reflective sheen that accentuates the structure's light-hued spandrels.

The buildings' curved facades and tall glass windows maximize views of the Cascades, Lake Washington, and the Seattle skyline, while post tensioned concrete supports lofty floor heights, staggered columns, and a refreshing variety of units. Floorplates extend well beyond the building envelope, with thin, concrete floor slabs at the buildings' corners, creating lengthy, dynamic balconies with views in all directions. Their diverse, sharply angled forms shape a dramatic, multipointed silhouette against the sky.

Four-foot six-inch-wide modules utilize a mosaic of glass types to complete the building skin. A higher percentage of vision glass is employed at living spaces and corners. The rigorous order of the modules repeats every third floor yet provides an appearance of randomness.

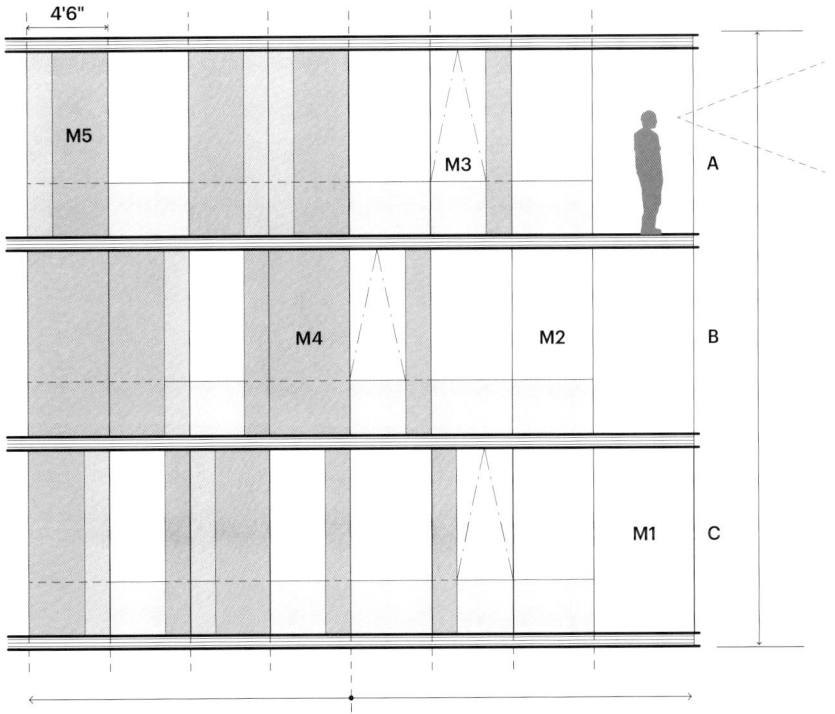

M1 Vision Glass
M2 Vision Glass; Black Spandrel
M3 Vision Glass; Black Spandrel;
    100% Gray Spandrel
M4 100% Gray Spandrel
M5 100% Black Spandrel;
    60% Gray Spandrel

The firm's collaboration with Su transformed what could have been a repetitive, monolithic structure into a balance of technical rigor, structural audacity, and poetic intuition. The building's subtle shifts in form and surface mask the towers' significant sizes and render their volumes softer and thinner—almost transparent.

"We've gotten a lot of praise from people around the city," noted Su, who is now embarking with the firm on a second residential tower a few blocks north of SOMA. "It has really helped us in terms of reputation."

Oblique unit layouts yield a rich variety of spaces, each with unique views.

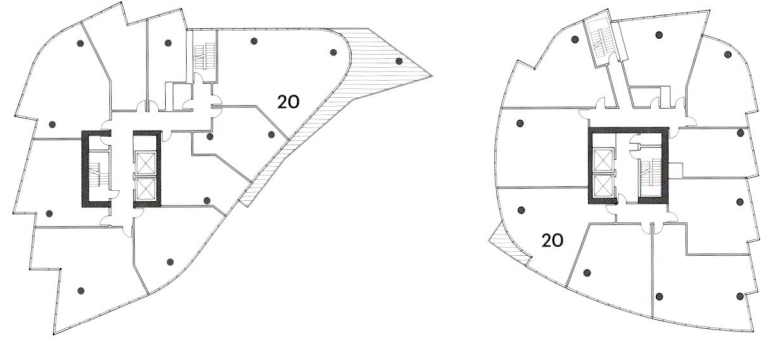

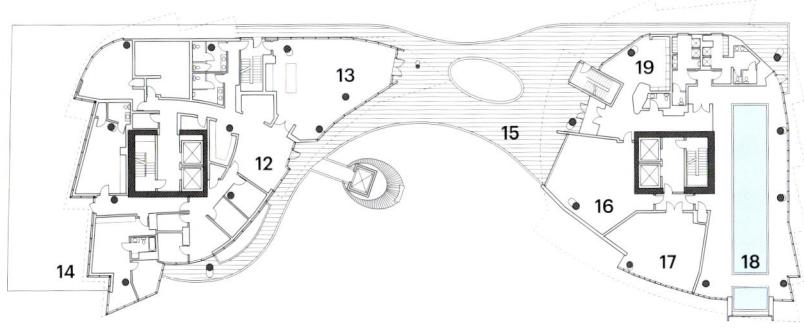

1	Parking Entry
2	Coffee Shop
3	Restaurant/Bar
4	Marketplace
5	Vertical Circulation
6	Exterior Seating
7	Loading
8	Glass Canopy
9	Offices
10	Performance Space
11	Commercial Space
12	Leasing Office
13	Community Room
14	Dog Walk
15	Amenity Deck
16	Media Room
17	Gym
18	Pool
19	Mail
20	Residential Units
21	Public Deck

Level 7

Level 3

Level 2

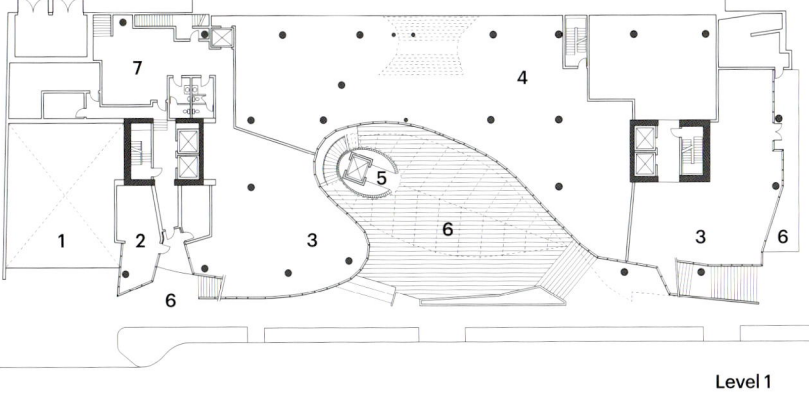

Level 1

0   16   32   64

Soma Towers

Frick Environmental Center

The Frick Environmental Center, a collaboration between the City of Pittsburgh and the Pittsburgh Parks Conservancy, merges building, landscape, and a palpable sense of civic and environmental advocacy. Thanks to rigorous planning and sensitive design, it has become a new Pittsburgh landmark and a valuable environmental teaching tool.

Nestled into a sloping hillside within the 644 wooded acres of Frick Park, just east of the city's center, the structure received LEED Platinum certification, an AIA Committee on the Environment (COTE) Top Ten Plus award, and is the first free, public building to receive Living Building certification. This is a highly rigorous performance standard that requires buildings to address sustainable design in a holistic fashion.

To envision the Conservancy's new home, the team worked with over one thousand community members—from park visitors to city officials—discussing and crafting potential uses and design concepts.

Location
Pittsburgh, Pennsylvania

Dates
2011–2016

Client
Pittsburgh Parks Conservancy and the City of Pittsburgh

Size
15,500 SF

Community members participated in the decade-long planning process. Outreach and engagement included planning meetings, focus groups, hands-on design workshops, and park walks. The process helped to define the ambitious vision for the Center: to advance Pittsburgh's position as a national leader in green design.

Implicit in the design philosophy is the belief that sustainability, resiliency, and functionality are at the heart of truly beautiful buildings, a holistic design approach exemplified by this Living Building.

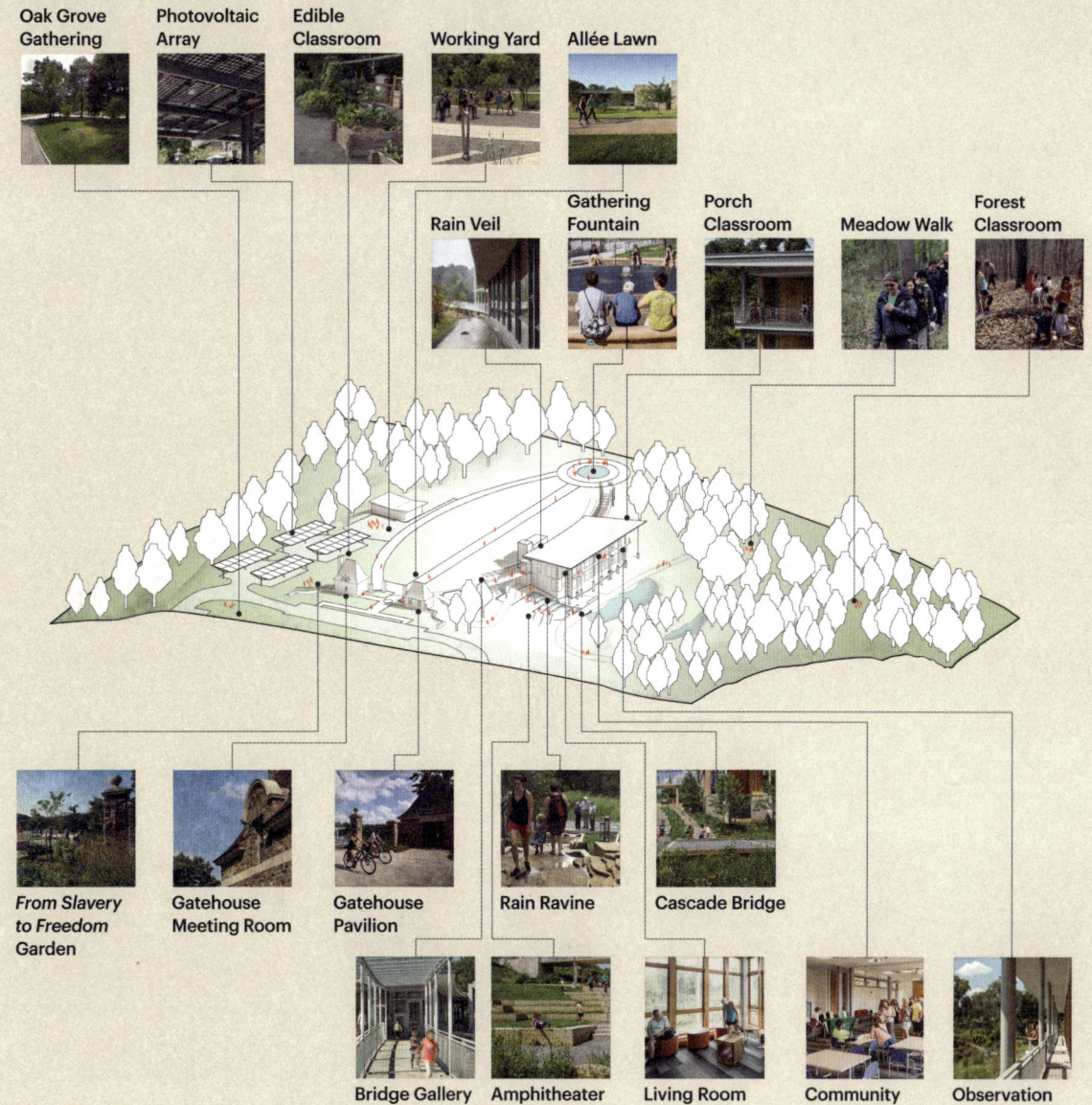

Oak Grove Gathering

Photovoltaic Array

Edible Classroom

Working Yard

Allée Lawn

Rain Veil

Gathering Fountain

Porch Classroom

Meadow Walk

Forest Classroom

From Slavery to Freedom Garden

Gatehouse Meeting Room

Gatehouse Pavilion

Rain Ravine

Cascade Bridge

Bridge Gallery

Amphitheater

Living Room

Community Classroom

Observation Balcony

The building and surrounding site are educational ecosystems for both immersive outdoor education and hands-on lessons in sustainability. The programs and events hosted on site serve the dual purpose of enriching the educational experience of local student and neighborhood populations, as well as improving public awareness and thus, the health and vitality of the park.

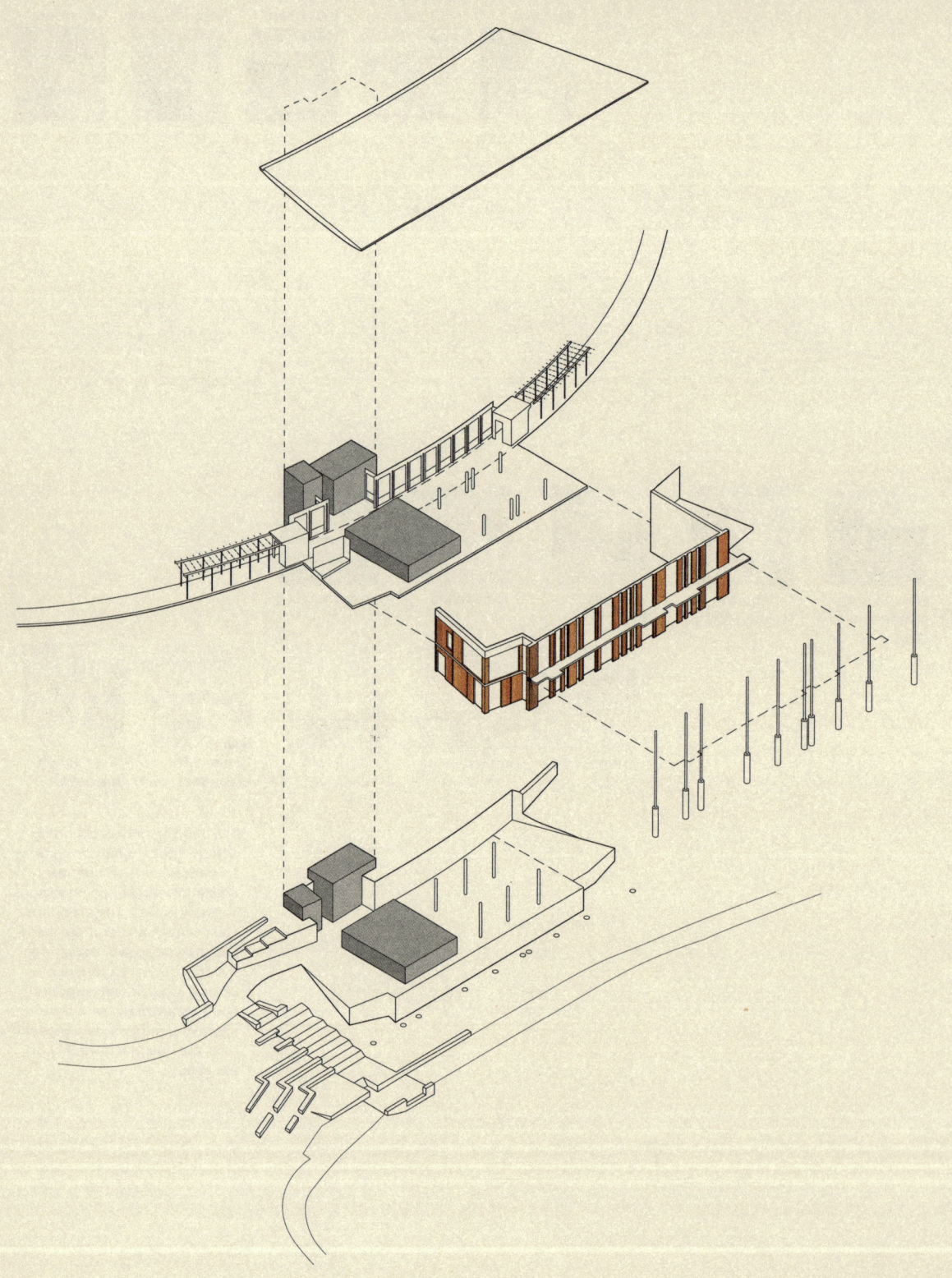

"We talked a lot about wanting the Center to feel like a home for everyone. We were immediately drawn to Bohlin Cywinski Jackson because they offered a feeling of sophistication and warmth," notes Marijke Hecht, who led the project for the Conservancy. The building includes Conservancy offices and public educational spaces, combined in a structure that acts both literally and symbolically as a bridge between the built and natural worlds.

The three-story structure, clad in locally harvested black locust, blends gracefully with the surrounding woods. It is approached via scalloped granite paths and a raised bridge that shepherd visitors from John Russell Pope's restored 1930s gatehouses toward the ridge-side Center, which unfolds views to the rest of the park; a perch in the forest.

1 Restored Gatehouses
2 Allée
3 Gathering Fountain
4 Service Bam
5 Photovoltaic Array & Parking
6 Main Building

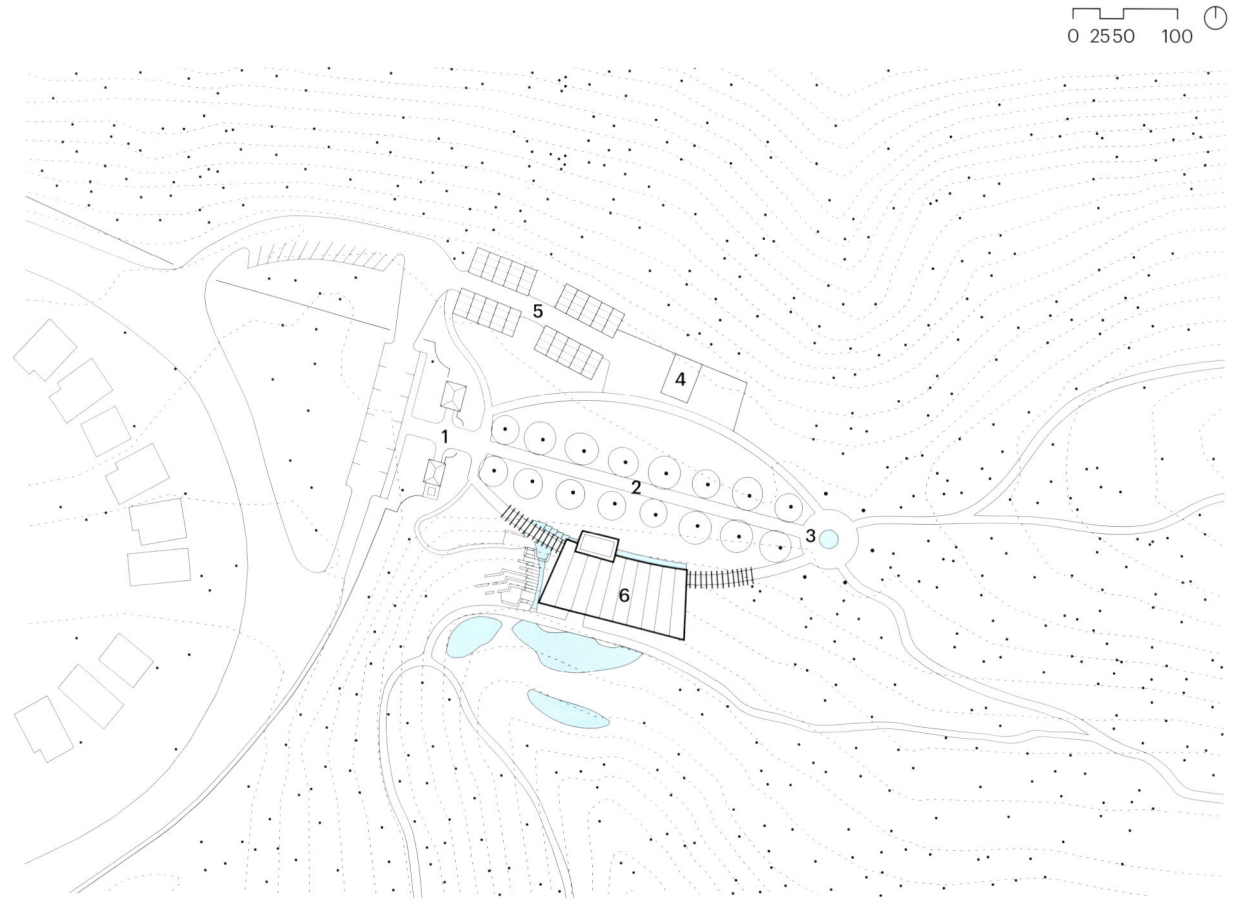

Frick Environmental Center

Just before the entry, the southward sloping land is carved by meandering sandstone spillways, designed by artist Stacy Levy, which make visible the building's water conservation mission. The curved pathway continues through the building, informally pulling people inside. To the south, the structure's full-height wood windows provide expansive vistas of the park, while its staggered, exposed steel exterior columns emulate the forest. A steel grate balcony allows views both downward and outward, while a soaring canopy projects ten feet, acting as a rain veil, and shading internal spaces which are naturally lit and ventilated through operable windows.

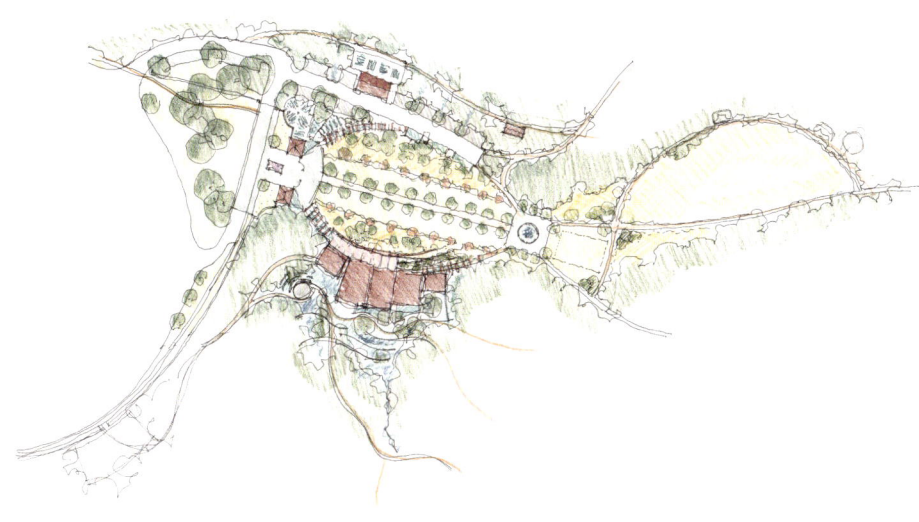

The historic gatehouses and fountain establish the axis of entry.

The master plan completed by Innocenti & Webel in the 1930s informs the park's curved circulation paths.

LaQuatra Bonci Associates worked with Bohlin Cywinski Jackson and the Parks Conservancy to realize a new plan for equitable public access while honoring the history of the site.

Frick Environmental Center

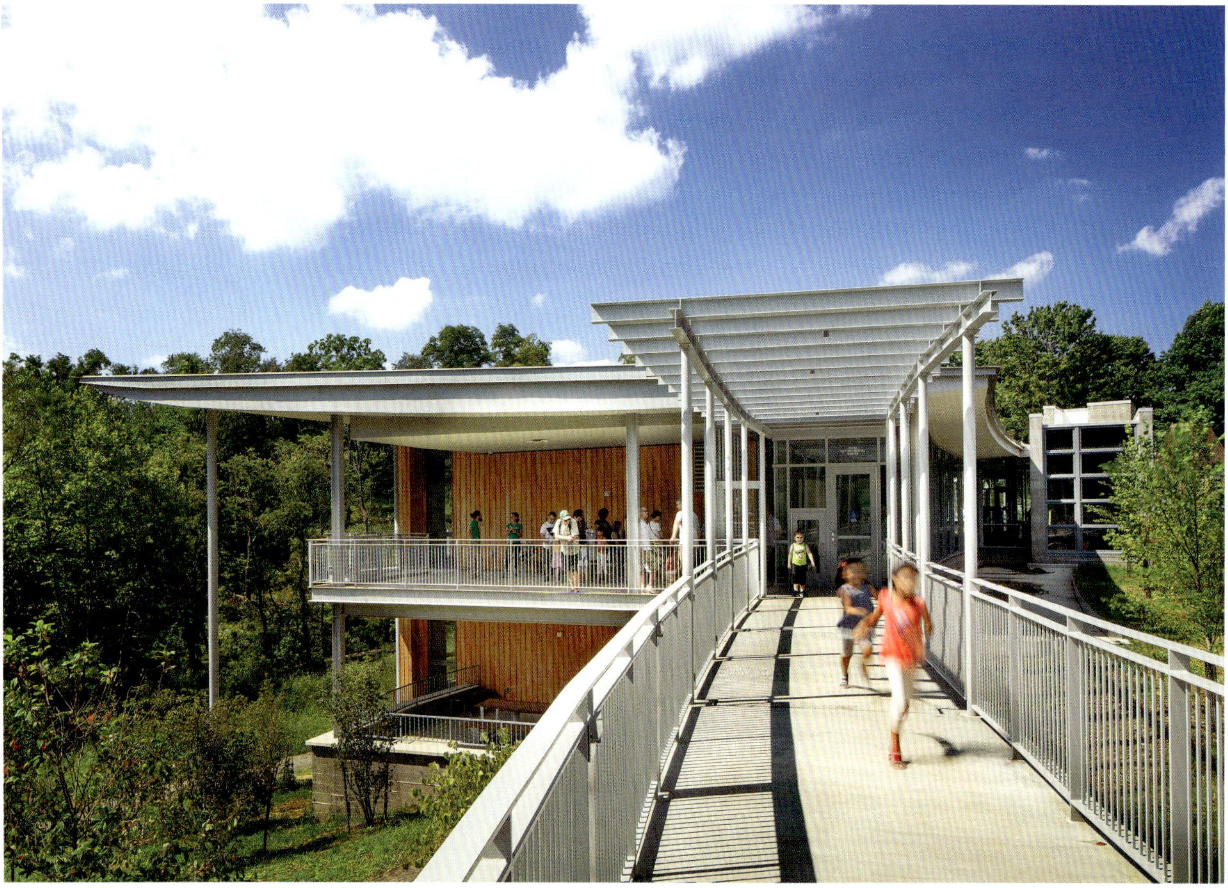

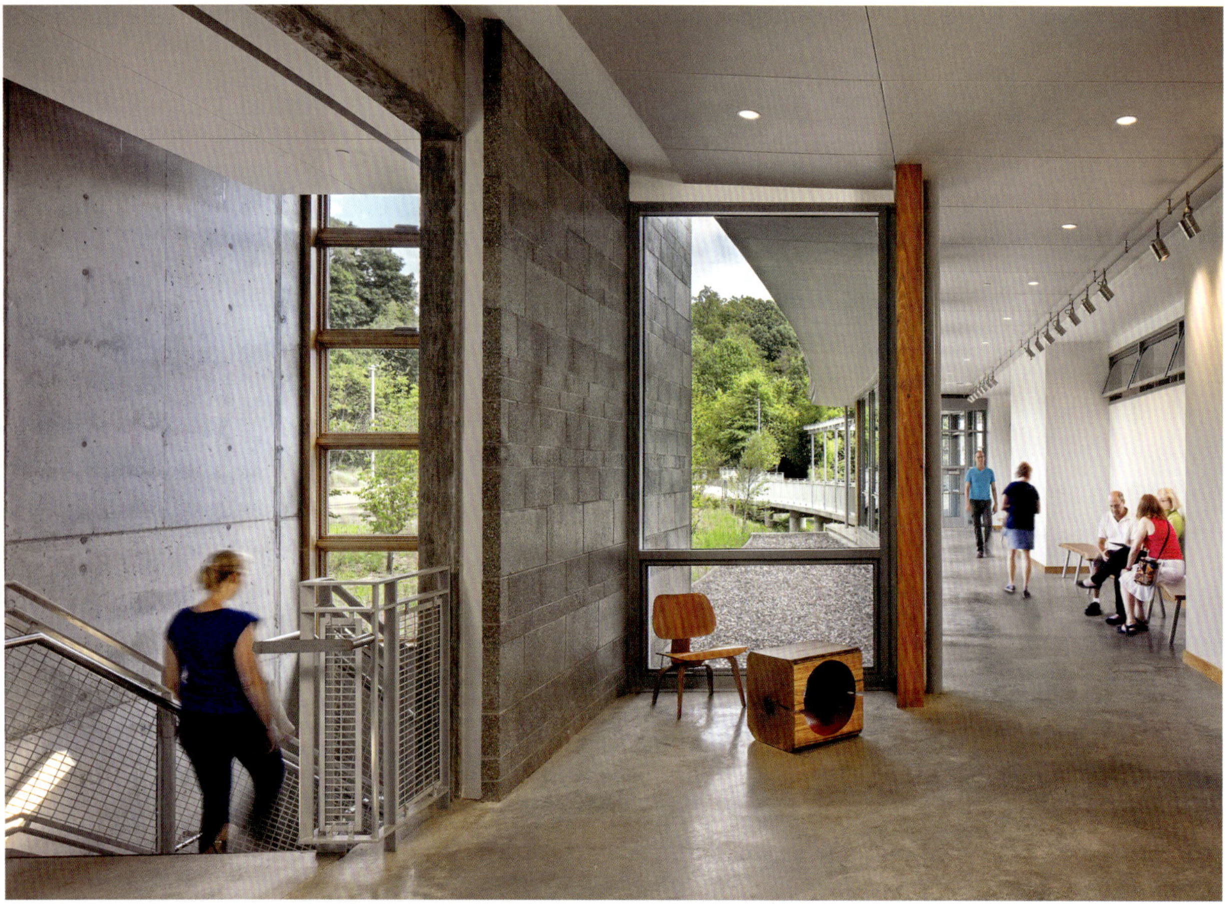

These are just a few of the many sustainable strategies incorporated into the project; others include nontoxic building materials, a geothermal heating and cooling system, photovoltaic arrays, a UV water filtration system, and drought-tolerant landscaping. These help the building achieve both on-site net-zero energy and net-zero water.

"They make an impression on us even when we're not conscious of them," notes Hecht, of the many sustainable building blocks. "The level of thought for each detail was absolutely amazing."

In a feature called the Rain Veil, rainwater cascades in a dynamic curtain of water from the roof, visible from inside and out. From there, the rainwater channels into the Rain Ravine— a stepped sandstone water feature. The water playfully meanders down the hillside of the amphitheater, continuing its journey to the wetlands below.

Frick Environmental Center

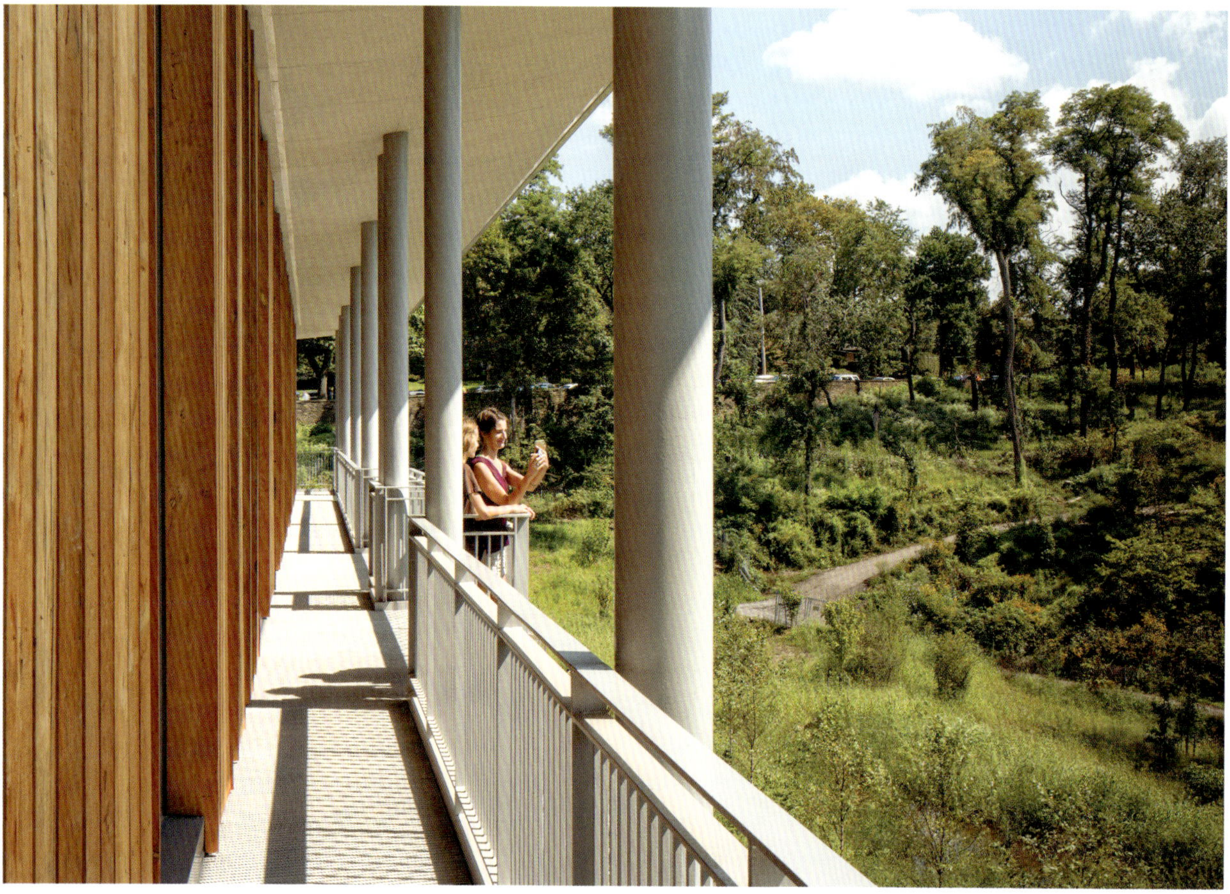

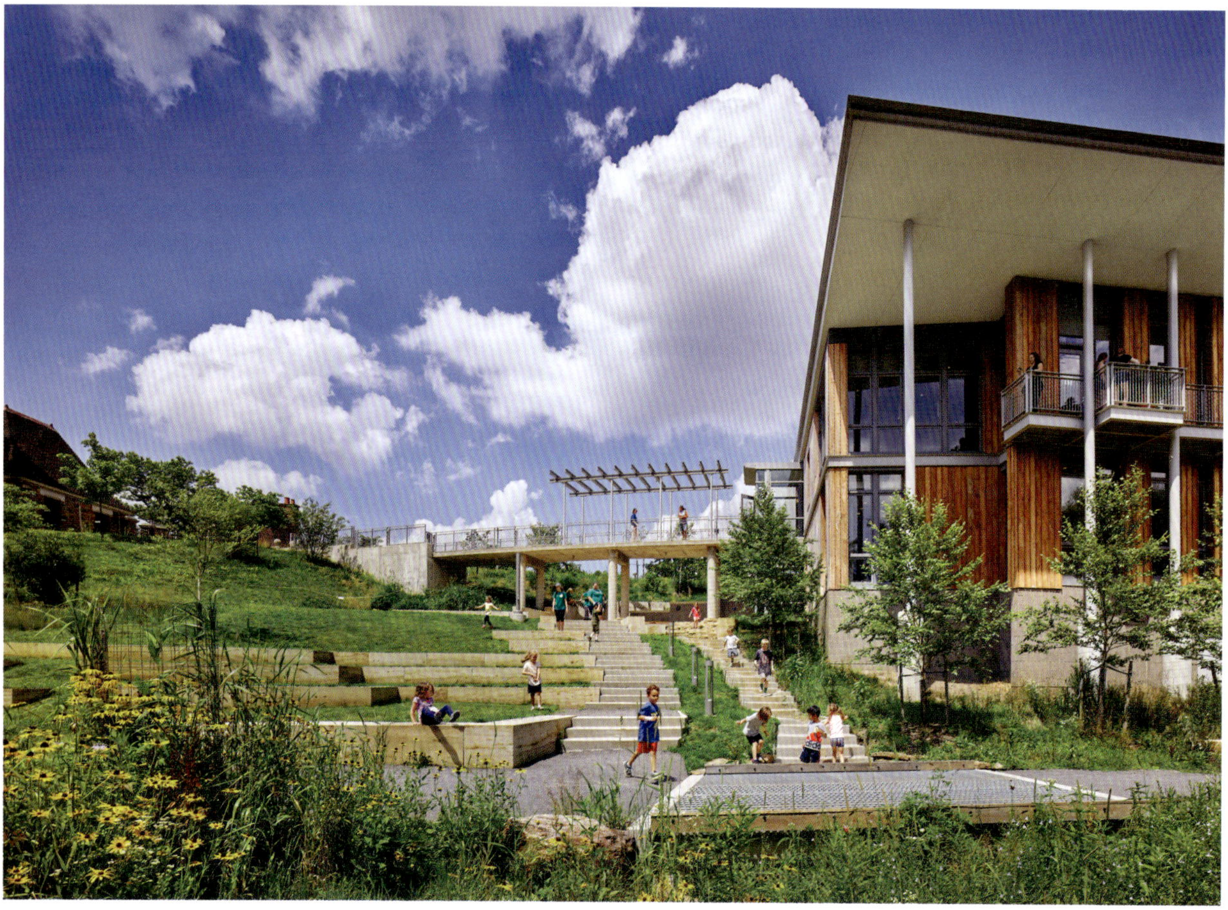

Once visitors pass through the building's curved concrete hallway and past its classrooms, environmental gallery, public living room, and locally-milled reception desk, they continue into the park via another bridge, leading to Pope's historic stone fountain. The design team has reimagined this important marker, preserving its outer ring as a seat wall, while making it more compact and sustainable. From here one is set to explore the city's largest municipal park, which includes winding trails, wildflower meadows, steeply sloped valleys, and wooded slopes.

The project, which also includes parking, a service barn, and extensive landscaping and ecological restoration, carefully balances sustainability, historic preservation, and a modern spirit to create a beacon that both blends into and stands out from its pastoral setting. It's not just a place of learning, but a living classroom that serves as an architectural teaching lab and inspiration.

"It's always been about how we're able to work together in order to be able to produce something that we can hand to the next generation," noted Pittsburgh Mayor, Bill Peduto at the Center's grand opening. "We celebrate not only a Center, but the collaboration of a city coming together to make it happen."

At almost every planning exercise during the process, an outdoor place to host programs, concerts, and lectures was at the top of the list of public priorities. An amphitheater was designed into the hillside for a variety of community gatherings.

Marquez Hall

Golden, Colorado, is home to one of the most prestigious engineering schools in the world, Colorado School of Mines. Bohlin Cywinski Jackson, working in collaboration with Anderson Mason Dale, was selected to design Marquez Hall, home to the college's petroleum engineering program, which allowed them to showcase not only the department's innovative new curriculum—focusing as much on renewable energy as drilling—but to promote a new level of architecture on campus.

The four-story, L-shaped structure, located near the east end of the university, introduces a contemporary and architecturally ambitious aesthetic to the traditional architecture of the campus. Changing this condition had become a priority for Bill Scoggins, School of Mines President at the time, and his campus architect, Chris Cocallas.

In association with
Anderson Mason Dale Architects

Location
Golden, CO

Dates
2006–2012

Client
Colorado School of Mines

Size
87,000 SF

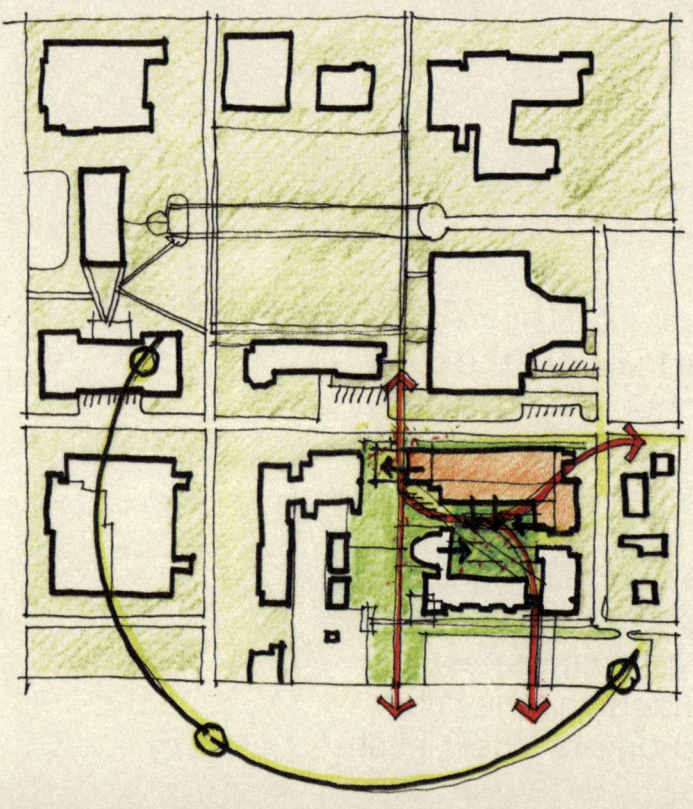

The School of Mines 2010 master plan established the opportunity to incorporate more open spaces and to link pedestrian ways—main entries, gateways, and important paths and intersections activating the new quads—throughout the campus.

Open Space / Student Life

The extended front porch of Marquez's west lobby creates a gateway (1) along the primary established pedestrian path of Cheyenne Way (2). Jalili Plaza (3), an intimate, open space includes a lawn, tree groves, and native plants, and covered study areas with custom concrete and steel furniture.

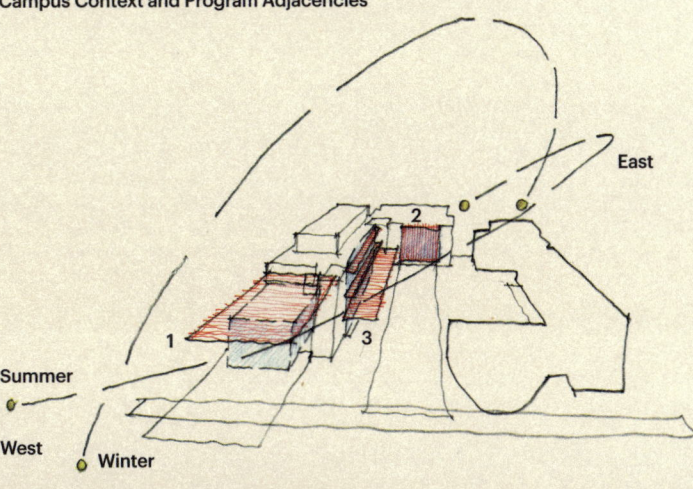

Campus Context and Program Adjacencies

Marquez Hall bounds the open space adjacent to the existing Center for Technology and Learning Media (CTLM) to create a shared plaza that provides access to and is energized by Marquez's south study spaces (1), general classroom lecture hall (2), and CTLM's entry (3) and auditorium (4), while providing a new connection to the south campus (5).

Solar Control and Daylighting Strategies

The west lobby's deep cantilever and south overhang (1) work in tandem with an integral top down shading system. Layered glass frits protect classrooms while allowing oblique views (2). Light colored, horizontal shades of steel grating bounce indirect daylight (3) while the deep canopy protects indoor/outdoor study spaces and a primary circulation path.

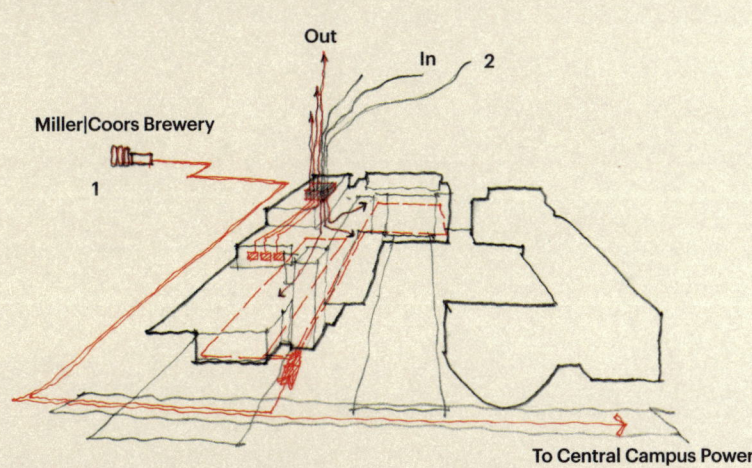

Building Energy and Waste Heat Recycling

Waste steam from the brewery production process is piped to Mines and used for the campus' hydronic heat system (1). Laboratory and fume hood exhaust pre-heats mechanical system's intake air (2).

Marquez Hall

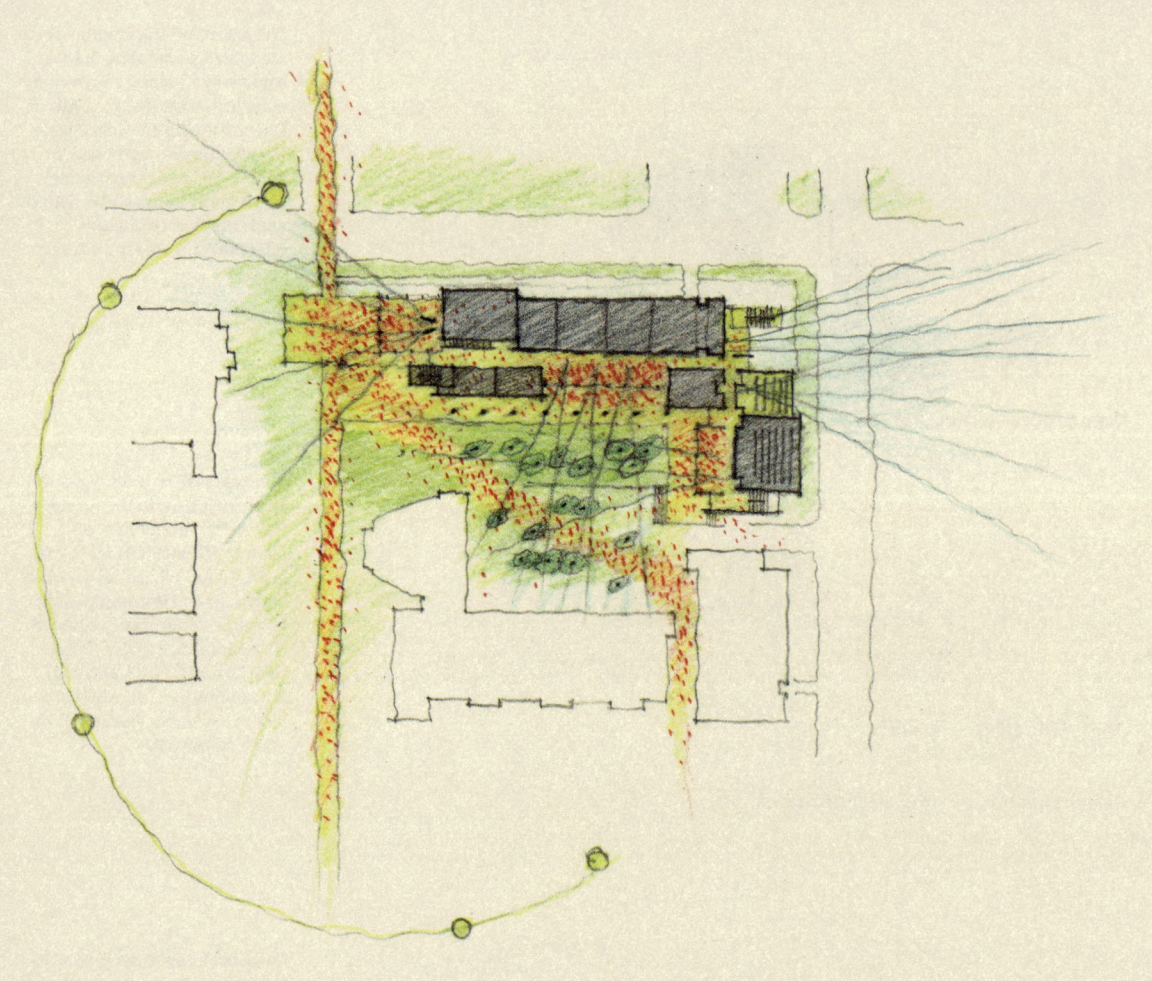

The building wraps around a new quadrangle, Jalili Plaza—a bold combination of lawn, trees, and native grasses whose staggered diagonal axis creates a new flow from Cheyenne Way toward a growing part of campus to the south-east. Along this path the firm installed a loose gradient of playfully scattered steel-plate seating, planters, and linear concrete benches.

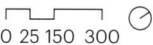

0 25 150 300

For Marquez's skin, the team updated the campus's beige-brick palette with rectangular, blond terra-cotta panels, lending it a more modern, streamlined feel. Large metallic canopies project from the structure's lateral sides, while classrooms cantilever over Jalili, providing shade and walkways underneath.

The most ambitious element is the cantilevered entrance canopy, held in place by steel-plate box beams buried into the building itself. The dramatic projection juts westward a full sixty feet over the building's west portal, clad with walls of low-e glass, marking an important position on one of the school's main pedestrian thoroughfares, Cheyenne Way.

Moving through the glazed foyer, under the shimmering metal-paneled soffit and muscular LED light bands, a view into the school's drilling simulator, framed by two V-shaped columns, becomes another natural showcase for the school.

Aluminum panels clad the tapered steel box columns and beams that provide a spring point for Marquez's grand gesture. The cantilevered roof's backspan utilizes the full frame of the building structure.

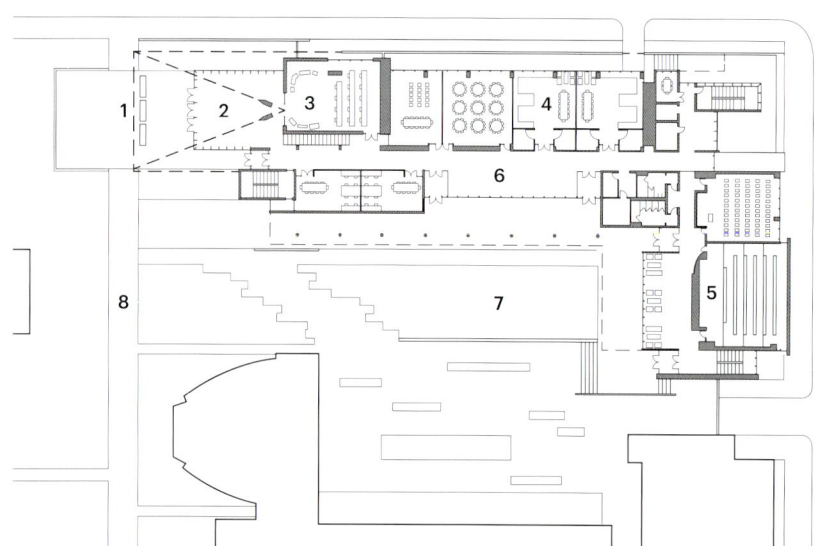

Floor Plan
1   West Plaza
2   Lobby
3   Science-in-Sight Lab
4   Lab
5   General Classroom
6   Student Gallery
7   Courtyard/Plaza
8   Cheyenne Way

0 10 20 40

Marquez Hall

Marquez Hall

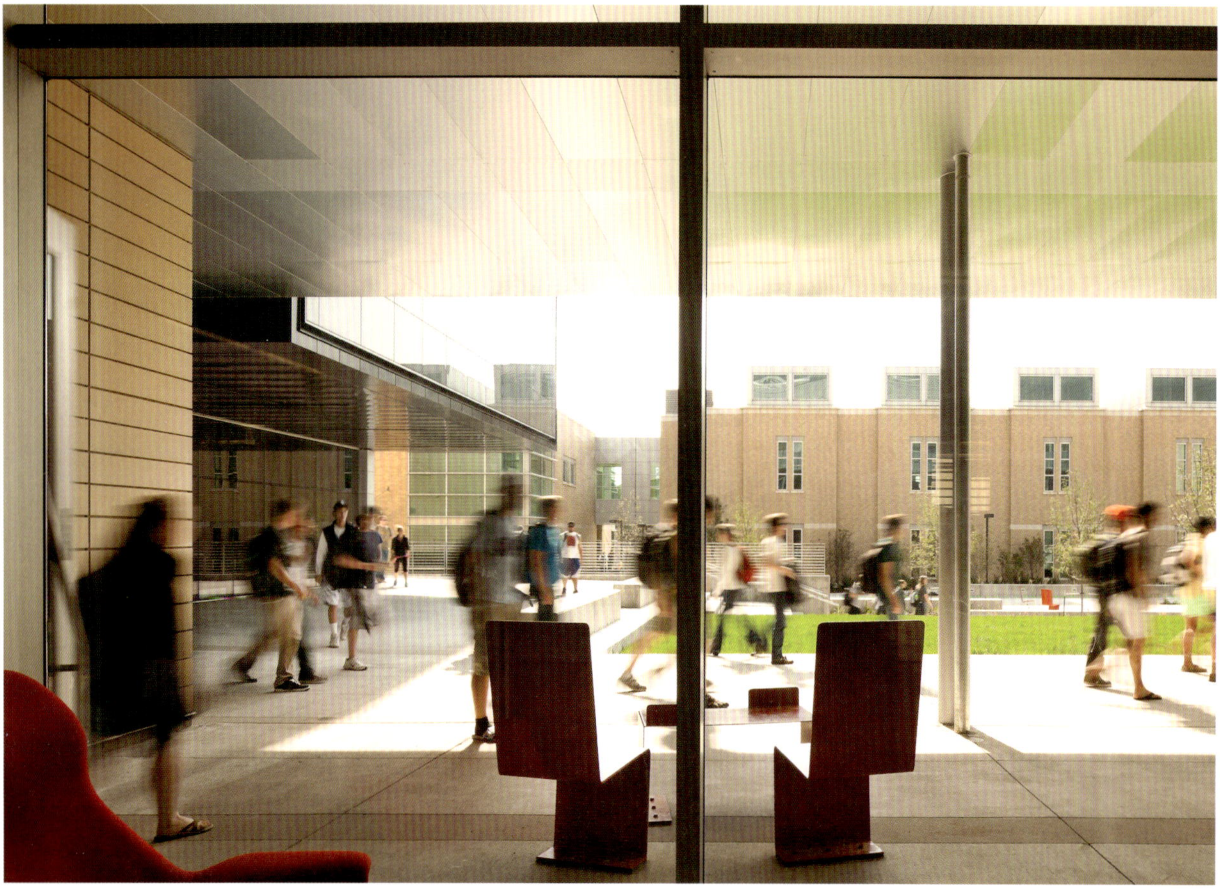

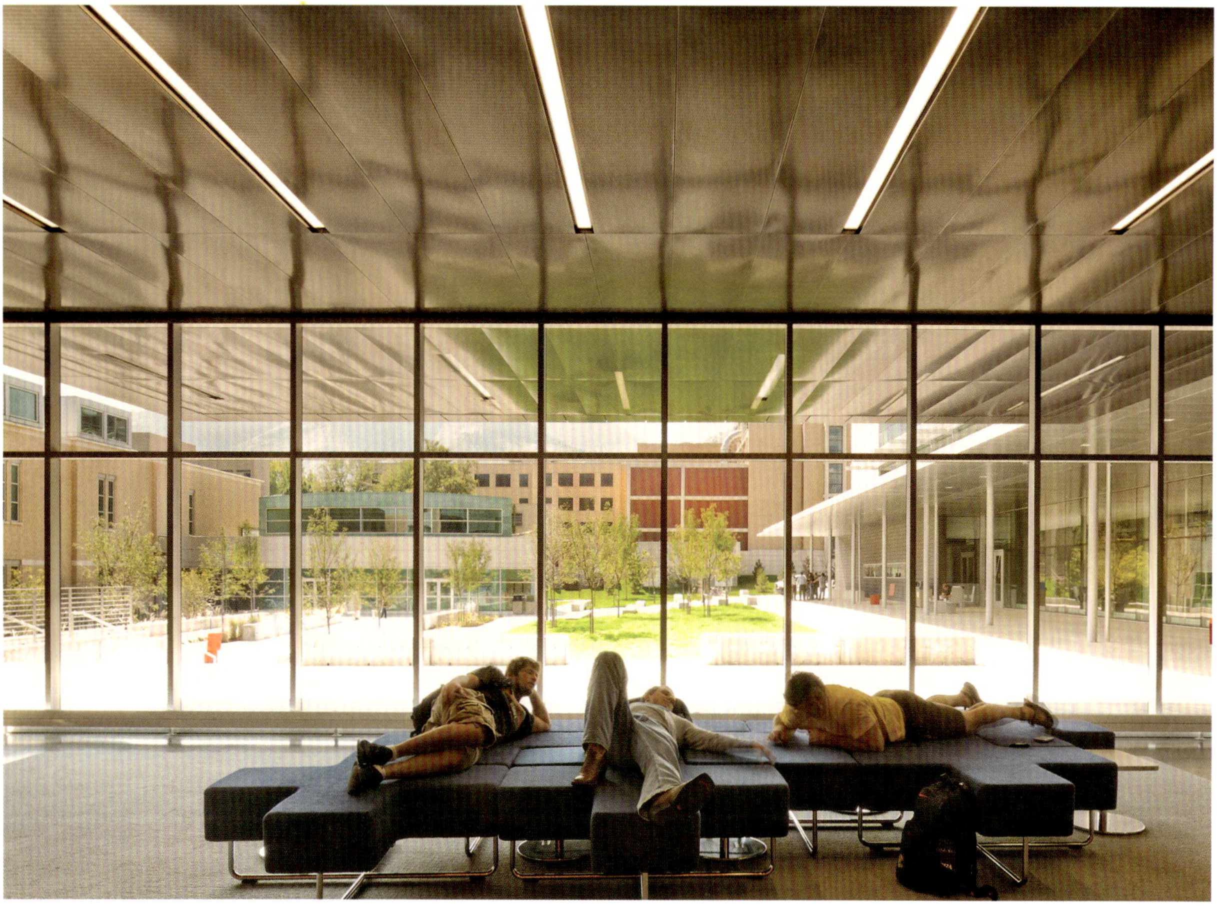

As visitors progress through the interior, the facade's terra-cotta and aluminum palette extends inside, ushering them through an open core full of lower-level public spaces and into a more rigorous series of labs and classrooms. Bridges cross above open metal-clad stairs. Exposed aluminum slat ceilings maintain the high tech, engineering-inspired aesthetic.

Framed views northward toward Golden's rugged landscape, including rocky mesas like Table Mountain, orient the building in its dramatic Colorado setting. And tall glass walls—shaded by metallic canopies and louvers—bring the outside in and connect the building to the rest of campus.

While Jalili Plaza's southwest orientation offers sunny places to sit, a deep ground-level canopy shades the exterior seating and study areas and protects a primary circulation path as a semi-formal colonnade—Marquez Hall's south porch. Expressive shades protect Level 2 and 3 offices, a striking horizontal highlight to the operable butt-glazed curtain wall.

To combat the extreme temperature swings of the Rocky Mountain Front Range, the terra cotta and glass building envelope was tested for air infiltration during construction. Building pressure testing, infrared camera analysis, and spray testing for air and water infiltration, led directly to in-field fine tuning to maximize envelope efficiency.

Marquez Hall

The building has already had a significant effect both on campus energy and recruitment.

"It has really activated the area," says Cocallas, who lauds the firm's crafting of architectural energy and deft balance of solidity and lightness. "When visitors come to campus they really see a difference. We've really raised the level of architecture and the quality of the experience."

Marquez Hall

CoorsTek Center for Applied Science and Engineering

In 2014, the Colorado School of Mines selected Bohlin Cywinski Jackson, working in collaboration with Anderson Mason Dale, to design a new physics facility on the school's main green, Kafadar Commons, that would become both a welcoming focus for campus life and an instigator of interdisciplinary learning. The firms' study process included meetings with school administrators, faculty, staff, and students. As they gained familiarity, the team began suggesting inventive solutions that went far beyond the nuts-and-bolts needs of faculty.

"As scientists we were thinking pragmatically," notes Jeff Squier, professor of Physics at the School of Mines. "We wanted classrooms and labs. They brought in a much more human element: suggesting ways for people to interact and flow."

In association with
Anderson Mason Dale Architects

Location
Golden, Colorado

Dates
2014–2018

Client
Colorado School of Mines

Size
95,000 SF

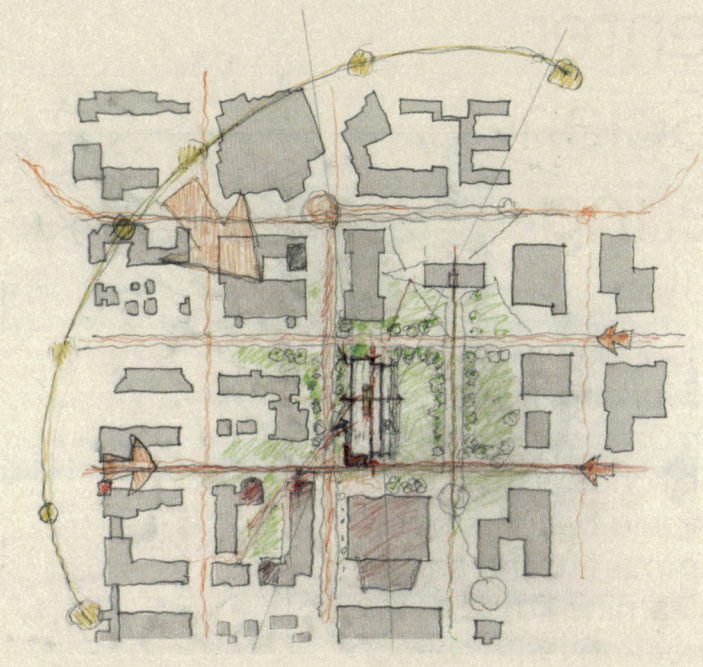

Initial sketches established the Center's priorities as a transformative campus building: engagement with existing pedestrian pathways via multiple entries; a dialogue across 16th Street with Marquez Hall and the southeast campus; acknowledgment of scale and proportion with adjacent historic campus buildings such as Guggenheim and Berthoud Halls; and, most importantly, an uncompromised commitment to the Kafadar Commons as the emotional heart of Mines.

Study models early in the process helped develop the site diagram into three dimensions. The three-story vertical cut capped by a skylight (left, in yellow) connects departments, both figuratively and literally.

Stair cores anchor a sectional relationship—between offices and labs, which float above public spaces, and the Commons (foreground)—diagrammatically enhancing the building's openness to the green. Models led the design team to prioritize the horizontal lengthening of these upper levels.

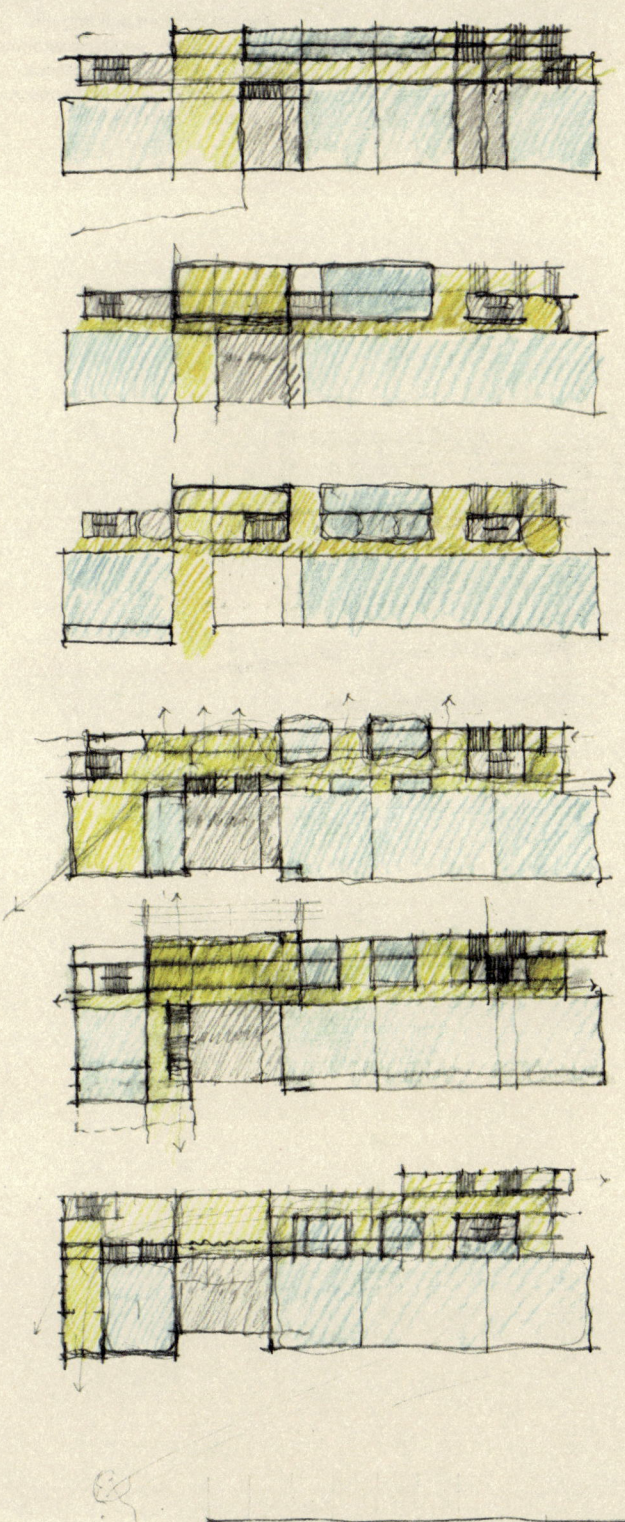

The program represents a dynamic mix of scientific disciplines and requirements. Focusing on the users and studying the spirit of the various departments and campus culture, the design team started asking questions: Are there unexpected spatial adjacencies that might make sense? What are the subtleties of public and private, open and closed, light and dark spaces? How might a lobby, corridor, or stair be arranged to bring about an impromptu discussion between a Physicist and a Chemist? And how might all of this be in service of the greater campus through relationships with adjacent paths, buildings, and open spaces?

The established building diagram includes south classrooms and labs, north social spaces, and a ground level that engages Kafadar Commons.

0   150 300 450

The four-story building—home to physics, applied sciences, and varied laboratories—has become a favored place on campus for students of many disciplines. Its glass facade, facing the quad to its north, is highly variegated, breaking down its mass and clearly delineating the uses inside. Two levels of offices float on thin columns above the transparent, set-back entrance, behind which lie the active internal public space, classrooms, and an event and conference space.

The double-height common space, accentuated by an open stair, is filled with furniture, changes of levels, and built-in socializing facilities. Visitors encounter this focal point on the way to each classroom—there are no double-loaded corridors on the ground level—encouraging interaction and cooperation. Natural light and views to the green make the space somewhere students want to frequent—and they do.

The Center's textured, pale-brick panel cantilevers toward Cheyenne Way, marking its intersection with 16th Street, and engaging Marquez Hall's shimmering metal soffit in a compositional dialogue of material planes.

The existing grade change of ten to twelve feet longitudinally through the building, between entries at Illinois Street and Cheyenne Way, presented a challenge to the lab requirements of a sixteen-foot floor-to-floor dimension. The solution places the lowest level partially below grade at Cheyenne Way, an ideal location for lab spaces with specific lighting, sound, and vibration requirements.

From the Cheyenne Way entry, an open stair along the green leads up to the promenade, providing a place for students to gather and study.

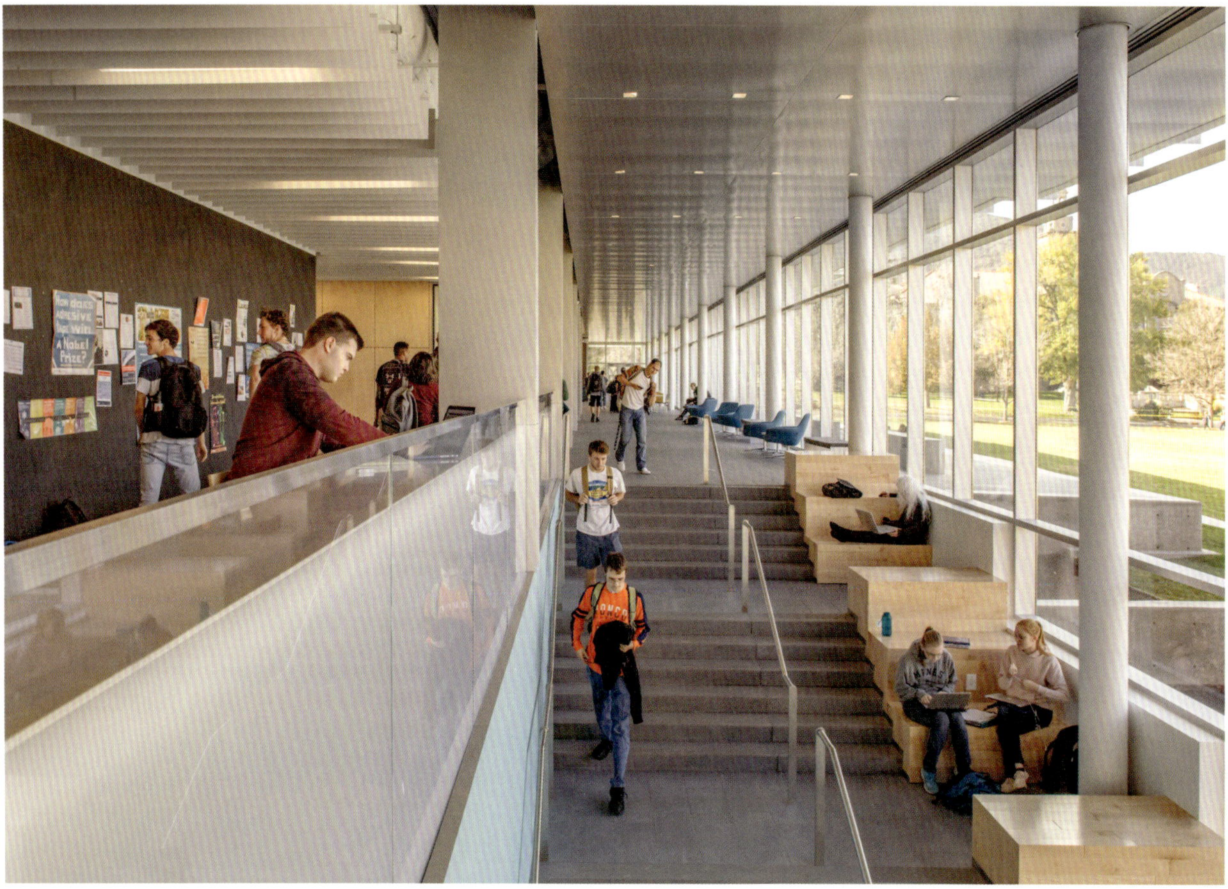

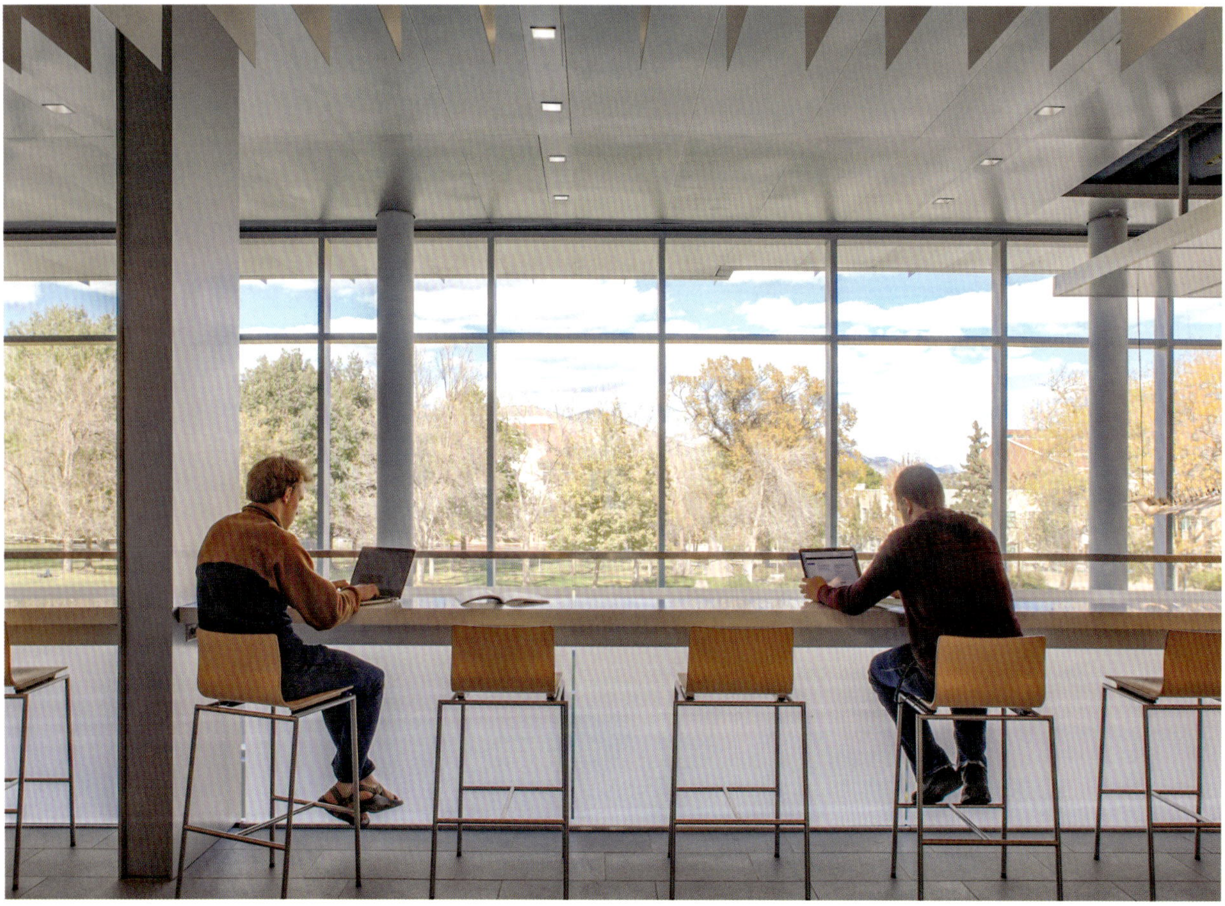

"For the first time ever, students hang around. They love to be here," notes Squier. "You can find places to interact everywhere, and even on gray days it's filled with light. The building is always full, all day."

The promenade offers a variety of study spaces to meet individual preferences. Bar seating at classroom entries fulfills transitory demands before and after classes, while semi-private booths offer extended stay opportunities to individuals or groups. Each share a visual connection to the Kafadar Commons landscape, and ample access to diffused north daylight.

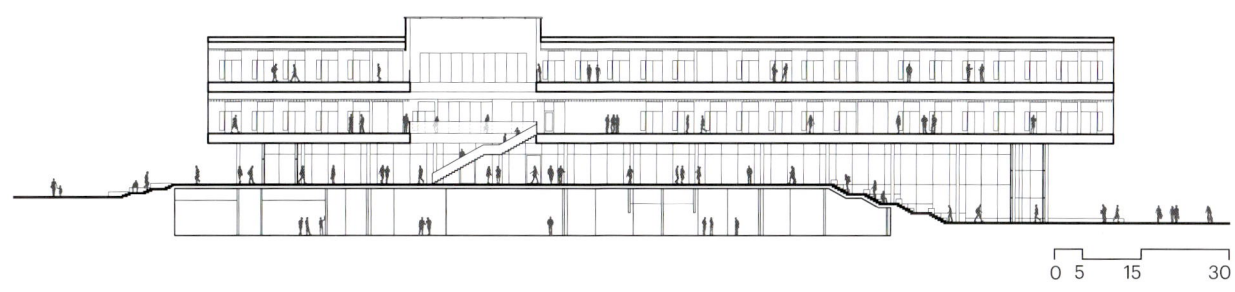

0 5   15   30

A tour of CoorsTek's manufacturing facilities inspired the design team to integrate the donor's ceramic products into an art installation for the main event space. The design team worked with faculty, administrators, and CoorsTek representatives to develop the sculptural installation that integrates color, donated ceramic tubes, and stainless-steel rods, all composed as an abstraction of molecular structure.

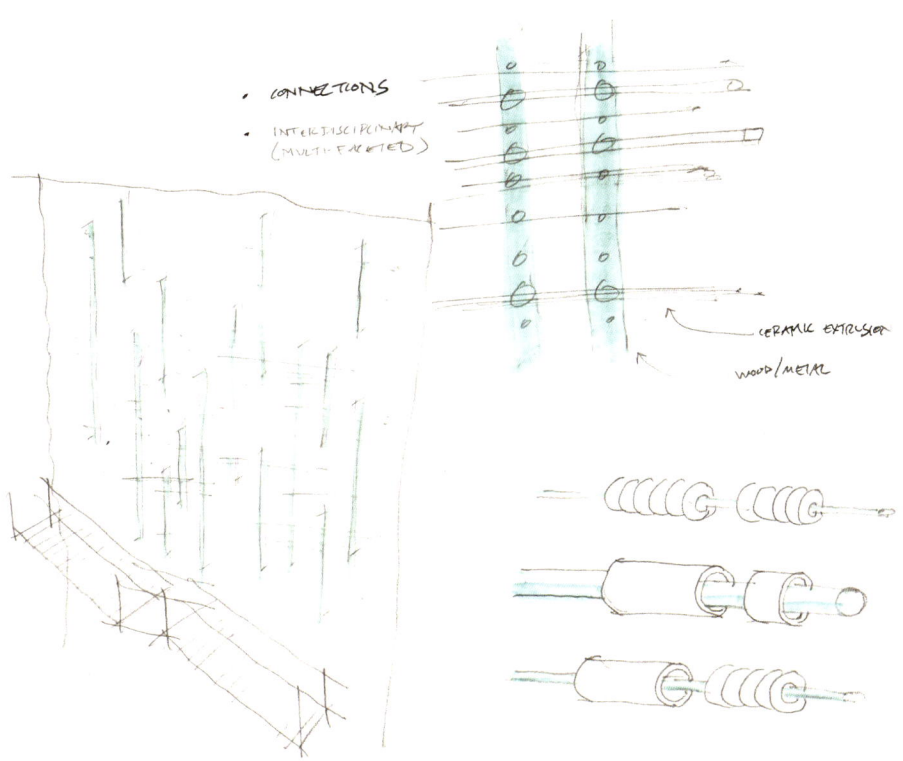

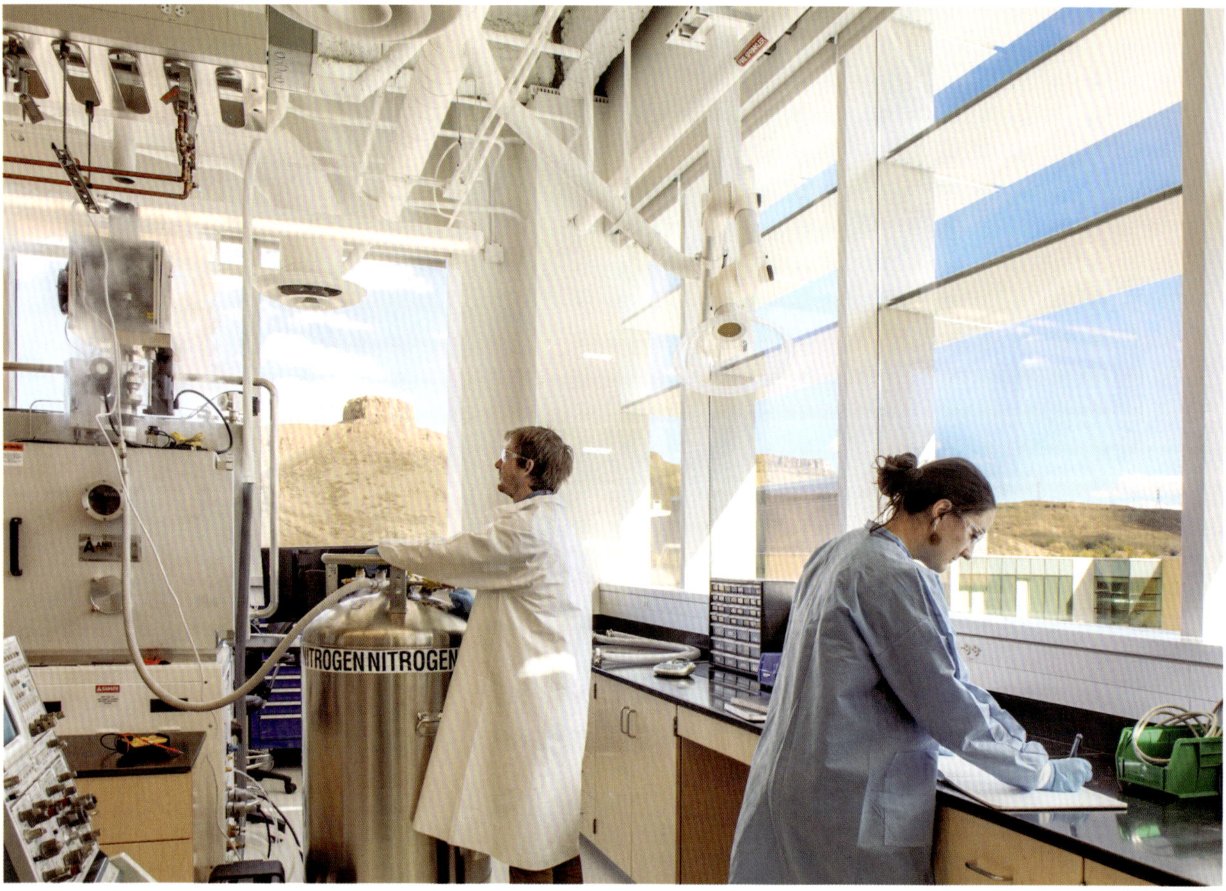
NITROGEN NITROGEN

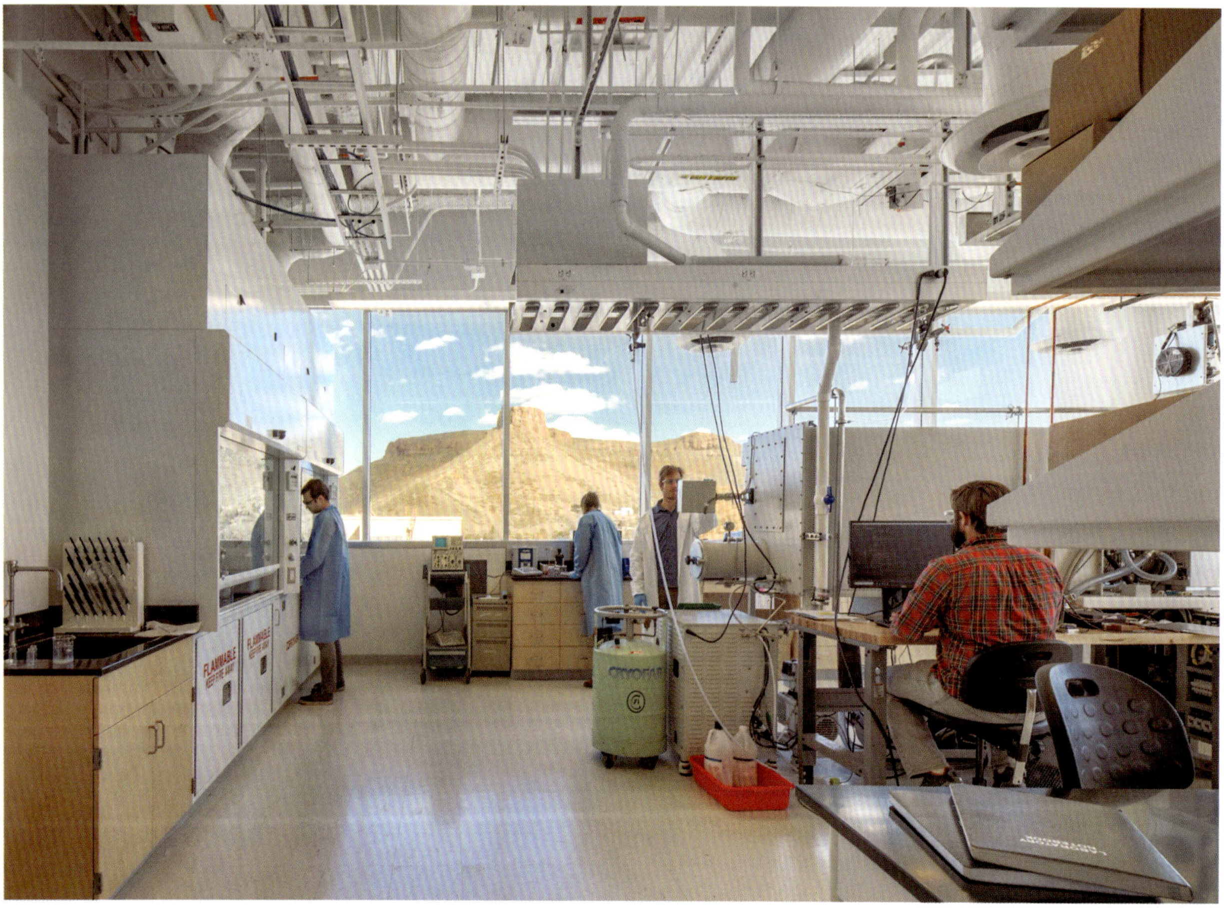
FLAMMABLE
CRYOFAB

9

10

8

11

7

Level 3

1 Gathering Space
2 Gallery
3 Collaboration
4 Classrooms
5 Active Learning Studios
6 Labs — Interdisciplinary
7 Labs — Physics
8 Lab Support
9 Faculty Offices
10 Grad Student Offices
11 Administration
12 Support Spaces
13 Service

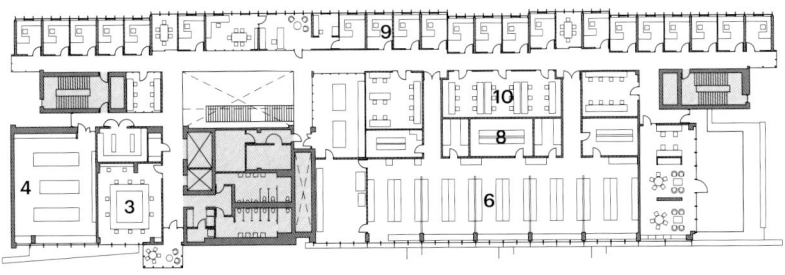

9

10

8

4

3

6

Level 2

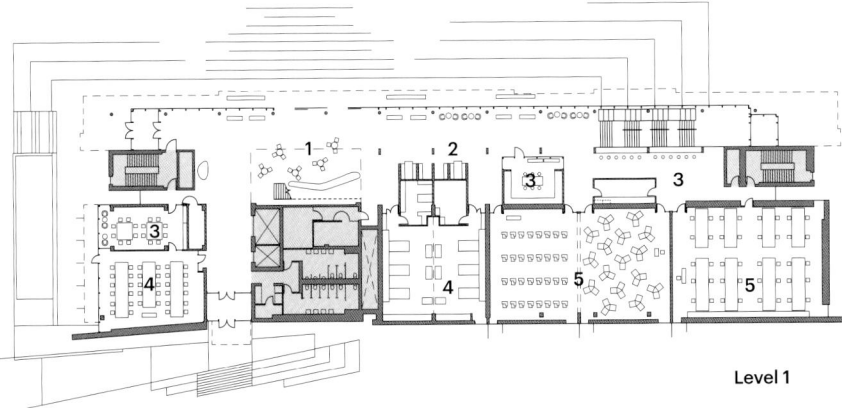

1

2

3

3

3

4

4

5

5

Level 1

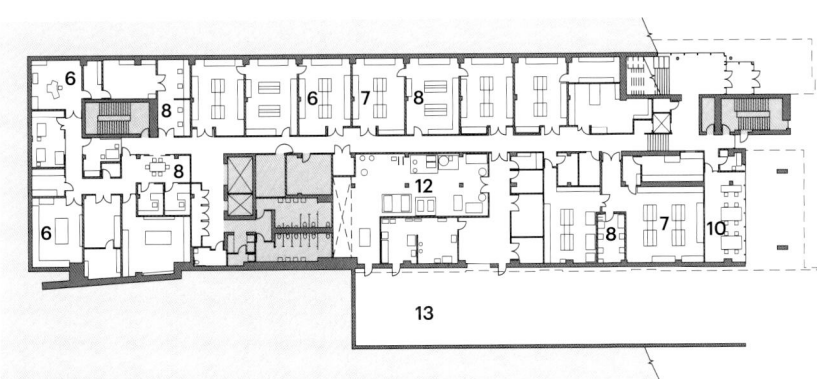

6

8

6

7

8

8

12

7

8

10

6

13

Basement Level

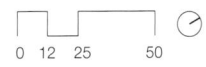

0 12 25   50

Classrooms are light-filled, flexible, and similarly full of light and framed views—many projecting out toward the campus and providing lateral transparency. Expanses of glass curtain wall provide sweeping connections to the landscape, while slot windows bring framed views and controllable sunlight. The building's faces are clad in pale brick, glass, and aluminum panels, responding to the surrounding context and lending variety to the envelope. Metal shades and an integrated metal support system provide solar control for the labs.

Squier adds that the facility has become a major attraction for top-caliber students and faculty. It already hosts international conferences and has indeed become a focus of the campus.

"People no longer flow around our building—
they flow through it," notes Squier. "They find
places to interact in every possible corner, and
most are thrilled that they've found an environment [in which] to be inspired and to create."

Mountain Lake
Park Playground

Mountain Lake Park Playground—a neighbor-hood park bordered by the eclectic townhomes of the Richmond District and the undulating southern edge of Presidio National Park—had last been renovated in the 1980s and was in dire need of an update.

Bohlin Cywinski Jackson spearheaded the effort with the San Francisco Recreation and Parks Department and a passionate neighborhood association, Friends of Mountain Lake Park Playground. Several public meetings revealed that residents were seeking much more than the typical city playground.

"We wanted different equipment, we wanted it to appeal to a large age range, and we wanted diverse experiences so kids would keep wanting to try new things," notes Jen Fetner Booth, one of the founders of Friends of Mountain Lake Park Playground. Fetner Booth, who stud-ied architecture, spent innumerable hours brainstorming imaginative concepts with Bohlin Cywinski Jackson associate Aaron Gomez, a former classmate who, as a local resident, had more at stake than the usual designer.

Location
San Francisco, CA

Dates
2011–2017

Client
Friends of Mountain Lake Playground

Size
23,000 SF

The previous play structure at the upper terrace of Mountain Lake Park Playground included pressure treated timbers and surrounding sand, features common to 1980s vintage playgrounds, which did not meet current safety and accessibility guidelines.

Similar to Koret's Children's Quarter in Golden Gate Park, Mountain Lake Park Playground features one of the city's unique concrete slides that takes advantage of the hills of San Francisco. The centerpiece of the playground, the slide has been preserved, anchoring the updated playground to the cherished memories of the community's past.

Mountain Lake Park Playground is nestled amidst mature evergreen trees and gently slopes down to the shore of Mountain Lake on the southern edge of Presidio National Park.

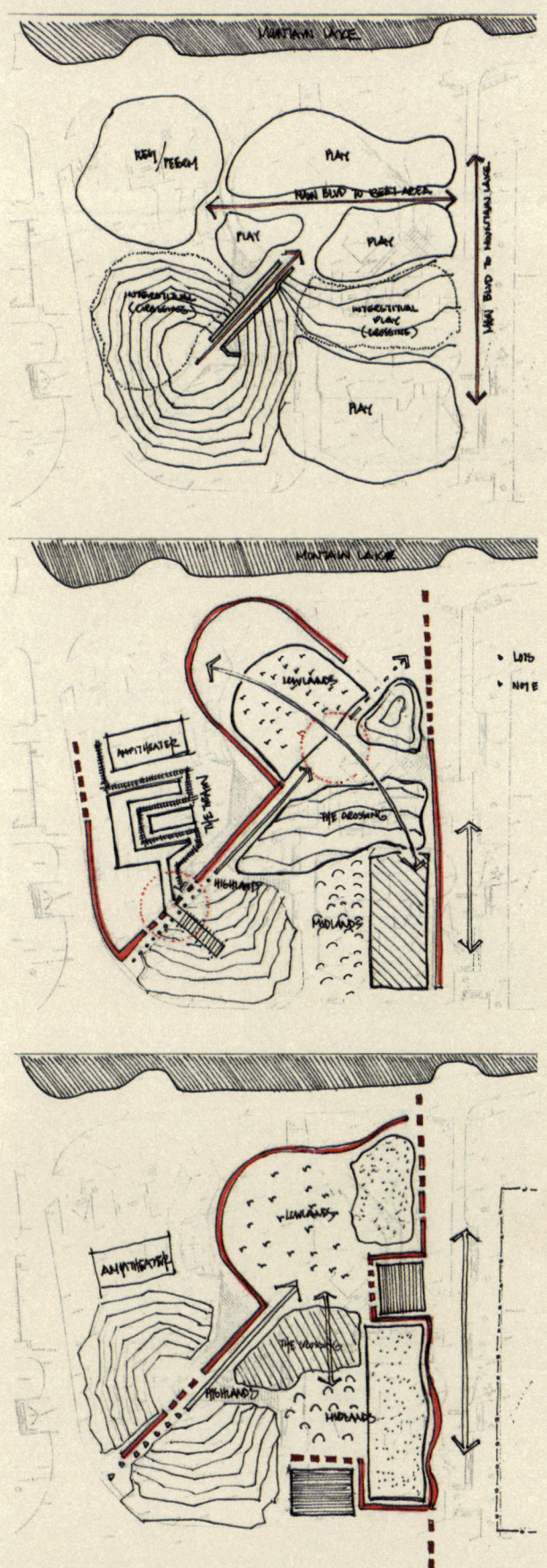

Sketches from early design and programming phase establish organizing principles of the design. The renovated playground takes advantage of the site's topography, with separate play areas on terraces organized according to age and playability.

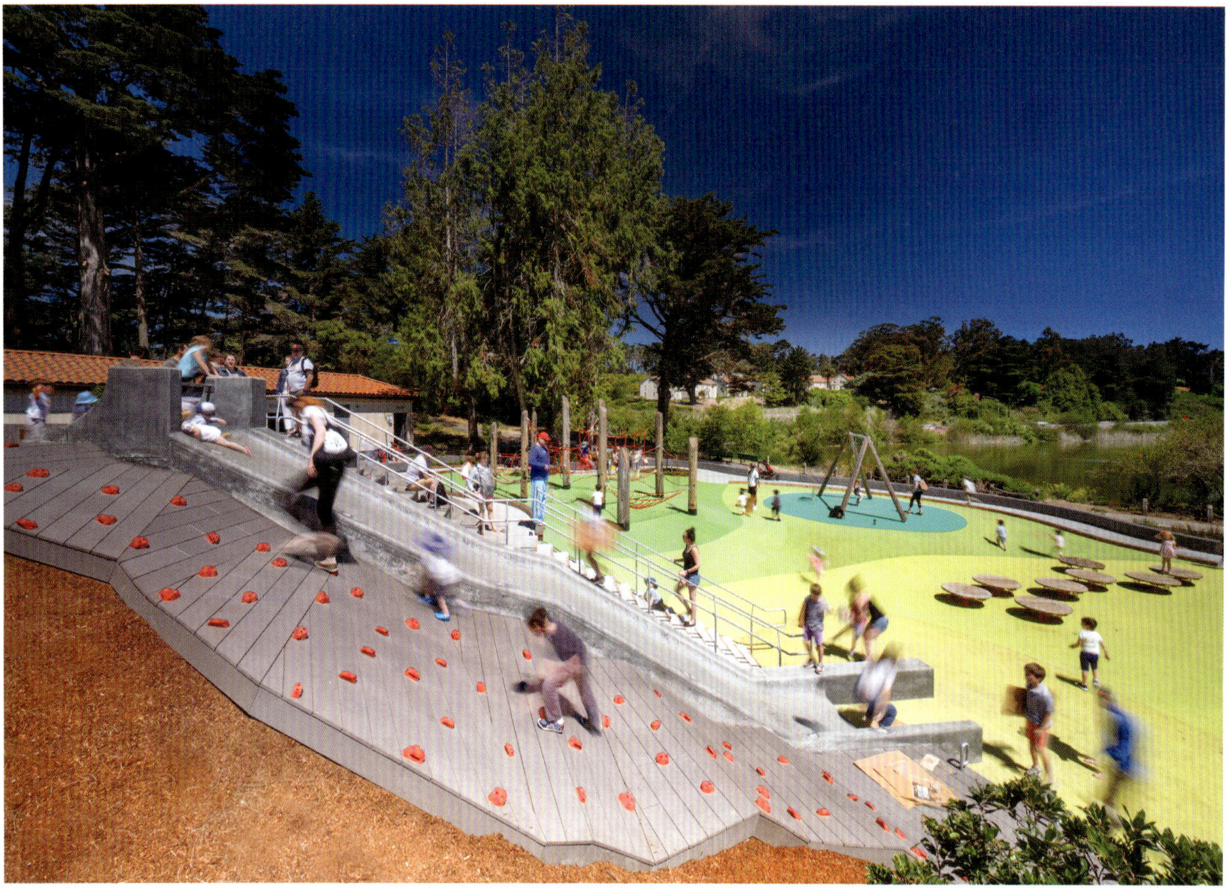

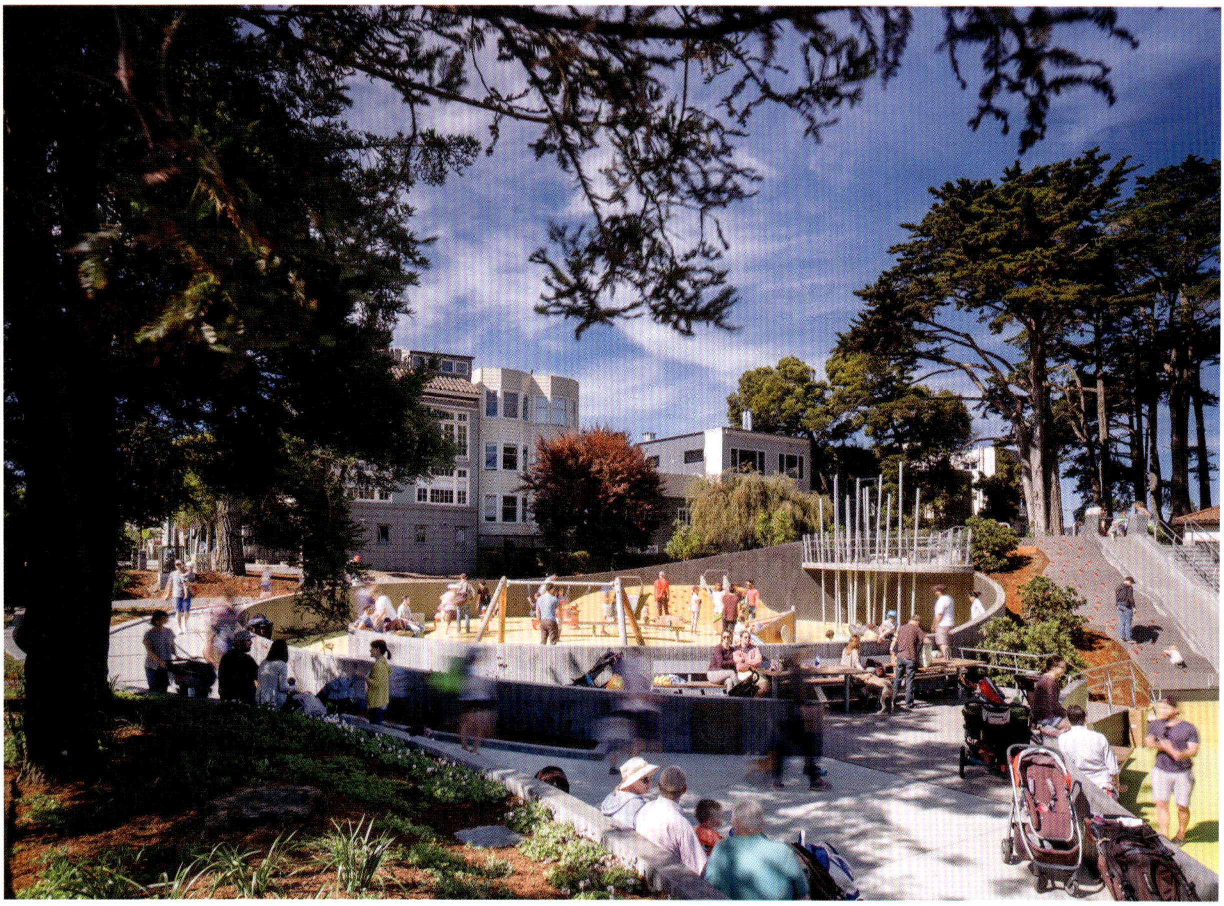

Rather than leveling off the site, the design team took advantage of its hilly topography, creating colorful, terraced play areas, organized according to ability and threaded by a series of meandering pathways. No tall fences separate the playground from the neighborhood, and each zone flows into the next, maintaining continuity of the experience.

The centerpiece of the park, a beloved concrete slide that had long cascaded down the side of a large earthen mound, was preserved. But to increase accessibility and safety, colorful plastic hand-holds along its meandering left edge—similar to those of a climbing wall—replace hulking boulders and create an equally invigorating ascent. Adjacent to this ramble, an observation platform perches on slender, slightly skewed steel columns, evoking the tapestry of surrounding trees and their freckled shadows.

Virtually every design element draws on the site's history and topography. The rippling "sand dunes" of the preschool area represent the seaside landscape that once dominated the city; the ribbed pattern of the concrete retaining walls is an abstraction of the thick reeds that line the shores of adjacent Mountain Lake; tracks of native birds and animals imprint wall surfaces; and large sculptures, including a frog and turtle, acknowledge the lake's aquatic life. The permeable granulated rubber surfaces allow rainwater to filter through the site, successfully recharging the lake below.

The ensemble is emboldened by zigging, zagging, bouncing, swinging, hovering, and curving play structures—procured from a European play structure manufacturer—that mix the tactile elements of the forest with a childlike spirit of imagination and exploration.

The park has been a success in every way. It's regularly full, and has become a yearlong destination for residents, who stop by on both planned and unplanned excursions. Children of all ages return again and again to explore areas that don't simply provide fun, but continually challenge them in new ways as well.

Midway on the journey to the top of the slide, an observation platform sits perched on a forest of steel-pipe columns. The platform overlooks the preschool area below while facilitating expansive views of Mountain Lake. Apertures in the platform provide framed moments of intrigue for the users both above and below.

"We have climbing, we have scrambling, we have running, we have problem solving, we have balancing pods. We have a little bit of everything," notes Fetner Booth, who shares her excitement that the site has become a local hub. Perfect for catching up with neighbors and participating in local events, the park is used by schools, by individuals teaching tai chi classes, and by other groups in unexpected ways.

"I underestimated that it would become such a focus of the community," she adds. "My kids beg to stop here on the way home. There's always someone here for them to see."

Mountain Lake Park Playground

Project Credits

High Meadow at Fallingwater
Client: Western Pennsylvania Conservancy

Design Team
Principal: Peter Bohlin, FAIA
Project Manager: William James
Project Team: William Loose, Kent Suhrbier

Consultant Team
General Contractor: Fairchance Construction Company
Structural Engineer: K2 Engineering
Mechanical, Electrical, and Plumbing Engineer: Iams Consulting

Newport Beach Civic Center and Park
Client: City of Newport Beach

Design Team
Principals: Gregory Mottola, FAIA; Peter Bohlin, FAIA
Project Manager: Steven Chaitow, AIA
Project Architects: Joshua Keller, RA; Daniel Lee, AIA
Project Team: Joseph Bridy, Yung Chang, Christopher Dobosz, Brian Driska, Christopher Eastman, Lulu Fang, Archer Firouzi, Helene Gregoire, Ashley Hinton, Karolina Kaczmarczyk, Trish Kahler, Brigham Keehner, Tom Kirk, Jennifer Kishi, Sandy Lam, Jeff Lew, Erika Miele, Dominique Price, Yvonne Riggie, Nicholas Ruiz, Lena Shah, Ryan Simpson, Reggie Stump, Michael Waltner

Consultant Team
General Contractor: C.W. Driver
Landscape Architect: PWP Landscape Architecture
Civil/Structural/MEP/Lighting/ Telecommunications/ Sustainability: Arup
Acoustics and AV: Charles M. Salter Associates
Cost Estimating: C.P. O'Halloran
Waterproofing: Allana Buick & Bers
Security: TransTech Systems
Code: The Fire Consultants
Food Service: HDA Pacific
Wayfinding/Signage: Ph.D

Nu Skin Innovation Center
Client: Nu Skin Enterprises

Design Team
Principal: Ray Calabro, FAIA
Project Managers: Sergei Bischak, AIA; Kirk Hostetter, AIA
Project Team: Mark Adams, Peter Bohlin, Kyle Boyd, Christian Evans, Eryn Gaul, Alexander Hale, Michael Hatcher, Michael Henderson, Nick Hons, Nate Lambdin, Heather Michael, Emma Nowinski, Bo Steadman, Glenn Timmons, Karen Zellner

Consultant Team
General Contractor: Okland Construction
Landscape Architect: Gustafson Guthrie Nichol Ltd.
Civil and Structural Engineer: Magnusson Klemencic Associates
Mechanical and Plumbing Engineer: Colvin Engineering Associates
Electrical Engineer: Spectrum Engineering
Lighting Design: Fisher Marantz Stone
Environmental Design: Atelier Ten
Interpretive Design and Exhibits: Ralph Appelbaum Associates
Acoustics: The Greenbusch Group, Inc.

Sawyer Library
Client: Williams College

Design Team
Principals: Frank Grauman, FAIA; William Loose, AIA
Project Manager: Lee Alison Clark, AIA
Project Architects: Gabriel Hodge, AIA; Jason Kilgore, RA; Chris Sutterer, RA
Project Team: Jacklyn Bacon, Charles Cwenar, Justin Harclerode, Collyn Hinchey, David Koschak, Jeremy Little, Pamela Mahoney-Casey, Kara Mann, Heather Morehead, Erika Parker, Jesse Pointon, Dana Reed, Russell Roberts, Gregory Spaw, Lindsay Renee Sutterer, Theresa Thomas, Derek Thome, Gina Volpicelli, David Weaver, Adam Wise, Charles Young

Consultant Team
General Contractor: Consigli Construction Management
Landscape Architect: Michael Vergason
Structural Engineer: Christakis VanOcker Morrison (CVM)
Civil Engineer: Guntlow & Associates, Inc.
Mechanical, Electrical, and Plumbing Engineer: Altieri Sebor Wieber, LLC

Geotechnical Engineer:
    Haley & Alrich, Inc.
Code Consulting Engineer:
    R.W. Sullivan Engineering
Site Utility Engineer: VanZelm
    Heywood & Shadford, Inc.
Architectural Restoration:
    Frens & Frens LLC
Acoustics/IT/AV: The Sextant
    Group, Inc.

Square, Inc. Headquarters
Client: Square, Inc.

Design Team
Principal: Gregory Mottola, FAIA
Project Manager:
    Christopher Orsega, AIA
Project Architect:
    Michael Kross, RA
Project Team: Sergei Bischak,
    Peter Bohlin, Christina Cho,
    Helene Gregoire, Alexander
    Gregor, Ashley Hinton, Ryan
    Keerns, Joshua Keller, Brian
    Padgett, Nicholas Ruiz, Helen
    Seldin, Lena Shah, Rosa Sheng,
    Carlo Sturken, Shawn Wood

Consultant Team
General Contractor:
    BCCI Construction
Construction Manager:
    projectFOCUS
MEP: CB Engineers
Structural Engineer: Tipping
    Structural Engineers
Lighting Design (phase I):
    Banks|Ramos Architectural
    Lighting Design
Lighting Design (phase II):
    Niteo Lighting
Acoustics: Charles M. Salter
    Associates
AV/Security/Telecom: RLS
Food Service: Presidio Design
    Group
Life Safety: The Fire Consultants

Cherie Flores Garden Pavilion
Client: The Hermann Park
    Conservancy

Design Team
Principal: Peter Bohlin, FAIA

Project Manager: Tom Kirk, AIA
Project Architect: Daniel Lee, AIA
Project Team: George Murphy,
    Christopher Renn

Consultant Team
General Contractor:
    Tellepsen Builders
Structural Engineer:
    Cardno Haynes Whaley
Mechanical, Electrical,
    and Plumbing Engineer:
    Infrastructure Associates, Inc.
Landscape Architect: Hoerr
    Schaudt; White Oak Studio

Apple Stores Worldwide
Client: Apple Inc.

Apple Fifth Avenue, New York — Original Store (2006)
Design Team
Principals: Karl Backus, FAIA;
    Peter Bohlin, FAIA
Project Manager: Rosa Sheng, AIA
Project Team: Nick Anderson,
    Anastasia Congdon, Maria
    Danielides, Jon Jackson, Joshua
    Keller, Cherie Lau, Rachel Lehn-
    Antin, Christopher Orsega,
    Brian Padgett, Lydia So

Consultant Team
Plaza Design in collaboration
    with: MdeAS
Associate Designer: Eight Inc.
General Contractor: Shawmut
    Design and Construction
Structural Engineer: Eckersley
    O'Callaghan; GL&SS
MEP Engineer: WSP
Lighting Design: ISP Design
Elevator: Edgett Williams
    Consulting Group

Apple Fifth Avenue, New York — Remodel (2011)
Design Team
Principals: Karl Backus, FAIA;
    Peter Bohlin, FAIA
Project Manager:
    George Bradley, AIA
Project Architect:
    Brian Padgett, RA
Project Team: David Murray

Consultant Team
General Contractor: Shawmut
    Design and Construction
Structural Engineer:
    Eckersley O'Callaghan
MEP Engineer: WSP
Lighting Design: ISP Design

Apple SoHo, New York
Design Team
Principals: Peter Bohlin, FAIA;
    Jon Jackson, FAIA
Project Manager: Karl Backus, FAIA
Project Architect: Rosa Sheng, AIA
Project Team: Colleen Caulliez,
    Peter Kreuthmeier, Ben
    McDonald, Brian Padgett,
    Nicholas Ruiz, Michael Waltner

Consultant Team
Associate Architect: Ronnette Riley
    Architect
Associate Designer: Eight Inc.
General Contractor: JT Magen &
    Company Inc.
Historic Preservation: Higgins
    Quasebarth & Partners
Civil Engineer: Langan Engineering
    & Environmental Services
Structural Engineer: GL&SS
MEP Engineer: WSP
Lighting: ISP Design

Apple SoHo, New York — Remodel (2011)
Design Team
Principals: Karl Backus, FAIA;
    Peter Bohlin, FAIA;
Project Manager:
    Maria Danielides, AIA
Project Team: David Andreini,
    George Bradley, David Murray,
    Nicholas Ruiz,

Consultant Team
General Contractor: Shawmut
    Design and Construction
Historic Preservation: Higgins
    Quasebarth & Partners
Civil Engineer: Langan Engineering
    & Environmental Services
Structural Engineer: Eckersley
    O'Callaghan
MEP Engineer: WSP
Lighting Design: ISP Design

Apple Covent Garden, London
Design Team
Principals: Karl Backus, FAIA; Peter Bohlin, FAIA
Project Manager: David Andreini, AIA; Christopher Orsega, AIA
Project Team: Stephanie Grandjacques, Michael Kross, Jon Jackson, Megan Johnson, Tina Lindinger, Priyanka Mara

Consultant Team
Associate Architect: MPA Architects; Gensler
General Contractor: Faithdean Plc
Historic Consultant: Julian Harrap Architects
Structural Engineer: Eckersley O'Callaghan
MEP Engineer: BuroHappold Engineering
Lighting Designer: ISP Design
Vertical Transportation Consultant: Dunbar and Boardman

Apple Upper West Side, New York
Design Team
Principals: Karl Backus, FAIA; Peter Bohlin, FAIA
Project Manager: George Bradley, Jr., AIA
Project Architect: Maria Danielides, AIA
Project Team: Christopher Hockenberry, Joseph Holsen, Jon Jackson, Karolina Kaczmarczyk, Joshua Keller, Michelle Lopez, Ariane Mates, Scott Newland, Nathan Owdom, Brian Padgett, Tanner Pikop, Jessica Rafferty, Alexandra Rich, Lauren Ross

Consultant Team
General Contractor: Shawmut Design and Construction
Civil Engineer: Langan Engineering & Environmental Services
Structural Engineer: Eckersley O'Callaghan
Structural Engineer of Record: Robert Silman Associates
MEP Engineer: BuroHappold Engineering
Lighting: ISP Design

Apple Upper East Side, New York
Design Team
Principals: Karl Backus, FAIA; David Murray, FAIA
Project Manager: David Andreini, AIA
Project Architect: Brigham Keehner, AIA
Project Team: Maria Danielides, Carson Davis, Sagar Desai, Sarah Estephan, Sarah Harkins, Alexandra Harvey, Jeffrey Lew, Megan Padalecki, Corey Schnobrich, Megan Strenski, Chenglong Tsai

Consultant Team
General Contractor: Shawut Design and Construction
Restoration Architect: CTS Group Architects
Historic Preservation: Higgins Quasebarth & Partners
Civil Engineer: Langan Engineering & Environmental Services
Structural Engineer: Eckersley O'Callaghan
MEP Engineer: WSP
Lighting: ISP Design
Acoustical: Arup
Elevator: Edgett Williams Consulting Group
Conservator: Jablonski Building Conservation, Inc.
Exterior Restoration Contractor: Nicholson & Galloway, Inc.

Apple Stanford, Palo Alto
Design Team
Principal: Karl Backus, FAIA; Peter Bohlin, FAIA
Project Manager: Michael Waltner, RA
Project Team: David Andreini, George Bradley, Joseph DiNapoli, Andrew Hamblin, Heather Kastern, Ryan Keerns, Tina Lindinger, Priyanka Mara, Gregory Mottola, Jessica Rafferty, Chenglong Tsai, Daniel Yoder

Consultant Team
General Contractor: Pepper Construction
Civil Engineer: BKF Engineers

Structural Engineer: Eckersley O'Callaghan; Umerani Associates
MEP Engineer: WSP
Lighting: ISP Design

Apple Pudong, Shanghai
Design Team
Principals: Karl Backus, FAIA; Peter Bohlin, FAIA
Project Manager: David Andreini, AIA
Project Architect: Brian Padgett, RA
Project Team: Christopher Hockenberry, Megan Johnson, Karolina Kaczmarczyk, Michael Kross, Ariane Mates, Jessica Rafferty, Sylwia Rewienska, Denis Schofield, Justin Trigg

Consultant Team
General Contractor: Rich Honour Design Group
Structural Engineer: Eckersley O'Callaghan
MEP Engineer: Arup
Lighting Design: ISP Design
Project Manager: MB Projects & Interiors

Apple Puerta del Sol, Madrid
Design Team
Principal: Karl Backus, FAIA
Project Manager: Christopher Moore, AIA
Project Team: Reuben Alt, Tina Lindinger, Scott Newland, Jessica Rafferty, Kristen Smith, Ming Thompson, Chenglong Tsai, Sonia Villanueva

Consultant Team
Executive Architect: SPI – Società Progettazioni Integrali
Local Architect: Bt/G4 Arquitectura
Executive Structural Engineer: MC2 Estudio de Ingeniería
Design Structural Engineer: Eckersley O'Callaghan
MEP Engineer: ESA Engineering
Lighting Design: ISP Design
Acoustical: Arup
Environmental Design: Atelier Ten

Manetti Shrem Museum of Art
Client: University of California, Davis

Bohlin Cywinski Jackson Team
Principal: Karl Backus, FAIA
Project Manager: Sergei Bischak, AIA; Ryan Keerns, RA
Project Team: Joseph Bridy, Yung Chang, Maria Danielides, Samantha Ensch, Rachel Estes, Alexander Gregor, Alexandra Harvey, Karolina Kaczmarczyk, Ashley Morgan, Rosa Sheng, Travis Shockley, Victor Tzen

SO – IL Team
Florian Idenburg, Ilias Papageorgiou, Jing Liu, Danny Duong, Kevin Lamyuktseung, Alvaro Gomez-Selles Fernandez

The Whiting-Turner Company Team
Jack Stackalis, Drew Roberts, Dave Rupert, Matt Burnie

Consultant Team
Landscape (Competition): The Office of Cheryl Barton
Landscape (Design and Construction): Lutsko Associates
Structural Engineer: Rutherford + Chekene
Lighting Design/Daylighting: Fisher Marantz Stone
MEP/Security: WSP
Sustainability: WSP
Civil Engineer: Cunningham Engineering
Acoustics: Charles M. Salter Associates
Canopy Engineer: Front Inc.
Graphic Design: Tim McNeil

New College House
Client: The Trustees of the University of Pennsylvania

Design Team
Principals: Bernard Cywinski, FAIA; Frank Grauman, FAIA
Project Manager: Dana Reed, AIA
Project Architects: Anthony Pregiato, AIA; Erin Roark, AIA
Project Team: Monica Barton, Thomas Breslin, Joseph Bridy, Nora Chase, Christian Didra, Alfred Dragani, Rebecca Esau, Tina Cheng Faust, Matthew Huber, Ryan Keerns, Jeffrey Lew, Charles Nawoj, Crista McDonald, Samuel McNutt, Virginia Melnyk, David Murray, Lauren Powers, Ryan Simpson, Bryan Sistino, Kristen Smith, Ngoc Tran, Kelly Vresilovic, Brian Yachyshen

Consultant Team
Construction Manager: Intech Construction
Landscape Architect: Michael Vergason Landscape Architects
Structural Engineer: CVM Engineers
MEP Engineer: AHA Consulting Engineers
Civil Engineer: Pennoni
Sustainability Coordination: AHA Consulting Engineers
Food Service: Hammer Design Associates
Lighting Design: Atelier Ten
Hardware: Jack Soeffing Consultant

Soma Towers
Client: Su Development

Bohlin Cywinski Jackson Team
Principals: Peter Bohlin, FAIA; Robert Miller, FAIA
Project Manager: Ethan Kushner, AIA; Kirk Hostetter, AIA
Project Team: Campie Ellis, Christian Evans, Jeremy Evard, Michael Hatcher, Adam Pazan, Glenn Timmons, Matt Wittman

Su Development Team
John Su, Linda Abe, Maria Hui, Tim Zielke, Sean Haste, Zoe Wang, Evette Yu, Patricia Chen

Consultant Team:
General Contractor: CDG Workshop, LLC
Structural & Civil Engineer: DCI Engineers
HVAC & Plumbing: Ocean Park Mechanical
Electrical Engineer: Stateside Power
Landscape: Weisman Design Group

Frick Environmental Center
Client: City of Pittsburgh; Pittsburgh Parks Conservancy

Design Team
Principal: Roxanne Sherbeck, FAIA
Project Manager: Robert Aumer, AIA
Project Architect: Patricia Culley, AIA
Project Team: Thomas Beatty, David Bostak, Jason Brody, Matthew Conti, Jon Funari, Natalie Gentile, Mark Hensler, Matthew Huber, Jon Jackson, Darrell Kauric, Gregory LaForest, Michael Maiese, Louis Markovic, Michele Mercer, Matthew Plecity, Gina Rossi, Kent Suhrbier, Paula Suhrbier, Zachary Weimer, Karen Zellner

Consultant Team
Construction Manager: PJ Dick
Landscape Architecture: La Quatra Bonci Associates
Structural Engineer: Barber & Hoffman
Civil Engineer: H.F. Lenz Company
MEP+FP Engineer: RAM-TECH Engineers
Sustainability Consultant: Atelier Ten
Stormwater Management Consultant: Nitsch Engineering

Marquez Hall
Client: Colorado School of Mines

Bohlin Cywinski Jackson Team
Principals: Peter Bohlin, FAIA; Robert Miller, FAIA
Project Manager: Kirk Hostetter, AIA
Project Team: Patricia Culley, Jeremy Evard, Natalie Gentile, Monika Gibson, Jon Jackson, Christian Kittelson, Nate Lambdin, David Miller, Atsuko Mori, Matt Wittman

Anderson Mason Dale
    Architects Team
Principal: Paul Haack, AIA
Project Manager:
    David Houston, AIA
Project Team: Gabe Comstock,
    Todd Townsend, Dan Bishop,
    Dan Craig, Jim Miller, John
    Graham, Julie Zurakowski,
    Kevin Keady, Laura Muniz,
    Sean Jursnick, Cathy Bellem,
    Heather Doster

Consultant Team
General Contractor: Adolfson
    and Peterson Construction
MEP Engineer: Shaffer Baucom
    Engineering & Consulting
Civil Engineer: Martin/Martin
    Consulting Engineers
Structural Engineer: Studio NYL
Landscape: studioINSITE
Acoustical: D.L. Adams Associates,
    Inc.
Cost Estimating: Parametrix, Inc.
Energy Consultant: Architectural
    Energy Corporation
Energy Modeling: The Weidt Group
Exhibit Design: ArtHouse Design

**CoorsTek Center for Applied
Science and Engineering**
Client: Colorado School of Mines

Bohlin Cywinski Jackson Team
Principals: Peter Bohlin, FAIA;
    Robert Miller, FAIA
Project Manager:
    Kirk Hostetter, AIA
Project Team: Torrence Campbell,
    Natalie Gentile, Nate Lambdin,
    Kevin Lang, Emma Nowinski,
    Brooke Thompson, Michael
    Waltner

Anderson Mason Dale
    Architects Team
Principals: Paul Haack, AIA;
    David Pfeifer, AIA
Project Manager:
    David Houston, AIA
Project Team: Dan Bishop,
    Mike Bucher, Peter Koehler,
    Beth Mosenthal, Hanna Kato,
    Suzanne Minear, Kevin Ilaoa,
    Luc Bamberger

Consultant Team
General Contractor:
    FCI Constructors
Landscape Designer:
    Lime Green Design
Mechanical Engineer:
    Shaffer Baucom
    Engineering & Consulting
Structural Engineer: Martin/Martin
    Consulting Engineers

Mountain Lake Park Playground
Client: Friends of Mountain Lake
    Park Playground, San Francisco
    Parks Alliance, City and County
    of San Francisco

Design Team
Principal: Gregory Mottola, FAIA
Project Manager:
    Aaron Gomez, AIA
Project Team: Laing Chung,
    Lauren Ross, Helen Seldin,
    Rebecca Wood, Daniel Yoder

Consultant Team
Contractor: CF Contracting
Landscape: Lutsko Associates
Structural Engineer: Holmes
    Structures
Civil Engineer: Lea & Braze
    Engineering
Geotechnical Engineer:
    Murray Engineers
Construction Engineer:
    Department of Public Works

Acknowledgments

We are grateful for the opportunities and the encouragement we've received from our clients and friends to make extraordinary architecture. Much like designing a building, *Gathering* is the result of a long process of reflection, collaboration, and hard work.

We are indebted to the talent and vision of Peter Bohlin, who founded our practice fifty-four years ago and whose deep influence is felt in these projects. His generous insights and encouragement have helped to guide the process for this book.

The projects here reflect the collective talents of the principals, associate principals, senior associates, associates, architects, interns, and staff at Bohlin Cywinski Jackson. We are deeply grateful to the project leaders for their tireless commitment in making this work a reality.

Special thanks go to our Publications Manager Sierra Haight, who took the lead in expertly coordinating the process. Thanks to our internal book team, especially Karl Backus, Gabe Hodge, Ryan Keerns, Josh Keller, Shannon Krick, Jennifer Varner Sadinsky, and Nick Snyder, for their energy and care in guiding the design and format. Katherine Acheson-Snow, Peter Bohlin, Bernard Cywinski, Jendy Edgerton, Chris Garland, Aaron Gomez, Frank Grauman, Kirk Hostetter, Bill James, Christian Kittelson, Daniel Lee, Leah Libow, Robert Miller, Greg Mottola, Chris Orsega, Davis Richardson, Elizabeth Smith, Andrew Thies, and Zach Wignall helped to produce and refine the sketches, drawings, and text.

We applaud the efforts of architectural writer Sam Lubell who diligently visited our projects, interviewed the designers, and shared his thoughtful impressions of our work in the introduction and in the text for each chapter.

Putting together *Gathering* has been an exceptional experience thanks to Dung Ngo, whose editorial insights were instrumental in developing the themes of the book, as well as Gordon Goff and his team at ORO Editions, whose support and enthusiasm have been remarkable. Special thanks go to Adam Michaels and Siiri Tännler at IN-FO.CO, whose skill in graphic design enhanced the book immeasurably. Photographers have captured the spirit of our buildings in exceptional images and graciously shared them for this collection.

Ray Calabro, 2019

Contributors

Sam Lubell

Sam Lubell is a writer based in New York. He has written ten books about architecture for ORO Editions, Phaidon, Rizzoli, Metropolis Books, and Monacelli Press. He writes for the *New York Times,* the *Los Angeles Times*, *Wallpaper*, *Dwell*, *Wired*, the *Atlantic*, *Metropolis*, the *Architect's Newspaper*, *Architectural Record*, *Architect Magazine*, *Contract*, *Architectural Review*, and other publications. He co-curated the exhibition *Never Built New York*, at the Queens Museum, and the exhibitions *Never Built Los Angeles* and *Shelter: Rethinking How We Live in Los Angeles* at the A+D Architecture and Design Museum > Los Angeles. Upcoming projects include *Never Built Central Park* at the Museum of the City of New York, and *Never Built Paris* at the Pavillon de l'Arsenale. He is currently an adjunct professor at Columbia GSAPP.

Dung Ngo

Dung Ngo is the founder and editor in chief of AUGUST: A Journal of Design + Travel; he was the creative director and senior editor at Rizzoli International Publications.

IN-FO.CO

Founded by Adam Michaels and Shannon Harvey, IN-FO.CO (Inventory Form & Content) is an independent design and editorial studio based in Los Angeles. IN-FO.CO's work encompasses graphic design, spatial design, strategy, content development, and publishing (including in-house imprint Inventory Press), with a focus on art, architecture, education, and culture.

Photography Credits

Images and drawings by Bohlin Cywinski Jackson unless otherwise noted.

Foreword
Nic Lehoux: 6

The Seeds of Grace
Peter Aaron/OTTO: 12; Benjamin Benschneider: 10 (top); Nic Lehoux: 10 (bottom), 15; Ed Massery: 11 (bottom); Matthew Millman: 13; Joseph Molitor: 8 (bottom); Sandy Nixon Taylor: 8 (center); Michael Thomas: 8 (top); Courtesy of Poconos Environmental Education Center: 11 (top)

High Meadow at Fallingwater
Denmarsh Photography, Inc.: 28 (top), 33; Nic Lehoux: 22–23, 26 (bottom), 28 (bottom), 29–32; Christian Phillips: 16, 26 (top), 34–35

Newport Beach Civic Center and Park
Tim Griffith: 36, 48, 56 (bottom); Nic Lehoux: 43 (bottom), 44–45, 47, 50, 51 (bottom), 52–55, 56 (top), 57, 58 (top), 60–61; Charles LeNoir: 43 (top); Fernando Pa: 51 (top), 58 (bottom), 62–63; David Wakely: 46, 49, 59; Historic American Engineering Record, Creator, Peter Dreher, Julia Salazar, Contractor Eip Associates, Brad Brewster, and Sponsor Claremont Redevelopment Agency, Hill, Dennis, photographer. *College Heights Lemon Packing House, 519–532 West First Street, Claremont, Los Angeles County, CA.* California Claremont Los Angeles County, 1968. Documentation Compiled After. Photograph. https://www.loc.gov/item/ca3253/.: 38 (center); "San Francisco City Hall from east end of Civic Center Plaza" by Mike Hoffman is licensed under CC-BY-SA-2.5.: 38 (top)

Nu Skin Innovation Center
Jeremy Bittermann: 64, 82 (bottom), 84 (bottom), 89 (bottom); Nic Lehoux: 70–71, 73–76, 79–80, 82 (top), 83, 84 (top), 85–88, 89 (top), 90–91

Sawyer Library
Peter Aaron/OTTO: 92, 101, 103–105, 107–109, 111, 113 (top), 114; Courtesy of Williams College: 100; Nic Lehoux: 98–99, 110, 116–119

Square, Inc. Headquarters
Matthew Millman: 120, 126–139 ; Wayne Thom Associates: 122 (top); Herman Hertzberger: 123 (top); Louis I. Kahn Collection, The Athenaeum of Philadelphia: 123 (bottom); Kirsten Sparenborg Brinton/Turn-of-the-Centuries: 123 (center)

Cherie Flores Garden Pavilion
Casey Dunn: 148 (bottom), 156; Nic Lehoux: 140, 146–147, 148 (top), 149–155, 157–159; Hoerr Schaudt: 142–143 (bottom); Sky Cam Aerial Photography Inc: 142 (top)

Apple Stores Worldwide
Peter Aaron/OTTO: 160, 166–170, 178, 180–187, 190–193, 194 (Row 1: left; Row 2: left center, right; Row 3: right; Row 4: left, right), 195 (Row 1: left; Row 2: right; Row 3: left, right; Row 4: center, right) Courtesy of Apple: 172 (bottom); Hufton + Crow: 188–189, 195 (Row 2: left); Nic Lehoux: 172 (top), 173, 176–177, 195 (Row 1: center); M. Nicholson: 195 (Row 3: center); Koji Okumura: 194 (Row 4: center), 195 (Row 4: left); Christian Renz: 175; Roy Zipstein: 174, 194 (Row 1: right; Row 2: left, right center; Row 3: left), 195 (Row 1: right)

Manetti Shrem Museum of Art
Iwan Baan: 196, 203; Nic Lehoux: 204–206, 208–210, 211 (bottom), 212–215; David Wakely: 211 (top); David Rumsey Map Collection, www.davidrumsey.com: 198 (center); SO-IL + Bohlin Cywinski Jackson, Associated Architects: 198 (top, bottom), 199

New College House
Greg Benson: 222; Nic Lehoux: 223–224, 229, 230 (bottom), 232, 235; Jeffrey Totaro: 216, 225, 227–228, 230 (top), 231, 233–234; Lawrence S. Williams Inc. Collection, The Athenaeum of Philadelphia: 219 (top)

SOMA Towers
Benjamin Benschneider: 236, 242, 245–246, 248–250, 252, 254–255

Frick Environmental Center
Elliott Cramer for Denmarsh Photography, Inc.: 268 (top), 269, 272 (top); Denmarsh Photography, Inc.: 268 (bottom), 274–275; Nic Lehoux: 270; Ed Massery: 256, 263 (top), 272 (bottom); Christian Phillips: 263 (bottom), 264–267; Renee Rosensteel: 271

Marquez Hall
Nic Lehoux: 276, 283–295

CoorsTek Center for Applied Science and Engineering
Nic Lehoux: 296, 306, 309, 312, 318–319, 322–323; Ron Pollard: 303–305, 307–308, 310–311, 314, 316–317, 320–321

Mountain Lake Park Playground
Nic Lehoux: 324, 326 (bottom), 330, 332–335; Gisela Steber: 326 (center)

ORO Editions
Publishers of Architecture, Art, and Design
Gordon Goff: Publisher

www.oroeditions.com
info@oroeditions.com

Published by ORO Editions

Text by Sam Lubell
Contributions from Dung Ngo
Design: IN-FO.CO (Adam Michaels, Siiri Tännler)
Project Manager: Sierra Haight
Managing Editor: Jake Anderson

10 9 8 7 6 5 4 3 2 1 First Edition

ISBN: 978-1-943532-18-6

Color Separations and Printing: ORO Group Ltd.
Printed in China.

ORO Editions makes a continuous effort to minimize the
overall carbon footprint of its publications. As part of this goal,
ORO Editions, in association with Global ReLeaf, arranges to
plant trees to replace those used in the manufacturing of the
paper produced for its books. Global ReLeaf is an international
campaign run by American Forests, one of the world's oldest
nonprofit conservation organizations. Global ReLeaf is American
Forests' education and action program that helps individuals,
organizations, agencies, and corporations improve the local and
global environment by planting and caring for trees.